TABLE OF CONTENTS

ACRONYMS

(J)ASDF	(Japan) Air Self-Defense Force
(J)GSDF	(Japan) Ground Self-Defense Force
(J)MSDF	(Japan) Maritime Self-Defense Force
(J)SDF	(Japan) Self-Defense Force
ACSA	Acquisition and Cross-Service Agreement
AFB	Air Force Base
ASO	Air Staff Office
BMD	Ballistic Missile Defense
CENTCOM	Central Command
CIC	Cabinet Intelligence Council
CIRO	Cabinet Intelligence and Research Office
CRF	Central Readiness Force
CSICE	Cabinet Satellite Intelligence Center
DCI	Director of Cabinet Intelligence
DIH	Defense Intelligence Headquarters
DIO	Defense Intelligence Officer
DPJ	Democratic Party of Japan
DPRI	Defense Posture Review Initiative
GHQ	General Headquarters
GPR	Global Posture Review
GSO	Ground Staff Office
HUMINT	Human intelligence
IAEA	International Atomic Energy Agency
IGS	Information-gathering satellite
ISAF	International Stabilization Force
JCG	Japan Coast Guard
JDA	Japan Defense Agency (now MOD)
JIC	Joint Intelligence Council
JMA	Japan Meteorological Agency
LDP	Liberal Democratic Party (Japan)
MAP	Military Assistance Program
METI	Ministry of Economy, Trade and Industry
MITI	Ministry of International Trade and Industry (Now METI)
MLIT	Ministry of Land, Infrastructure, Transport and Tourism
MOD	Ministry of Defense
MOF	Ministry of Finance
MOFA	Ministry of Foreign Affairs
MSA	Maritime Safety Agency
MSO	Maritime Staff Office
MTDP	Mid-Term Defense Program
NATO	North Atlantic Treaty Organization
NDPG	National Defense Program Guideline
NDPO	National Defense Program Outline
NPA	National Police Agency
NPT	Nuclear Non-Proliferation Treaty
NSC	National Security Council
OEF	Operation Enduring Freedom

Japan's National Security Policy Infrastructure

Can Tokyo Meet Washington's Expectation?

Yuki Tatsumi

November 2008

ISBN: 0-9770023-9-X
Photos by the Ministry of Defense in Japan and the Japan Ground Self-Defense Force
Cover design by Rock Creek Creative.

The Henry L. Stimson Center
1111 19th Street, NW 12th Floor Washington, DC 20036
phone: 202-223-5956 fax: 202-238-9604 www.stimson.org

OIP	Operation Iraq Freedom
PCO	Provincial Cooperation Office
PLA	People's Liberation Army (China)
PLAAF	PLA Air Force
PLAN	PLA Navy
PLO	Provincial Liaison Office
PKO	Peace-Keeping Operations
PMO	Prime Minister's Office
PPH	Prefectural police headquarters
PPSC	Prefectural Public Safety Commission
P-REX	Police Team Rescue Units
PRTs	Provincial Reconstruction Teams
PSI	Proliferation Security Initiative
PSIA	Public Security Investigation Agency
RPBs	Regional Police Bureaus
SAM	Surface-to-air missile
SCAP	Supreme Commander of the Allied Powers
SCC	Security Consultative Committee
SIGINT	Signal intelligence
SOFA	Status of Forces Agreement
TMD	Theater Missile Defense
TMD-WG	Theater Missile Defense-Working Group
TMPD	Tokyo Metropolitan Police Department
UN	United Nations
UNMIS	UN Mission in Sudan
WMD	Weapons of Mass Destruction

PREFACE

Dear Colleagues,

It is with pleasure that I present *Japan's National Security Policy Infrastructure: Can Tokyo Meet Washington's Expectation?* by Yuki Tatsumi, Senior Associate at the Stimson Center. This is the latest volume in a series of works on Japan and its critical security alliance with the United States. In an era when we are focused on the rise of Asian powers and the realignment of geopolitical relationships in Asia, it is important to not lose sight of the central role that Japan, the most advanced economy in Asia, continues to play. From deployments in the Indian Ocean in support of coalition operations in Afghanistan and Iraq to an attempt to enhance the decision-making capability of the country's leadership, Japan's national security policies and practices have been trying to respond and adapt to new 21st century missions, after decades of self-imposed constraints on Japan's external engagements.

Ms. Tatsumi's new book is a unique contribution to our understanding of Japan's security policy community. It examines the core realities of how security policies are formulated and presented to decision-makers, and implemented once political choices are made. Ms. Tatsumi examines systematically all the key players in the Japanese system: the civilian agencies, the military services, the intelligence community, as well as the legal factors, including the prospects for constitutional reform. Her book concludes with important reflections on how the United States perceives these changes in Japan's security community, and whether mutual expectations in this key alliance relationship are satisfied.

The Stimson Center expresses special thanks to Allan Y. Song and the Smith Richardson Foundation for their support to this project. We hope that this volume will contribute to greater knowledge of Japan and its changing security community, in the interests of devising effective policies that promote peace in the vital East Asian region.

Sincerely,

Ellen Laipson

Ellen Laipson
President and CEO

ACKNOWLEDGMENTS

First and foremost, my deepest gratitude goes to the Smith Richardson Foundation for their generous support for my work. In particular, I am thankful that Allan Y. Song, the Foundation's senior program officer, had faith in me to support my project idea throughout the project period.

I also would not have been able to complete this book without the professionally nurturing environment at the Henry L. Stimson Center. I thank Ellen Laipson and Cheryl Ramp for supporting me with my efforts at the Center to develop its Japan program; Jane Dorsey and Alison Yost deserve enormous credit for providing valuable assistance at the final stage of the project. I also owe Junko Kobayashi special acknowledgement for helping me write a proposal that launched this project. And I am extremely grateful for Alan D. Romberg, Distinguished Fellow and Director of the Center's East Asia Program, for allowing me to pursue my own analytical interests. The Japan project interns—Aaron Young, Arthur Lord, Brian Clampitt, and Leslie Forgach—for spending endless hours proofreading my manuscript must be thanked for their efforts. In particular, Brian and Leslie have my respect for spending hours reading through my chapter drafts, helping to shape it into a publishable manuscript.

I can never thank enough those in the government, militaries, and academia in both the United States and Japan whom I have had the privilege to call my mentors. Throughout the project, they shared their insights with me in a way that I could not have hoped otherwise. I am particularly grateful to Masahiro Akiyama, Rust M. Deming, Michael J. Green, Mike M. Mochizuki, Andrew L. Oros, James J. Przystup, Robin "Sak" Sakoda, Nicholas Szechenyi, and Akihiko Tanaka for providing constructive criticism to improve my work.

Finally, my deep personal gratitude goes to Hideaki. As always, he was a master at keeping me in good spirit even through my thickest writer's blocks. I can never thank him enough for his confidence in me and support for my work.

Yuki Tatsumi
Senior Associate, East Asia Program
November 2008

— Introduction —

When I began to work on my first edited volume, *Japan's New Defense Establishment: Institutions, Capabilities and Implications,* in January 2005, expectations had been rising among policymakers in the United States that Japan would be a more engaging actor in international security affairs. Japan, following the 9-11 terrorist attacks in 2001, had made several unprecedented decisions under then Prime Minister Junichiro Koizumi. First, Japan decided to dispatch Maritime Self-Defense Force (JMSDF) vessels for a refueling mission in support of Operation Enduring Freedom (OEF) in November 2001. Then, in March 2002, it dispatch Ground Self-Defense Force (JGSDF) troops to East Timor. Finally, in November 2003, Japan dispatched the Air Self-Defense Force (JASDF) to Kuwait to provide transport support (as well as liaise with the US Central Command (US CENTCOM) headquarters in Qatar) and the Ground Self-Defense Force (JGSDF) to Iraq, both in support of Operation Iraqi Freedom (OIF). For Japan, the decision to send the JSDF to the overseas missions that do not have an explicit mandate from the United Nations (UN) was unprecedented. They were made possible largely thanks to the strong political will demonstrated by Prime Minister Koizumi.

Furthermore, Japan watchers in Washington—many of whom are proponents of Japan playing a greater role in security affairs as a US ally—were encouraged to witness certain developments in Japan that unfolded in tandem with these decisions. To start, in the first press conference after becoming prime minister, Koizumi argued that Japan should depart from the short-sighted habit of labeling proponents of constitutional revision as right-wing hawks. He further suggested that it is the responsibility of political leadership to establish legal and other frameworks in which the Japan Self-Defense Forces (JSDF) would receive the respect it deserves.[1] In December 2003, Japan decided to co-develop a ballistic missile defense (BMD) system with the United States, departing from its previous position that it was only willing to engage in "joint study" of BMD with the United States. In October 2004, the Council on Defense Capability and Security, a private advisory group for the prime minister that included former senior government officials and prominent scholars, issued its final report (better known as the Araki Report in the United States) that advocated Japan's more proactive role in international security affairs and realignment of the Japan Self-Defense Forces (JSDF) to that end. Drawing largely from the recommendation made in the Araki Report, Japan revised its *National Defense Program Guidelines* in December 2004. These decisions were interpreted in the

United States as signs that Japan, after six decades of hesitance, was finally willing to engage more internationally in the security arena, with the JSDF having a greater role therein.

By the time *Japan's New Defense Establishment* was published in March 2007, it seemed as though Washington's expectation of the trajectory of Japan's national security policy would grow even higher. The two allies completed the Defense Policy Review Initiative (DPRI) which they launched in December 2002. Under the framework of the DPRI, Tokyo and Washington sought to discuss ways to further expand and deepen alliance cooperation. The first joint document, announced on 19 February 2005, best reflected the sense that the US-Japan alliance was reaching a new level of depth and breadth. In this document, the two countries identified a number of "common strategic objectives" that included both regional and global goals.[2] The document signaled that the two countries were determined not only to adjust their bilateral alliance to face the security challenges of the new era, but also to grow the alliance into a global strategic partnership that reached well beyond the Asia-Pacific region.[3] The DPRI reached a critical juncture when the two sides agreed on one of the largest US force realignment packages in the history of the US-Japan alliance in May 2006 that included a large-scale relocation of US Marines out of Okinawa. The euphoric mood that surrounded the US-Japan relationship was coined in the phrase "one of the most accomplished bilateral relationships in history," in the joint statement adopted when Koizumi visited Washington for the last time as prime minister in June 2006.[4]

Shinzo Abe succeeded Koizumi as prime minister in September 2006. Abe's rise to the premiership was celebrated among the alliance managers in the United States as the first real chance for Japan to liberate itself from the institutional and legal legacy of the World War II and the Cold War that constrained Japan's national security policy. The prospect of constitutional revision in Japan began to be discussed with a certain sense of reality. No one in Washington thought that the revision would come easily, but at least the debate over constitutional revision appeared to have been placed on the political calendar and Abe appeared committed. While in office, Abe continued Koizumi's efforts to strengthen the prime minister's leadership in Japan's national security policy-making. Utilizing the provisions in the Cabinet Law, he appointed the Special Advisor in charge of National Security Affairs for the first time. He also began a serious study on establishing an American-style National Security Council in Japan as an organization to shape Japan's strategy and provide policy support for the prime minister. Further, Abe was determined to address the constitutional question. The National Referendum Law was one of the few major bills that Abe became personally involved in ensuring the Diet's approval, paving the way for eventual constitutional revision. While embattled with domestic issues and the scandals of his cabinet members, he also launched a study group that looked into the legal framework for Japan's national policy security, specifically eyeing the prospect of changing the Japanese government's standing interpretation of Japan's inability to exercise the right of collective self-defense at all times. When Abe proudly spoke that Japan would "not shy away from carrying out overseas activities involving the SDF, if it is for the sake of international peace and stability"[5] at his visit to the North Atlantic Treaty Organization (NATO) in January 2007, it was received by many in Washington as an indicator that Japan's national security policy was indeed on the cusp of the greatest transformation since 1945. Or, at least, so it was hoped.

I, however, felt uncomfortable with such an overjoyed characterization of the US-Japan alliance. Such statements often seemed to stand on two premises. First, it seemed premised that Japan was solidly on the path to become a more active player in security affairs under decisive leaders such as Koizumi and Abe. Second, such an outlook of a more proactive Japan also seemed to assume that Japan, at the end of the day, will find it in its interest to continue on a path that brought the US-Japan alliance closer to the US-UK alliance, just like the October 2000 Institute for National Strategic Studies (INSS) Special Report (better known as the first Armitage-Nye Report) visualized.

On the one hand, it was understandable why many experts in Washington made such assessments. The developments in Japan's national security policy between 2001 through 2007 demonstrate Japan's will to make an attempt to depart from its national security policy practices of the Cold War and to recast its fundamental organizing principle to better reflect the changes in the security environment and nature of security threats in the post-9/11 world. Both Koizumi and Abe seemed committed to strengthening the policy- and decision – making functions of the prime minister. They were also interested in strengthening Japan's national security policy institutions so that Japan could be more responsive to the evolving security environment in Japan for the 21st century. Internally, initiatives taken under Koizumi and Abe seemed to reflect good-faith efforts by senior security policy experts both inside and outside the Japanese government in this regard.

On the other hand, I detected signs that suggest the changes Japan has been making to its national security policy institutions and its policies may have not taken deep roots. The DPRI process turned out to be protracted and painful. Fraught with the bureaucratic infighting in Japan, with the Ministry of Defense (MOD) determined—perhaps over-determined—to take the lead vis-à-vis the Ministry of Foreign Affairs (MOFA) in the negotiation, it revealed insufficient institutionalization for the coordination among Japan's national security policy agencies.[6] The MOD's unwillingness to coordinate with the other agencies, particularly its tendency to reject other agencies' engagements in the discussion within the Japanese government on the DPRI, was often criticized not only by MOFA officials, but also those in the Cabinet Secretariat. A senior MOFA official once criticized MOD representatives who were on the DPRI negotiation team by saying that "no one in the MOD delegation seems to understand the DPRI-related issues as a total package… they only study the talking points that matter to the specific issues that they work on."[7] A Cabinet Secretariat official also lamented that while the DPRI was the classic case in which the negotiation position needed to be shaped through interagency discussion under the facilitation of the Cabinet Secretariat, it had not been able to play the facilitator's role because the MOD too often kept them out of the loop.[8]

Of particular concern were two factors that remained constant while the changes were being made in Japan. For one, Japanese leaders had not invested much effort in institutionalizing a process to shape national security strategy. Not only does the prime minister not have intellectual, institutional and personnel support to help plan Japan's national security strategy, the interagency coordination process continues to be influenced by the personalities that are involved in the process and their personal relationships with one another.[9] Moreover, although policies were changing and institutions seemed to be evolving, not much progress had been made in identifying Japan's national security interests and discussing its vision of its role in the world. In particular, there has been very little discussion on how Japan should use its enforcement organizations—the Japan Self-Defense Forces (JSDF), Japan Coast Guard (JCG) and police forces—in an integrated manner in order to defend the country from various threats at home and promote its national security interests abroad.[10] With these two factors changing very little, it was doubtful to me how sustainable the changes that Japan underwent after 2001 would be in the post-Koizumi, post-Abe Japan.

Reflecting on the developments since then, I cannot help but be humbled by the turn of events, and how much has considerably changed in the landscape for Japan's national security policy infrastructure. Shinzo Abe's unexpected resignation in September 2007 was met with a resounding sense of disappointment in Washington—there was a distinct sense that political leaders who were willing to champion a more active Japan in the security arena suddenly disappeared. When Prime Minister Yasuo Fukuda took office in September 2007 after Shinzo Abe's resignation, it was clear that Fukuda wanted to take a more cautionary approach to national security policy. Many of the initiatives launched by Abe—including the creation of a US-style National

Security Council in the Cabinet Secretariat and the discussion by the Advisory Committee on the right of collective self-defense—were either suspended or hastily terminated with very little impact on the government's policy and no concrete prospect to be resurrected. Consequently, despite the efforts under Koizumi and Abe, some of the most critical institutional changes necessary for Japan's national security policy infrastructure are still left unaddressed today. Many of the changes that were made since 2001 remain incomplete, and still need to be either legislated or equipped with a more effective enforcement mechanism in order to survive the leadership change and have a sustainable impact. Being preoccupied with domestic issues, and its political landscape looking as uncertain as the early 1990s, all Japan can do seems to be the bare minimum so that it will not be completely isolated from the world and damage the US-Japan alliance. It looks as though today's Japan is at a standstill in the process of strengthening its national security institutions.

The change of mood in Japan also began to affect the tone of the alliance relationship. Frustration mounted as Washington and Tokyo faced slower-than-expected progress in US force realignment in Japan. Equally slow progress in bilateral discussions on the divisions of roles and missions between the US forces and the JSDF also made Washington question Tokyo's willingness to take the necessary steps to realize deepening alliance cooperation at a military-to-military level. There was a great sense of disappointment and frustration when the Japanese government had to suspend the JMSDF vessels' refueling operation in the Indian Ocean after the Anti-Terror Special Measures Law expired on 1 November 2007. Taken together, there is a growing sense of uncertainty in Washington about where Japan is going in its national security policy, what can and cannot be expected from Japan, and whether what can be expected from Japan will be enough for the United States to maintain its national interests in Asia and beyond.

From Washington's perspective, it is easy to blame a certain group—politicians, bureaucrats— it does not matter who—for the lack of progress in the way that Japan conducts its national security policy, and to criticize Japan for not being able to carry its share of responsibility. But if one pauses for a moment, it seems the United States has always been complaining about Japan's inability to meet US expectations. From the very beginning of the US-Japan alliance, Japan has been placed in a position of having a constitution that essentially banned Japan from having any form of military force on the one hand, yet feeling constant pressure to become a more reliable ally for the United States on the other. For instance, when the United States first began to discuss rearmament with Japan in the outset of the Korean War, despite the fact that the constitution that banned Japan from having armed forces was enacted only a few years prior,

Washington envisioned that Japan would ultimately rearm itself to include a ground force of approximately 350,000 personnel. When the Self-Defense Forces was officially established in 1954, however, Japan had a ground force of 130,000.[11] Furthermore, when the United States asked Japan to allow the SDF to participate in the multinational force during the 1990-91 Gulf War, Japan was only able to dispatch SDF minesweepers after the conflict was declared to be over. Additionally, when the United States wanted Japan to send SDF troops to Iraq, it took the Japanese government months to reach a decision despite then Prime Minister Koizumi's immediate expression of support for the US war in Iraq. Thus, one can argue that US experience with Japan has been characterized as a history of US expecting more than Japan can deliver.

This begs one question: why does Japan "fail to meet" US expectations? Is it because Japan has not tried hard enough, or is because US expectations of Japan have simply been unrealistic? This question is especially relevant today, when there are growing questions regarding Japan's future course in its security policy after US-Japan relations reached an all-time high under Koizumi.

There is no question that the policy statements coming out of Tokyo regarding its national security policy and vision of the US-Japan alliance has undergone considerable evolution, particularly in the last five years. Today, Japan openly acknowledges that the US-Japan alliance is one of the core pillars of Japan's national security policy. Japan also acknowledges that it needs to strengthen its own efforts to defend the country.[12] Furthermore, as of March 2007, Japan has deployed the JSDF overseas over twenty times for disaster relief, humanitarian assistance, peacekeeping operations, and other multinational operations (including Operation Enduring Freedom and Operation Iraqi Freedom) since 1991.[13] Considering that Japan once had a prime minister that refused to characterize the US-Japan alliance as a military alliance[i] and a major opposition party that considered the Self-Defense Forces unconstitutional,[ii] this is a change whose significance must not be overlooked. However, any policy statement that suggests a significant change in Japan's national security policy needs to be examined from the perspective of whether appropriate changes in policy infrastructure accompany the proposed policy.

---

[i] Zenko Suzuki, who served as Japan's prime minister 1980-82, responded to the Japanese press' question by saying that the word "*doumei* (alliance)" that was referred to in the joint declaration during his visit to Washington in May 1981 had no "military meaning" Tanaka, *ibid.* 289-290.

[ii] It was not until 1994 when Tomiichi Murayama, then the leader of the Social Democratic Party of Japan (SDPJ), became the prime minister that the SDPJ, the biggest opposition party throughout the Cold War, abandoned its position that deemed the JSDF as unconstitutional.

This volume intends to provide a "close-up" look of Japan's national security policy infrastructure. "Infrastructure," in general terms, can be defined in the following three ways:

- The underlying foundation or basic framework (of a system or organization);
- The permanent installations required for military purposes; or
- The system of public works of a country, state, or region; *also*: the resources (such as personnel, buildings, or equipment) required for an activity.[14]

When applied to the government, the term "policy infrastructure" can be defined as *an organizational arrangement that supports the government shaping and executing the policies to achieve its goals.*[15] Given this definition, Japan's national security policy infrastructure in this volume will cover the following institutions:

- Civilian government agencies that set national security policy priorities;
- Uniform institutions that enforces the policies;
- Intelligence community that provides information critical for the leadership and civilian agencies to develop policies and make decisions, and for the uniform institution to take action on; and
- Legal framework that provides legitimacy in the government's policy decision and enforcement actions.

By closely examining each element of Japan's national security policy infrastructure, this volume attempts to assess the capacity that the Japanese government has to implement its current policy and to identify where structural challenges remain. Then, it will match its assessment with current expectations held by the United States to see if they are realistic or not. This volume will also contemplate what policies the United States can take to ensure that its interests in the Asia-Pacific region are ensured in the event that US current expectations of Japan are unrealistic.

Chapter 1 will provide a general overview of postwar Japan's national security policy. Based on analysis of policy documents that emerged as part of Japan's efforts to reorient its security policy in response to changes in the security environment after 9/11, this chapter seeks to examine how Japan's national security policy priorities got to where they are today. Following the establishment of Japan's national security policy priorities in the era of 9-11, the chapter ends with the identification of the requirements for Japan's national security policy infrastructure in order for Japan to accomplish its security policy goals.

Chapter 2 will question whether the civilian national security institutions in the Japanese government have sufficient institutional capacity to support Japanese security policy goals. This chapter will attempt to evaluate how civilian agencies that have responsibilities within national security policymaking in Japan—namely the Ministry of Foreign Affairs (MOFA), the National Policy Agency (NPA), the civilian side (the Internal Bureau) in the Ministry of Defense (MOD), the Cabinet Secretariat—currently work with one other in executing national security policy decisions.

Chapter 3 will examine how the entities that employ physical force in implementing the national security policy are organized and interact with one another. The focus of this chapter will be on the Japan Self-Defense Forces, the Japan Coast Guard (JCG), and the police forces in Japan's forty seven prefectures. Implications of the recent reorganization proposal by the Defense Minister Shigeru Ishiba—namely the merger of the Internal Bureau and the staff offices of the three JSDF services—will be examined here as well.

Chapter 4 will look at Japan's intelligence community. Each agency that is a member of Japan's intelligence community will be examined on its organizational and institutional characteristics. The chapter also explores the challenges that Japan's intelligence community face as it reorganizes itself to become more centralized, focused on providing policy-relevant intelligence to the prime minister.

Chapter 5 will trace developments in the legal framework that supports Japanese national security policy. Which laws apply to what scenarios, where gaps in the current legal framework may be, and the measures to fill such gaps will be examined. Furthermore, the status and future prospects of the debate on constitutional reform and other legal constraints limiting proactive security policies (such as the self-imposed ban on the right of collective self-defense, the effectively total ban of arms export and the prohibition of using space for national security purposes) will be discussed in detail.

Chapter 6 will assess whether the recent changes to the existing institutions, as well as the developments in the legal framework, amount to the progress in the key elements of Japan's national security policy infrastructure identified in Chapter 1. The chapter essentially offers a "report card" on Japan's effort to develop its national security infrastructure in order to meet its policy goals. The chapter also examines whether the political dynamism in Tokyo today and the near future will facilitate the progress.

Chapter 7 looks at the evolution of US expectations of Japan. It particularly focuses on the changes in Washington's expectations of Tokyo in the area of national security policy in the post-Cold War era. The purpose of the chapter is to explore what the United States really expects of Japan as its ally. Further, it attempts to evaluate if there is a gap between the actual US expectation of Japan and what Japan can actually accomplish.

Summing up the observations made in the preceding chapters, the volume concludes with analyses and observation on whether Japan has the capacity to meet the expectations of the United States. Particularly drawing on the assessments in Chapters 6 and 7, this chapter will present a list of factors that US policymakers should keep in mind as the United States continues its efforts to further deepen its security relationship with Japan.

This volume builds on *Japan's New Defense Establishment: Institutions, Capabilities and Implications,* which I worked on with Andrew Oros of Washington College. As pleased as I am with the year-long collaborative project, it also left a number of areas, mostly internal to Japan's national security policy-making and policy-execution system, unexplored. This book attempts to reach into some of these untapped territories.

At the same time, the volume is by no means an exhaustive study of Japan's national security policy infrastructure. There are a couple of areas that were left outside of this volume which demand further study. One example is the issue of resources for national security in Japan. The last few years witnessed the consecutive decline of Japan's national defense budget. However, while cutting the MOD budget, the Japanese government has invested in, for instance, the Japan Coast Guard.[16] Further, Japan's information-gathering satellite, while pronounced to be multi-purpose, has been predominantly used for intelligence collection for national security purposes,[17] but its operating budget for the system is included in the Cabinet Secretariat's annual budget. How Japan allocates its fiscal resources for national security is still an unexplored area which goes well beyond the conventional discussion of defense procurements. This is one area in which future analyses is called for.

Another area that remains unexplored is Japan's arms export policy. It is widely known that Japan self-imposed a stringent set of restrictions that essentially prohibit arms exports. The rising cost of advanced defense systems recently encouraged the debate on whether this practice should be revised. However, less discussed is the real impact in case the current interpretation of the Three Principles of Arms Exports is revised to allow Japanese industries to export technologies and items for weapons. How does that affect the current defense industry in Japan, which essentially only includes heavy industry? How does it affect the current defense industrial cooperation between Japan and the United States? Again, these are unexplored areas that beg further study.

An equally important issue to be explored in the future is Japan's arms procurement practices. In fact, when the project was first conceived, the defense acquisition was included in the area of examination. However, several months into the project, the theme of defense acquisition in Japan became a politically sensitive topic when former Vice Defense Minister Takemasa Moriya was arrested for exercising favoritism in some of the acquisition decisions made by the MOD. Following the outbreak of the charge, the efforts began both inside and outside the MOD to re-examine the acquisition process altogether. Provided that these efforts are still ongoing, I determined that it is best to wait until more studies come out to tackle this issue.

As in *Japan's New Defense Establishment,* the term "national security" focuses very much on the dimension of security that protects a nation state from physical threats, whether they may be external or internal, conventional or non-conventional. Its scope is similar to what Christopher W. Hughes defines as the "military dimension" of security,[18] or what Akihiko Tanaka describes as *kokka anzen hosho* (national security).[19] It is my hope that this book, even with its flaws, will offer a peeking window into the often opaque Japanese national security policy infrastructure.

— 1 —
EVOLUTION OF JAPANESE NATIONAL SECURITY POLICY

In June 2006, at the time of then-Prime Minister Junichiro Koizumi's visit to the United States, the United States and Japan issued a joint statement in which Koizumi and President George W. Bush described the US-Japan alliance as "a global alliance."[20] This was reaffirmed when former Prime Minister Shinzo Abe visited Washington in April 2007.[21] It is true that the expansion of the scope of the US-Japan alliance—particularly the series of events following the September 2001 terrorist attacks—is remarkable. Given that the US-Japan alliance began as a bulwark against the communist threat embodied by the Soviet Union, its evolution since the 1990s is a fascinating phenomenon. Today, the two countries not only coordinate their approaches to traditional national security issues (both regional and functional) but also seek to cooperate in combating non-traditional security challenges. The areas of bilateral cooperation go well beyond what the alliance originally intended to respond to, such as invasion attempts against Japan and large-scale security crises in East Asia. In fact, Tokyo and Washington both reaffirmed publicly that they share a partnership based on mutual values and interests, with the US-Japan alliance having a global reach.

Such a change would not have been possible without the evolution of Japan's national security policy. Indeed, the changes in Japan's national security policy, particularly following the end of the Cold War, have been remarkable—it was only two decades ago that Japanese leaders rejected the notion that the US-Japan alliance had a military element.[iii] Several factors contributed to this evolution occurring in the 1990s and onward.

Japan's national security policy is difficult to identify. Rather, Japan's national security policy can only be identified by putting together the information in multiple official documents, legislative actions, and statements by Japanese leadership. Doing so reveals that Japan's national security policy can be divided into three periods—Cold War, post-Cold War, and post-9/11. This section

---

[iii] Zenko Suzuki, then Japanese prime minister, made the comment to this effect after his visit to the United States in 1981.

provides an observation on the basic principles of Japan's national security policy in each period.

COLD WAR

Japan's Cold War national security policy principles were based on what is known as the "Yoshida Doctrine." In the aftermath of World War II, Japan was wary of military power. Political leaders, the media and the public all blamed the military for leading Japan down the expansionist path, which ultimately resulted in Japan's unconditional surrender to the allied nations on 15 August 1945. Thus, it was almost instinctive for Japan to reject anything in its immediate postwar years that was in any way affiliated with the military. In those days, the military was not the area in which Japan wanted to invest its limited resources. In fact, it was the last. Shigeru Yoshida—who led the immediate postwar Japan through the occupation until Japan regained sovereignty in 1954—considered economic recovery the most important national agenda for Japan at that time. With the country's wariness toward military power, the "Yoshida Doctrine" focused primarily on the nation's economic recovery as a means to regain independence and status in the international community.

Instead, Japan sought the outside world for the source of its security. Japan expected that the United Nations (UN) would play the primary role in maintaining the world's peace and security in post-World War II. When it became clear, with the division during the Cold War, that such an expectation was unrealistic, Japan still did not reorient its national security policy to place a greater emphasis in security policy. Instead, it turned to the United States as its primary protector. The original *Security Treaty between Japan and the United States of America*, signed in 1951, was an unequal treaty.[22] On the one hand, it spoke to Japan's expectation of the United States: it states that a disarmed Japan would request the United States station some of its forces in Japan in order to protect Japan from external aggression. On the other hand, the original treaty allowed the United States to use its military stationed in Japan to maintain peace and stability in the Far East, as well as to respond to attempts to invade Japan and/or disrupt its domestic order.[23]

Japan signed *the Treaty of Mutual Cooperation and Security between Japan and the United States of America* (more commonly referred to as the US-Japan Security Treaty) in 1960. Although the inequality in the original treaty was corrected and the US-Japan Security Treaty had become more reciprocal, Japan's military role in the alliance was still extremely limited. While Article Five of the treaty obligates the US military to respond when an armed attack against Japanese territory takes place, the JSDF does not have a treaty obligation to reciprocate when an armed attack against US territory occurs.[24]

Japan established achievement of its security through non-military means as the core principle of its national security policy. It is noteworthy that the US-Japan Security Treaty functioned to reinforce the low profile of the military element in Japan's national security policy. The Treaty essentially established the bilateral security system that is reciprocal yet asymmetrical: the United States would be committed to the defense of Japan, provide strategic guarantees and a nuclear umbrella, while Japan would develop the capability for national defense, host US forces, and provide host-nation support.[25] The military role for Japan, even under the alliance was strictly limited to the defense of Japan.

As Japan emphasizes the dominance of non-military (or perhaps even anti-military) elements in its national security policy, the concept "comprehensive security" (*sogo anzen hosho*) emerged as the notion to describe Japan's security policy strategy during the Cold War. Comprehensive security can be defined as the principle that links national security in terms of defense from aggression with others, broader non-military policy goals, and sets policies in such a way that optimizes non-military measures.[26] In other words, it was an antithesis to the notion that military power, as the central element in a country's national security policy, would enhance the nation's national security. In fact, it was believed that military power played very little visible role in Japan's national security policy during the Cold War. The Japan Self-Defense Forces (JSDF), originally established as the police reserve, was not considered a military. Unlike a regular military, it did not have military law or a court martial. Further, it was not organized with the prospect of overseas dispatches in mind, either. Its personnel did not have the status of a soldier or military officer—they were considered civil servants, like diplomats, policeman and other government employees. All in all, the JSDF was regarded as an organization that existed for defending Japan from external aggression, and helping police maintain public order—not a professional military organization.

The notion of comprehensive security was articulated most clearly by the Study group on Comprehensive Security, a private policy advisory council that was convened by then Prime Minister Masayoshi Ohira in 1979. Headed by Masamichi Inoki, then serving as the president of the Research Institute of Peace and Security, the study group consisted of a diverse set of former bureaucrats, academics, and non-government intellectuals, which deliberated on not only conventional military security, but also economic security, energy security and food security. The final report by the Study Group, submitted to

Acting Prime Minister Masayoshi Ito in July 1980,[iv] defined national security as "the means to protect people's lives from various threats." It then suggested that the efforts to maintain security have three components: (1) efforts to eliminate threats and thereby make the international environment more favorable; (2) self-help efforts to cope with threats; and (3) efforts to work with countries that share values and interests to ensure security and make the international environment favorable.[27]

The report suggested that Japan should pursue its national security policy goals by utilizing numerous means. Specifically, it proposed that the Japanese government pursue a comprehensive security strategy by tackling the national security institution reform that would include the following:

- Ensure that the Diet holds serious and substantive discussion on security issues, particularly at a newly-established Committee on National Security

- Establish a framework under which security issues can be seriously studied in academia ensure that a range of government agencies—not only the Japan Defense Agency (JDA), but also other agencies such as the Ministry of Foreign Affairs (MOFA), Ministry of Finance (MOF), Ministry of Agriculture, Forests and Fisheries, Ministry of International Trade and Industry (now METI), and the National Land Agency—maintain the perspective of comprehensive security as they formulate their respective policies

- Establish a "National Comprehensive Security Council" to replace the existing but dormant National Defense Council

- Establish a system that allows the prime minister constant access to information that ensures his/her to effectively exercise leadership and oversight.[28]

While stressing the importance of achieving national security policy goals by using military and non-military measures, the report was noteworthy in recognizing the potential challenge in the very small role Japan's military power played in Japan's national security policy. Specifically, the report was concerned about the low awareness on defense issues among the public, lack of an institutionalized process for the government to respond to national security challenges, and a near-complete reliance on the United States for Japan's

---

[iv] Prime Minister Ohira unexpectedly passed away in June 1980.

external security.[29] It is also notable that the report criticized the polarization of the security policy discourse between two extreme ideological groups; between the proponents for an autonomous and large-scale defense buildup and the supporters of complete disarmament. The report particularly blamed the Diet for its failure to have thoughtful discussion on security issues, aggravating the lack of discourse.[30]

While recognizing that there was not enough attention on the military element of the national security policy, the report asserted that Japan anticipated a minimal role for its military power during the Cold War. For instance, while lamenting that too few in Japan knew about national defense issues, the report did not recommend the provision of greater capability to the JDA and/or the JSDF. Even though the report discussed the undesirability of Japan continuing its over-reliance on the United States for its security, it did not propose concrete measures by which Japan could be a more equal security partner for the United States. Most of all, the recommendation to replace the National Defense Council with the National Comprehensive Security Council was evidence that national defense was a minor part in the country's national security policy. Given this background, Japan's national security policy during the Cold War had three basic principles—a limited role of military power, reliance on the US-Japan alliance to ensure its external security, and efforts to achieve its security through other means of national power such as diplomatic efforts to strengthen international institutions and economic measures.

Japan's commitment to the principle of keeping the role of military power limited is manifested in the Japanese government's decision to take a minimalist approach to its defense capability buildup. The 1957 Basic Principles of National Defense (*Kokubo no Kihon Hoshin*) is illustrative of Japan's such decision. It suggests that Japan's defense capability should (1) support the United Nations; (2) stabilize public life and acquire defense capabilities that are necessary for self-defense; and (3) address aggression attempts by using the US-Japan security system until the United Nations possesses the capacity to effectively intervene in conflicts.[31] While Yasuhiro Nakasone, when serving as Japan's prime minister between 1982–87, tried to stress the importance of Japan strengthening its autonomous defense capability, Japan's approach toward national security policy remained fundamentally unchanged in its emphasis on non-military elements as a means to protect peace for Japan.[v]

---

[v] For the comprehensive review of Japan's foreign policy under Prime Minister Yasuhiro Nakasone, see Thayer, Nathaniel B. 'Japanese foreign policy in the Nakasone Years" in Curtis, Gerald L. ed. *Japan's Foreign Policy After the Cold War: Coping With Change* (New York: M.E. Sharpe 1993) 90–104.

Further, Japan's decision to restrict the role of military in its security policy has led to its extremely strict interpretation of the constitution on when Japan could employ its military force. To begin with, Article Nine of the Japanese constitution states that Japan renounce war as a means to settle international disputes, forgoing the right to possess military forces as well as the right of belligerency.[32] This becomes an issue when Japan established the Japan Self-Defense Forces (JSDF) in 1954. The constitution unambiguously prohibits Japan from possessing a military force. How could, then, the Japanese government justify the creation of the JSDF? Simply put, the Japanese government opted to argue that:

- Even the constitution does not deny Japan the right of self-defense. However, since Japan renounced the use of force to settle international disputes, it can only defend itself. In other words, the Japanese constitution only allows Japan to exercise the right of individual self-defense, *not* the right of collective self-defense; and

- To have the JSDF is an organization of self-defense and therefore is not considered as war potential, the entity that the Constitution prohibits.[33]

The prohibition of the right of collective self-defense and related arguments were also utilized by the Japanese government to justify the US-Japan alliance to the Diet and to the Japanese public. The Japanese government argued that its obligations under the US-Japan Security Treaty would not require Japan to exercise the right of collective self-defense, referring to Article Five of the US-Japan Security Treaty in which both countries' commitments to the defense of Japan and the territory under the Japanese government's control are articulated.[34] The Japanese government even argued that the use of force by the JSDF to protect US military bases in Japan with the United States was considered the exercise of individual collective self-defense, because Japan would be under direct military attack when US military bases in Japan are physically threatened.[35] Even Japan's support for US efforts to maintain stability in the Far East—the situation provided in Article Six of the US-Japan Security Treaty—was explained as being consistent with Japan's self-imposed ban on the right of collective self-defense.

The third principle of Japan's national security policy—utilizes non-military means to ensure its security—was demonstrated primarily through its effort to become the world's major player in the international economy. Such an effort started at home: Japan focused on rebuilding its economy through the combination of an export-driven trade policy and the industrial policy that focused on nurturing advanced technology. These policies brought about a dramatic economic growth for Japan. Japan's exports experienced a 114-fold increase from 1955 to 1987.[36] The Japanese government sought to capitalize on the country's economic growth to increase Japan's international standing. It had done so by increasing the contribution to international institutions such as the UN, the World Bank, the Asian Development Bank, and the International Monetary Fund (IMF). It also considerably increased its foreign aid and official development assistance (ODA). By 1990, Japan had become not only the world's largest creditor, but also the world's largest foreign aid donor. Even in the UN, Japan had become the second largest contributor after the United Nations, shouldering approximately 11.5 % of the UN budget.[37]

In addition to these basic principles, Japan self-imposed additional restrictions to ensure the low-profile of its military. Three of such restrictions should be noted for its long-lasting impact on Japan's national security policy. First is the restriction on arms exports. It began first as a limited set of principles. Japan's Foreign Exchange and Foreign Trade Law only dictates that the exports of weapons require the approval by the Minister of International Trade and Industry (now the Minister of Economy, Trade and Industry). In 1967, the Japanese government under the Sato Cabinet then adopted the Three Principles of Arms Exports which banned arms exports to (1) communist countries; (2) countries that are subject to UN sanctions; and (3) countries at conflict, or those that are likely to be involved in conflicts.[38] This restriction was further tightened in 1976 when the Japanese government under the Miki Cabinet determined that Japan should stay away from exporting arms even to the countries that would not meet the conditions set forth in the Three Principles of Arms Exports.[39] This effectively has banned Japan from exporting arms ever since.[40]

The restriction on the use of outer space also began as a non-binding principle. In 1969, the Japanese Diet passed a non-legally-binding resolution that limited Japan's use of outer space to "non-military purposes."[41] Since then, the Japanese government has prevented itself from using outer space for national security purposes, including reconnaissance and surveillance. The principle was codified when the National Space Development Agency of Japan (NASDA, *Uchu Kaihatsu Jigyodan*), the agency responsible for space development in Japan until 2003, was established in June 1969[vi]: the agency was given a mandate to engage in the development of Japan's satellite technology that is to be used only for "peaceful purposes".[42] This limited the scope of Japan's space policy to that of scientific exploration with no national security application.

[vi] NASDA, the Institute of Space and Astronautical Science (ISAS) and the National Aerospace Laboratory of Japan (NAL) were consolidated into the Japan Aerospace Exploration Agency (JAXA) in October 2003.

While Japan has had an indigenous reconnaissance satellite system in operation since 2003, it is given the name "information-gathering satellite (ISG)" to downplay the degree of participation in the program by then Japan Defense Agency (JDA, now the Ministry of Defense, or MOD),[43] despite the critical role that imagery analysts seconded from the JDA to the Satellite Intelligence Center, have played in its ISG operation. Such a separation of space development and national security continued until the Japanese government enacted the Basic Law for Space (*Uchu Kihon Ho*) in 2008. The law provides that the Japanese government should be mindful of national security interest in the space development program.[44]

Finally, through policy and legislative decisions made in the 1950s and 1960s, Japan has established the principle that it would not acquire nuclear weapons. Possession of nuclear weapons is considered constitutional in Japan: in 1958, then Prime Minister Nobusuke Kishi stated that Japan had chosen a policy of not developing nuclear weapons although nuclear weapons with defensive characteristics would be considered constitutional.[45] Japan's commitment to not becoming a nuclear weapon state is codified by Japan signing *the US-Japan Cooperative Agreement on Nuclear Power* in 1955. The 1955 Nuclear Power Basic Law (*Genshi-ryoku Kihon-ho*), adopted following Japan's signing of *the US-Japan Cooperative Agreement on Nuclear Power*, declared Japan's intention to use nuclear energy only for "peaceful purposes."[46] While not legally binding, Japan's non-nuclear commitment was also expressed in the policy speech delivered by Prime Minister Eisaku Sato in 1968, in which he established the "four pillars of Japan's non-nuclear policy" as:

- Three Non-Nuclear Principles (no nuclear weapon possession, production, or introduction);[47]
- Nuclear disarmament and arms control;
- Reliance on US nuclear deterrence; and
- Peaceful use of nuclear energy.[48]

Finally, Japan's signing of the Nuclear Non-Proliferation Treaty (NPT) in 1974 solidified Japan's non-nuclear policy.

With these restrictions in place, Japan's postwar security policy has focused on minimizing the role of its conventional military power. When the United States entered a period of détente with the Soviet Union, however, Japan's external environment began to change. In his speech in Guam on 25 July 1969, US president Richard Nixon essentially abandoned the basic position of US national security strategy that the United States would more or less function as the world's policeman. Rather, Nixon declared that each US ally now held primary responsibility for its own national defense, and that the United States would come to its aid only when it failed to respond to the threat.[49] Even after attempts for détente failed and the tension between the United States and the Soviet Union rose again under the Carter administration, this shift in US strategy remained in place. If anything, as the US policy toward the Soviet Union hardened following the Soviet invasion in Afghanistan in 1979, the US demand on Japan to boost its own defense capabilities grew.[50]

In order to adapt to such a change in US strategy, rather than conducting a fundamental review of the premises of its security policy, Japan instead opted to respond by adjusting its military buildup. The notion known as the Basic Defense Capability Concept (*Kiban-teki Boueiryoku Kousou*) emerged while Japan attempted to adjust to the change in US global strategy. In essence, the Basic Concept was based on the idea that Japan's defense capability should be at the level where it would not create a power vacuum in East Asia, yet restrained enough to be considered exclusively defense-oriented. This approach was completely opposite to a threat-based approach to force build-up, as its primary focus was on what it takes for Japan not to become vulnerable to aggression rather than what type of capability Japan needs to develop to meet a certain threat.[51]

The National Defense Program Outline (*Bouei Keikaku no Taiko*) that was adopted in 1976 was a reflection of the Basic Defense Capability Concept. It affirmed that Japan contributes to the stability of the region by maintaining a posture that, combined with the US-Japan security system, (1) deters aggression, and (2) repels aggression when it occurs. The Outline argues that, given the ongoing efforts to stabilize the international security environment, Japan should anticipate no drastic change in the international or regional environment for the time being in assessing the appropriate level of defense capability.

The NDPO then articulates that the most appropriate defense posture for Japan is one in which Japan is

> *Equipped with various functions that are necessary for defense, well-balanced in its organization and deployment including its logistical support system, and is capable of providing sufficient defense during peacetime, responding effectively to limited and small-scale invasion, and being deployable for disaster relief and other missions that could contribute to the stability of public livelihood.*[52]

When the NDPO was announced, the Chief Cabinet Secretary stated that the document aimed at "maintaining the same quantitative size of Japanese defense capability while pursuing a qualitative improvement."[53]

The 1976 NDPO translated such policy aspirations into a concrete list of priority areas in which Japan should enhance its capabilities—namely, reconnaissance/surveillance, countermeasures for "indirect" acts of invasion (including penetration of foreign agents and illegal activities, and incursion to Japanese airspace) in the areas surrounding Japanese territory, repelling direct threats to territory, and logistical support, education and training, and disaster relief.[54] It also set specific force build-up goals for the JSDF, as outlined below:

- JGSDF: balanced deployment of divisions that would allow a timely and effective response to aggressions from any part of Japan; at minimum, one unit that is mobile and can operate flexibly; and surface-to-air missile capabilities that can take charge of lower altitude air defense in critical areas.

- JMSDF: at least one destroyer group that can be mobile and deployed flexibly at a moments' notice at all times; at least one surface ship fleet that can be readily available to counter incursion by submarines; submarines, anti-submarine fixed-wing aircrafts, and minesweeping units to patrol, defend and sweep mines as necessary; and anti-submarine fixed-wing aircrafts for reconnaissance, patrol, and maritime escort.

- JASDF: air patrol units that cover the entire Japanese airspace and its vicinity at all times; fighters and surface-to-air guidance missiles for high altitude air defense for the purpose of countering invasion of airspace; and units that can be deployed to repel ground invasion as well as support ground operations, aerial reconnaissance, early-warning systems and air transportation.[55]

Established without revising the Basic Principles of National Defense, the force build-up goals under the 1976 NDPO surely jump-started SDF modernization efforts. By the mid-1980s, the JSDF had become one of the most advanced militaries in the world at the time, with more than 200,000 personnel and state-of-the-art weapon platforms. Despite such a change in its defense posture, however, the core of Japan's security policy—relying to a great extent on the United States for its military security while trying to secure its place in the world through alternative means, such as the economy—remained unchanged throughout the Cold War. The role that the JDA played was restrictive, with many of its activities kept away from the public.[56]

POST COLD-WAR

The Cold War ended rather abruptly when the Berlin Wall came down in November 1989 and US president George H. W. Bush met with Soviet president Mikhail Gorbachev in Malta in December. The world celebrated the end of the Cold War, anticipating that an era of peace with an undivided world would finally arrive.

However, such a hope quickly vanished when Saddam Hussein invaded Kuwait on August 2, 1990. After painstaking efforts by the international community failed, the United States formed a multinational force based on UN Security Council resolution 687. The Gulf War broke out when the multinational force began bombing Iraq on 17 January 1991 and ended 100 days later when combat operations ceased on 28 February. In April 1991, the multinational force and Iraq reached an armistice. Through the Gulf War, the world learned that the end of the Cold War did not necessarily mean world peace—rather, it could mean that conflict and tension that had been suppressed in the bipolar world would emerge and make the security environment unpredictable and volatile.

For Japan, the Gulf War turned out to be a bitter pill to swallow: in fact, it was Japan's rocky introduction into the post-Cold War world. Even though Japan made a considerable financial contribution in the total amount of thirteen billion dollars, this contribution was largely unappreciated by the international community. To make matters worse, Japan's failure to allow the SDF to participate in the multinational force operation led the international community to criticize Japan's "checkbook diplomacy." Japan's belated dispatch of minesweepers in the Persian Gulf was for the most part considered "too little, too late." When the government of Kuwait passed a resolution to thank the members of the international community who helped liberate Kuwait, Japan was not included. To put it simply, the Gulf War showed Japan that its economic power alone would not be enough to gain respect from the international community and yield influence.[57]

Furthermore, several external incidents reminded Japan that albeit the Cold War had ended, the security situation surrounding Japan not only remained dangerous, but also far more unpredictable and fluid with the disappearance of an overarching Soviet threat. The first such incident was the 1993 North Korea nuclear crisis. The 1995 underground nuclear test by China, the 1996 Taiwan Strait crisis, the 1998 and 1999 North Korean missile tests, and the 1999 North

Korean spy ship incident followed. In particular, the inability of Japan and the United States to come up with a bilateral operational plan to respond at the time of the 1993 North Korean nuclear crisis exposed the vulnerability of the alliance. While an open military clash was averted at the last minute in both the North Korean and Taiwan crises, the bilateral consultations that took place during the crisis forced government officials of both countries to acknowledge that the existing defense cooperative mechanism would not be operational.[58] What particularly concerned the US and Japanese officials was that Japan seemed neither able nor willing to provide much in support for the US military under these circumstances.[59] Ironically, just as the global strategic environment began to change in a way that stressed non-traditional security challenges, these incidents in Japan's neighborhood began to make Japan focus more on conventional security threats.

Finally, the incompetence that the Japanese government showed in responding to domestic crises such as the 1995 Sarin gas attack by Aum Shinrikyo and the 1995 Hanshin-Awaji earthquake made many in Japan question whether the Japanese government was properly equipped with a system, legal or otherwise, to protect its people's lives. Global concerns for the stability of information systems at the turn of the century (the so-called Y2K problem) also raised awareness of the vulnerability of Japan's computer network.

All these factors had a compound effect on the discourse of security policy in Japan. The discussion within Japan had a single goal: to raise Japan's profile in international security affairs by making a "visible" (*menimieru*) contribution. As Michael J. Green noted, one can also argue that the debate centered around how Japan could depart from its Cold War practice of passive (almost utopian) pacifism and move toward what may be described as "reluctant realism."[vii]

The efforts to redesign Japanese security policy to better respond to security challenges began in earnest with the deliberation by the Advisory Group on Defense Issues (commonly referred to as the Higuchi Commission, named after its chairman), a non-government advisory group convened by Prime Minister Morihiro Hosokawa in 1994. The results of the discussion held by the Higuchi Commission were published as *Modality of the Security and Defense Capability of Japan: The Outlook for the 21st Century* (the so-called Higuchi Commission Report) in October 1994.

[vii] Reluctant realism can be described as a policy "that still converges with the United States on fundamental issues but it is also increasingly independent. While it remains low risk, it is more sensitive to balance-of-power considerations. And while it is still reactive, it is far less passive," See Green, Michel J. *Reluctant Realism.* (New York: Palgrave McMillan, 2000) 3.

The Higuchi Commission Report stressed qualitative changes in security threats in the post-Cold War world, alerting readers that Japan would face dangers that would be dispersed and unpredictable.[60] The report declared that Japan must pursue an "active" (and constructive) security policy to deal with post-Cold War security threats, arguing that Japan "should extricate itself from its security policy of the past that was, if anything, passive, and henceforth play an active role in shaping a new order."[61] The report further proposed that Japan, in order to fulfill its responsibility to this end, must pursue "a coherent and comprehensive security policy" that consists of embracing multinational security cooperation, enhancing US-Japan security relations, and equipping itself with a "highly reliable and efficient defense capability based on a strengthened information capability and a prompt crisis-management capability."[62] It was the first time that a commission gathered by the Japanese prime minister spoke openly about strengthening Japan's military capability as the core elements of Japan's national security policy.

Based on the recommendations in the Higuchi Commission Report, the Japanese government revised *the National Defense Program Outline* (NDPO) in 1995. The 1995 NDPO acknowledged the unpredictability and fluidity of the post-Cold War international security environment and proposed that Japan continue its effort to enhance its own security through strengthening its alliance with the United States and contributing to the stability of the international community. In this context, it clarified that Japan would use its defense capabilities to defend its homeland, respond to large-scale disasters and other emergencies, and contribute to a more stable international security environment.[63] The 1995 NDPO stressed the importance of having an efficient defense capability that takes full advantage of advanced technologies and could respond to diversified threats. The 1995 NDPO marked a clear departure from the original NPDO (which was solely focused on the defense of Japan), as it included "contribution to a more stable international environment" among the goals for Japanese security policy, indicating that the SDF would be used in Japan's engagement in international peacekeeping operations and other overseas humanitarian relief activities. Japan also paved the way to dispatch the SDF, albeit with tight restrictions, on overseas missions in support of peacekeeping operations led by the United Nations when it passed the Peacekeeping Operations Cooperation Law in 1992. These actions suggested that Japan, although slowly, was beginning to recognize that it could no longer focus only on defending its homeland if it wanted to enhance its security.

Further, consistent with the priorities set forth in the Higuchi Commission Report, Japan also proceeded to redefine and revitalize the US-Japan alliance. Efforts in this regard, which ultimately produced the 1996 Tokyo Declaration, the 1997 revision of the US-Japan Guidelines for Defense Cooperation, and the adoption of the Special Action Committee for Okinawa (SACO) Final Report, not only reaffirmed the significance of the US-Japan alliance, but also repositioned the alliance as "a cornerstone of stability in the Asia-Pacific region."[64] Through this process, the roles Japan would play within the framework of the US-Japan alliance in case of contingencies outside of Japanese territory were clarified and expanded. Such efforts, along with Japan's own efforts to expand its military security portfolio, signaled that Japan continued to consider the US-Japan alliance as the key pillar of its military security policy.

Still, while Japan tried to strengthen its position within the US-Japan alliance and looked to expand the role of the JSDF overseas, it continued to explore how it could play a role in defining security in non-military terms. For instance, Tomiichi Murayama, who served as Japan's prime minister between June 1994 and January 1996, spoke about his vision for Japan "that is kind to people" and suggested that Japan should devote greater efforts in addressing issues such as poverty, hunger, population, environment, resources, and HIV/AIDS in order to play "an appropriate" (*oubun no*) role to create peace as "a peaceful nation" (*heiwa kokka*).[65] His successor, Ryutaro Hashimoto, advocated a strong US-Japan alliance, but also spoke of Japan's need to boost its "Eurasia diplomacy" and to become a supporter of sustainable development.[66] Keizo Obuchi later discussed Japan's post-Cold War diplomacy in the context of "five bridges"—bridges to the world, prosperity, sense of peace (*anshin*), safety, and the future—and stressed that Japan should make "due" (*oubun no*) contribution to the world.[67] With Obuchi's leadership, Japan also established human security as one of the pillars of its foreign policy,[viii] leading international efforts to establish the Human Security Fund under the auspices of the United Nations in 1999.[68] These efforts by Japanese leaders throughout the 1990s are illustrative of Japan's inclination to continue the practice of not depending primarily on its military security policy for its national security. However, the tensions in East Asia and the public's concerns regarding the government's capacity in crisis management writ large forced the government to focus more on national security in more conventional terms.

Japan's extreme hesitance to allow the SDF to engage in overseas activities was particularly illustrated by the debate that eventually led to the enactment of the 1992 PKO Cooperation Law. When this law was

---

[viii] Human security is defined as "protecting vital freedoms…protecting people from critical and pervasive threats and situations, building on their strengths and aspirations…creating systems that give people the building blocks of survival, dignity and livelihood." See Commission on Human Security *Human Security Now*, 2003, http://www.humansecurity-chs.org/finalreport/English/FinalReport.pdf (accessed 25 January, 2008).

originally enacted, it came with the so-called "PKO five principles:" According to these principles, the SDF could only participate in a PKO if:

- A cease-fire agreement was in place;
- There was unanimous consent to the deployment of PKO forces (and Japan's participation therein) by all the parties;
- There was impartiality for the PKO forces;
- Japan had the right to withdraw if the conditions on the ground changed; and
- The JSDF had limits on its use of weapons.[69]

These principles essentially prevented a timely and effective SDF deployment to take part in the UN-led peacekeeping operations, as demonstrated by the difficulties in dispatching the SDF to East Timor. In particular, a severe restriction on the use of weapons placed the SDF in an awkward position in which they were not allowed to use their weapons to protect the other countries' PKO forces that were under attack. Furthermore, the freeze on SDF participation in the "core" PKO missions (*hontai gyomu*) (including cease-fire monitoring, cease-fire patrolling, transport inspection, disposal of weapons, and assistance for the exchange of prisoners) imposed by the Japanese government severely limited the scope of activities to which the SDF could be deployed.[ix]

Japan's preference for not expanding the role of the JSDF in Japanese security policy was also apparent in the debate that took place within the Japanese Diet at the time the US-Japan Guidelines for Defense Cooperation were revised in the mid- to late 1990s. The issues related to Japan's ban on exercising the right of collective self-defense came to the forefront of the debate. Japanese legislators focused on whether a certain type of cooperation that Japan would provide to the United States in contingencies outside Japanese territory would be regarded as the exercise of the right of collective self-defense. They also focused on whether a certain type of logistical support might constitute "integration with the use of force" (*buryoku koshi tono ittai-ka*). As early as 1959, the Japanese government argued that Article Nine of the Constitution prohibited Japan from engaging in activities that were so closely related to the use of force by other countries that they could be considered as an integral part

---

[ix] These limitations were not lifted until 2001 when the Japanese government decided to dispatch the SDF to East Timor.

of using military force.[70] The Japanese legislators who had reservations about Japan's deepening defense cooperation with the United States argued that if the JSDF provide logistical support for US forces in the situation in the areas surrounding Japan, such support could be considered as integrated with the use of force.[71] When the Diet deliberated the legislation that would enable the Japanese government to fulfill its responsibility under the *Guidelines for US-Japan Defense Cooperation* in case of the *shuhen jitai* (situation in the areas surrounding Japan, commonly interpreted as the regional contingencies), the legal definition of the geographical area that was covered under this concept was also an intense focus of the debate in the Diet.[72] Greater strategic issues such as Japan's proper role in a post-Cold War security environment or Japan's appropriate role as a US ally in the Asia-Pacific region were not debated.

In short, following the end of the Cold War, Japan found itself in a place in which it knew that it had to do more in security affairs in order to not only maintain its alliance with the United States, but also to enjoy respect from the international community it thought it deserved. However, its strong inclination of not wanting to engage militarily prohibited Japan from revising its security policy priorities in a more robust and comprehensive way.

POST-9/11

The 9/11 terrorist attacks against the United States in 2001 shocked the international system. The world was stunned by the degree of destruction that a loosely organized transnational terrorist group could bring to the world's sole superpower. This incident illuminated the dangers of non-traditional threats such as terrorism and the proliferation of weapons of mass destruction, and the considerable difficulty that nation-states have in dealing with them.

To put it simply, the 9/11 terrorist attacks dramatically broadened the types of security problems included in national security in the United States, shifting its approach to security issues. For example, prior to 9/11, while the danger of terrorism was certainly recognized, it was primarily considered a domestic security issue over which law enforcement agencies had primary jurisdiction. After 9/11, not only was terrorism counted as a national security concern, but other issues that were also traditionally not considered national security challenges (e.g., energy, environment) also came to be looked at in this context of national security. Concerns over transnational security challenges such as weapon proliferation, weapons of mass destruction, manipulation of technology, non-proliferation, and failed states, were intensified given the damage they could cause when these elements end up in the hands of terrorist groups.

Few would disagree with the proposition that such a dramatic shift in perspectives on national security, much of which was brought upon by the 9/11 terrorist attacks against the United States, served as another awakening for Japan to be reminded of the changed nature of security threats that the world faced. Further, as the crisis over North Korea's covert nuclear program intensified, Japan was again reminded that conventional security tension and threats continued to persist. The revelation in 2002 that North Korea was indeed involved in kidnapping Japanese citizens in the 1970s and the 1980s also gave Japan a renewed sense of vulnerability against non-military security threats. Other incidents, including the incursion of Chinese submarines into Japanese territorial waters, also contributed to a heightened interest in Japan in national security.

In such an environment, Japan initiated important domestic processes to (1) reassess the changes in the international security situation in the post-9/11 era and (2) revise the direction of Japanese security policy priorities. The process began with deliberations conducted by a task force called the Council on Security and Defense Capabilities (more commonly known in the United States as the Araki Commission). The Commission included former senior defense officials, retired senior SDF officers, business leaders, and academics who were influential in security policy debates in Japan. After several month-long deliberations, the Council submitted its report, *Japan's Visions for Future Security and Defense Capability* to Prime Minister Koizumi in October 2004.

The Araki Report had several elements that distinguished itself from preceding task force reports of this kind, including the 1994 Higuchi Report. For one, it clearly articulated the goal of Japanese national security policy for the first time. The report identified the defense of Japan and prevention of threats in the international security environment as the two goals that Japan's national security policy should pursue. The report further suggested that Japan should create a multi-layered security policy by flexibly combining three approaches: 1) developing Japan's own defense build-up plans; 2) cooperating with its ally, the United States; and 3) cooperating with the broader international community in its efforts to achieve these goals. The report also stood out as the clearest statement yet on how Japan seeks to strengthen the US-Japan alliance while cooperating with the international community (including the United Nations) in a complementary manner. It is worthwhile to note that, while the task force's deliberations did not go beyond the current constitutional framework, the report was more forthcoming in suggesting that Japan might be at the crossroads where the restrictions in Japan's military power should be revisited. In addition to stressing Japan's need to build up "multi-functional and flexible defense capability," the report, for instance, suggested the potential need for revising Japan's long-held principles on arms exports.[73]

In a process parallel to that of the mid-1990s, the Japanese government once again conducted a new round of revisions to the NDPO following the release of the Araki Report. Prior to its release, it was reported that the revised NDPO would set Japanese security and defense policies on a different path than in the past. After the Araki Commission Report, many Japanese security policy observers anticipated that these two documents, particularly the NDPO, would launch a new chapter in Japanese security policy.

The *National Defense Program Guideline* (NDPG), adopted in December 2004, incorporated some of the basic ideas that were put forward in the Araki Report. It mirrored the Araki Report by defining the basic principles of Japanese security policy for the first time. It also called particular attention to "new threats and various situations (i.e. terrorism, proliferation of weapons of mass destruction)"[74] as Japan's greatest security challenge in the post-9/11 security environment.

What is particularly notable in the 2004 NDPG was the degree of importance attached to SDF participation in international operations. Compared with the 1995 NDPO, in which SDF engagement in international activities was of secondary importance, the 2004 NDPG addressed it as a mission with equal significance as defense of the homeland and maintenance of a strong US-Japan alliance. The importance of inter-agency coordination and cooperation with nongovernmental organizations was also noted for the first time. As for defense capabilities, the 2004 NDPG called for Japan to have a "responsive, mobile, flexible, and multi-purpose" capability that is supported by "high technological and intelligence capabilities."[75] To achieve these goals, the 2004 NDPG dictated that Japan should have defense capabilities that not only respond to ballistic missile threats but also other security threats, including guerrilla attacks, the takeover of the distant islands, incursion attempts, and large-scale disasters.[76]

Furthermore, the 2004 NDPG suggested that Japan should move beyond an exclusively defense-oriented posture for the first time in Japan's postwar history. It strongly argued that Japan should revise its force structure in a fundamental manner by proposing that Japan should have a "multi-functional, flexible and effective force with a high level of readiness, mobility, adaptability and multi-purpose capability, and is equipped with state-of-the-art technologies and intelligence capabilities comparable to global military-technological level (sic)."[77]

Japan also launched a parallel effort to strengthen its alliance relationship with the United States. When the US-Japan alliance went through a period of redefinition and reaffirmation in the mid-1990s, bilateral efforts focused on finding a new meaning for the alliance. With the alliance having had its role redefined as the stabilizer of the Asia-Pacific region, the two governments took another step to both expand the scope of and deepen the US-Japan alliance, with an eye on growing it into a global partnership. The three documents issued by the US-Japan Security Consultative Committee (SCC) between February 2005 and May 2006 laid out the vision and concrete steps for the two countries to move toward that goal.

Taken together, these policy developments all seemed to point to Japan finally reconsidering its key principles based on national security policy of the Cold War. That is, Japan finally began to appear willing to allow greater space and profile for its military power as the major element of its national security policy. It certainly did not mean that Japan would pursue an autonomous assertive military capability. But it seemed to mean, at minimum, that Japan was more willing to put the JSDF as one of the major "faces" of its national security policy, utilizing it more robustly in the context of national defense, its alliance with the United States, and international efforts to respond to global transnational security threats.

Prime Minister Abe, shortly after coming into the office in September 2006, took several important steps to continue the overall trend of reconsidering the role of military power in its national security policy. Shortly after assuming the office, Abe convened three advisory commissions, all of which had a great deal of relevance in how Japan shapes its national security policy, how it implements them, and what kinds of constitutional parameters the government could operate within in the future. In November 2006, Abe launched the Committee on Strengthening the Function of Prime Minister's Executives on National Security (*Kokka Anzen Hosho ni kansuru Kantei Kinou Kyouka Kaigi*) to explore ways in which the prime minister could have stronger policy- and decision-making support independent from the bureaucracy, and served as the chairman. In December 2006, Abe established the Council on Strengthening Intelligence Function (*Jouhou Kinou Kyouka Kentou Kaigi*) to examine ways in which the prime minister and his staff could establish a more effective and streamlined intelligence community in the Japanese government. The Chief Cabinet Secretary was designated as the chairman of the committee. Finally, in April 2007, Abe launched the Council on Re-establishing the Legal Foundation for National Security (*Anzen Hosho no Houteki Kiban no Sai-kouchiku ni kansuru Kondankai*) to seriously discuss the prospect of Japan revising its current ban on exercising its right of collective self-defense.

Moreover, under Abe's watch, Japan enacted the so-called National Referendum Law to establish the specific procedure for constitutional revision. While its constitution states that the constitution can be revised with two-thirds majority of all the Diet members, followed by a simple majority approval of the public, Japan never had a law that specified actual steps through which the constitutional revision is put to a vote. With the National Referendum Law approved by the Diet, Abe created an environment in which Japan can now discuss the substance of constitutional revision.

REQUIREMENTS FOR AN EFFECTIVE "NATIONAL SECURITY POLICY INFRASTRUCTURE" FOR JAPAN

Today, Japan's national security policy is in transition. While not being able to completely depart from its low emphasis on military power, Japan continues to make policy and legislative decisions that suggest its intention to expand the role that its military power plays in national security policy. If one is to take the statements in the 2004 *National Defense Policy Guideline* as the document that defines the basic principles of Japan's national security policy, the goals of Japan's national security policy are: (1) to prevent any threat from directly reaching Japan and, in the event that it does, to repel the threat as well as to minimize the damage; and (2) to reduce the chances of any threat arising in various parts of the world in order to prevent it from reaching Japan.

In order for Japan to achieve its basic security policy goals, how do these organizations interact within and among themselves? Provided the aforementioned security policy goals, there are several key elements that have to exist in the national security policy infrastructure.[78]

First is the strong policy- and decision-making capability of the prime minister. The Japanese government, in essence, has a decentralized policy- and decision-making process. Even when agencies in the Japanese government argue their need to be more integrated and centralized in its policy/decision-making processes, such discussion usually takes place in the context of inside those particular agencies, and not necessarily among difference agencies. Thus, the prime minister is often the only actor in the process that can impose the bureaucracy to work together and be more responsive to the policy needs.

Second, the capability to collect, analyze, and appropriately share and distribute salient information is essential. As "domestic" and "international" security threats are becoming more difficult to distinguish, it is imperative that the institutions that handle domestic intelligence and those that handle foreign intelligence have an effective way of cooperation. Again, the prime minister is often the only actor that can demand a government-wide effort in this.

Third, as it becomes more important for Japan to deter security threats before they reach Japanese borders, the military capability to enable such efforts is imperative. Further, as the activities that used to be law enforcement concerns (e.g., terrorism, smuggling) are increasingly linked up with national security concerns, the coordination and cooperation between law enforcement and national defense institutions are critical. For instance, the potential disruption that can be caused by the terrorist activities inside Japan make it necessary that the intelligence community, the National Policy Agency (NPA), local police, the Ministry of Defense (MOD) and the JSDF establish a close-knit network of sharing necessary information and work together first to prevent such activities but secondly to respond to and manage the consequences should the deterrence effort fail. Similarly, as the increasing number of suspicious activities by the vessels of Japan's neighbors that mix security and law enforcement concerns take place within and/or near Japanese territorial waters, it becomes important that the Japan Coast Guard (JCG) and the Maritime Self-Defense Force (JMSDF) cooperate in responding to those challenges. Further, due to a lowering threshold between domestic and international security threats, it is also imperative that both law enforcement and national defense institutions improve their relationship with Japan's diplomatic community as well.

Fourth, the changes that are made to the missions of the institutions and other arrangements must be written into law in order to have a lasting effect. In Japan's case, however, a great deal of laws that have to do with national security policy stands on an unreasonably complicated interpretation of its constitution that was created during the Cold War. As a result, the current legal framework that justifies the Japanese government's current national security policy is supported by a very obscure and fragile compilation of one interpretation of the law after another. In order for Japan to meet the security challenges of the 21st century, the legal framework that supports national security policy needs to be streamlined and brought in line with today's reality.

Finally, many of these changes can be very unpopular to the public. In particular, the changes to the existing legal framework—especially the Constitution—are expected to be an uphill battle. Since the legal changes must be debated and approved by the Diet, political consensus on the key national security issues would be critical. At minimum, a serious discussion on the key national security issues needs to be taking place in a sustainable manner within the political circles in Japan.

Do the recent developments in Japan in the area of national security policy represent progress in these four elements? Or, are the changes all superficial, leaving the fundamentals in its national security policy infrastructure unchanged? How do they agree (or disagree) with what the United States envisions in Japan, and what are the implications for US approaches toward the US-Japan alliance? Attention is now turned to these questions.

—2—
CIVILIAN INSTITUTIONS

The institutional component of national security policy infrastructure can be divided into two groups—civilian and uniform.[x] In general, civilian institutions define a strategy based on broader national goals and interests and set the policy priorities. They also oversee the uniform institutions when the decisions are made to have the uniform institutions carry out their assigned missions, because civilian institutions usually have the authority over senior staff in uniform institutions as well as their budgets, the relationship between the two types of institutions are complex and often contentious.

As a general principle, Japanese bureaucracy has a "bottom-up" decision-making process. In the context of the government's structure, it specifically means that an issue is managed and policy approach is shaped primarily at the division (*ka*) level. The policies that are shaped are communicated to the outside world—especially to the general public and political leaders in Japan—most commonly through division directors (*ka-cho*), deputy director-generals (*shingi-kan*), and director-generals (*kyoku-cho*) of the bureaus (*kyoku*) to which the divisions belong to.[79] As such, organizational structure in these institutions and the distribution of the area of the responsibilities within them are both important factors in examining policymaking processes in Japan. Japan's national security policy is no exception. Further, when examining these institutions, checking the laws that authorize their establishment is key, as they often define the jurisdiction and authority of each institution.

Furthermore, wariness toward the uniform organization (particularly military) was paramount in Japan when it was rebuilding its national security establishment. One should remember that Japan had not planned to arm itself in the immediate postwar years—it was only at the strong request from the United States that Japan began the rearmament, re-establishing its national defense organizations. As Japanese leaders reconstructed Japan's national defense institutions, they made sure that the uniform organizations (particularly the military) played very little role in the national security policymaking process. In other words, uniform organizations were given the role of a mere executioner/enforcer of the policy determined by the civilian leaders.[80] This

---

[x] I refrain from using the term "military" on the opposite side of the civilian, as the institutions in Japan that have enforcement capabilities include non-military organizations such as the Japan Coast Guard.

was institutionalized in two ways. First, the core national defense institution that was established at the end of the process was not granted a full ministerial status: The Japan Defense Agency (JDA) was positioned as one of the agencies that the Prime Minister's Office exercised administrative supervision. Within the JDA, the Self-Defense Forces (SDF)—a uniform institution that will be examined more closely in Chapter Three—was placed under the supervision of the Internal Bureau (IB) that consisted mostly of elite civil servants.[xi] Since then, the civilian institutions supervised and controlled uniform institutions in Japan's national security policy infrastructure by establishing policies, creating the budget and controlling the personnel.

The examination of the institutional component of Japan's national security infrastructure, therefore, has to start with civilian institutions. This chapter intends to examine how each of the "civilian" institutions in Japan's national security policy infrastructure has been organized, identifying key offices on national security issues in each institution. It also attempts to explain the institutional arrangements that organizations utilize to negotiate during the creation of decisions that eventually represent the whole Japanese government. Finally, the chapter tries to examine potential challenges to the improvement in institutional arrangement focusing on two issues—interagency coordination and the prospect of the Japanese-style National Security Council (J-NSC).

OVERVIEW OF EACH INSTITUTION

There are four main civilian institutions that form Japan's national security policy infrastructure. These are the Ministry of Foreign Affairs (MOFA), National Police Agency (NPA), Ministry of Defense (MOD) and the Cabinet Secretariat. This section provides a brief overview of each institution, identifying the specific bureaus/divisions within each institution that play a role in Japan's national security policy.

Ministry of Foreign Affairs: a traditional steward of alliance

The Ministry of Foreign Affairs (MOFA) is mandated to: contribute to the maintenance of a peaceful and secure international community; help create an atmosphere that is conducive to a positive international environment through proactive efforts; and attempt to promote the Japanese nation's interest, as well as that of its people, through maintaining harmonious external relations.[81] Pursuant to fulfilling these mandates, the MOFA Establishment Law further

[xi] See Akihiko Tanaka, *Anzen Hosho (Security)* (Tokyo: Yomiuri Shimbun-sha, 1997) for the process of establishing the Japan Defense Agency (JDA) and the Self-Defense Forces (JSDF).

grants MOFA the jurisdiction to manage issues of national security policy. MOFA continues to maintain the statutory primary jurisdiction over national security policy today.[82]

As of 2006, MOFA has 5,453 personnel (out of which 3,286 are assigned to the foreign embassies and consulates).[83] The MOFA headquarters in Tokyo is organized into ten bureaus—five regional affairs bureaus and four functional bureaus (Chart 2-1-1).

Chart 2-1-1. MOFA Organizational Chart

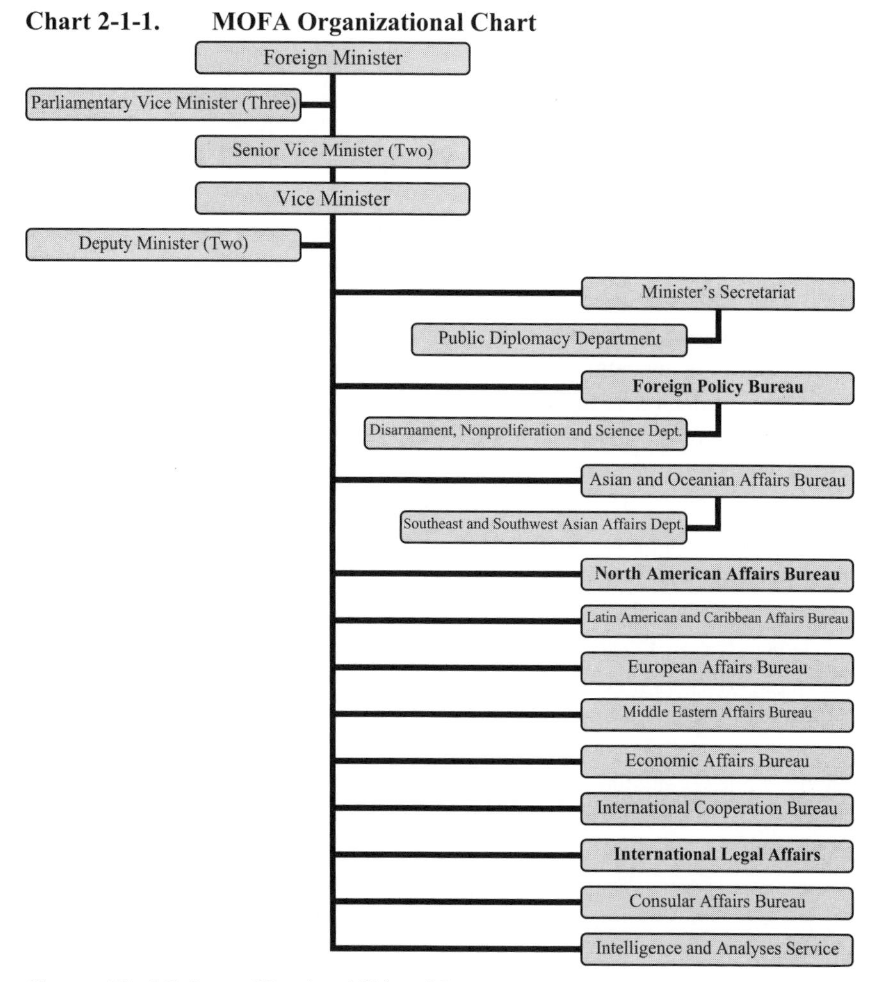

(Source: The Ministry of Foreign Affairs of Japan. http://www.mofa.go.jp/about/hq/chart.html (accessed 11 April 2008)).

Within MOFA, three bureaus have been directly involved in Japan's national security policymaking. The first is the Foreign Policy Bureau (*Sogo Gaiko*

Seisaku Kyoku). Responding to the recommendation by the Advisory Group for the Enhancement of Diplomacy (*Gaiko Kyoka Kondan-kai*), a private advisory group for the prime minister and foreign minister, the bureau was created in 1993 to (1) plans long-term policy in all areas of foreign policy and (2) oversees and coordinates among the regional as well as functional bureaus to reach the coordinated policy position that is shared within MOFA in December 1991.[84]

The Foreign Policy Bureau has nine divisions.[xii] Among them, two divisions are of particular importance: The Policy Coordination Division and the National Security Policy Division. Policy Coordination Division is expected to lead MOFA's effort to shape policies over the issues that require extensive coordination both inside and outside MOFA, such as G8 meetings. National Security Policy Division takes the lead in shaping the foreign policy that deeply involves Japan's national security policy interests.

Although eclipsed by the recent ascendance of the Foreign Policy Bureau, the North American Affairs Bureau (*Hokubei Kyoku*), having a long history of leading the Japanese government's consultation with the United States on the US-Japan alliance, continues to play an important role in bilateral alliance discussion. Two divisions in the North American Affairs Bureau need to be highlighted for their role in Japan's management of the US-Japan alliance. The Japan-US Security Treaty Division has led the Japanese government's negotiation with the United States on alliance issues. The Status of US Forces Agreement (SOFA) Division serves as a point of contact with the US Department of State and Defense as well as US forces in Japan when incidents arise concerning US military personnel and their families in Japan. For instance, whenever US service members commit a crime in Japan, the SOFA Division is responsible for coordinating the bilateral efforts to respond to the situation, including facilitating the communication between Japanese law enforcement and US military police.

Finally, while maintaining a low profile, the International Legal Affairs Bureau (*Kokusai-ho Kyoku*) is critical because of its responsibility to ensure that international legal agreements that the Japanese government sign does not violate Japan's domestic laws. The works by the Treaties Division is particularly important, because the division shoulders the responsibility of interpreting the international treaties signed by the Japanese government to ensure the treaty's legal consistency with Japan's domestic laws. The Division, for instance, played a critical role in interpreting the scope of the Japan-US Security Treaty

---

[xii] Headed by a senior diplomat with a title of ambassador, the Non-proliferation, Disarmament and Science Department is placed under the Bureau, although it functions as a *de facto* functional affairs bureau (e.g., Economic Affairs Bureau).

when Japan and the United States were negotiating the redefinition of the US-Japan alliance in the 1990s. More recently, it played an important role in identifying the international legitimacy on which Japan could dispatch the JSDF to the Indian Ocean or to Iraq.

During the Cold War, Japan had very little to offer in the area of national security policy. Beyond the fundamental principles of its defense policy (e.g., no exercise of the right of collective self-defense, exclusively defense-oriented posture), Japan's national security policy during the Cold War was by and large about maintaining its alliance with the United States. Because of Japan's exclusive focus on self-defense in its national security policy, even Japan's policy toward the US-Japan alliance revolved around questions such as "what area does 'Far East' in Article Six of the Japan-US Mutual Security Treaty cover?," "if Japan supports a US military operation in East Asia, does that constitute the prohibition of the exercise of the right of collective self-defense?," and so on. In other words, the context in which Japan's national security policy was discussed during the Cold War was more legalistic than strategic or policy-driven.

This made the North American Affairs Bureau (the Japan-US Security Treaty Division in particular) and the Treaty Bureau (*Joyaku-kyoku*), today's International Legal Affairs Bureau two key players within MOFA in Japan's national security policymaking during the Cold War. The Foreign Policy Bureau did not exist.[xiii] The leading role that the two bureaus played in the deliberation of national security policy within the Japanese government was demonstrated most vividly when Japanese lawmakers debated on Japan's security policy. For instance, when the Japanese Diet deliberated on Japan's contribution to the 1990-91 Gulf War, it was the senior officials from the Treaty Bureau who were at the frontline of answering the questions from Japanese legislatures.

Such a dynamic within MOFA began to change with the establishment of the Foreign Policy Bureau in 1993. Since then, whenever MOFA discussed reorganization to enhance its policy-making capability, the enhancement of the Foreign Policy Bureau was included in the recommendations that followed such a discussion. In response to a series of scandals that began with the embezzlement charges against its official and ended with the resignation of then Foreign Minister Makiko Tanaka, MOFA announced an extensive reform plan

---

[xiii] The Foreign Policy Bureau's current portfolio was placed under the United Nations (UN) Affairs Bureau (*Kokuren-kyoku*). Since Japan played very little role in the area of international security, particularly in the multinational framework such as the United Nations, the UN Affairs Bureau had a very little role in shaping MOFA's position on Japan's national security policy.

in August 2002.[xiv] The announced MOFA reform plan was the product of two private advisory groups that were formed between 2001-2002. One was MOFA Functional Reform Council (*Gaimusho Kinou Kaikaku Kaigi*), a group that was formed in February 2001 in response to the aforementioned embezzlement charge.[85] The other was the "Council for Change" in regards to MOFA Reform (*Gaimusho Kaikaku ni kansuru "Kaeru Kai"*) that was formed in March 2002. The plan, while largely focused on MOFA's internal administrative procedures (such as accounting and personnel management) and the enhancement of its consular services, also included the enhancement of the policy planning capacity in MOFA among its recommendations. In particular, the reform plan called for the enhancement of the Foreign Policy Bureau by: adding more mid-career personnel as policy coordinators; ensuring the Foreign Policy Bureau's participation in policymaking on critical issues; creating an office for policy evaluation and assessment; and giving the Bureau the mandate for mid-term and long-range policy planning.[86]

In July 2004, MOFA announced another reorganization plan, which had five major goals:

- Enhancement of the capacity of shaping diplomatic strategy;
- Strengthening of crisis-management and consular function;
- Improvement of intelligence collection and analyses;
- Establishment of new international frameworks; and
- Improvement of Japan's image abroad.[87]

When the reorganization took effect on 1 August 2004, the Foreign Policy Bureau was clearly designated as the "lead" bureau among all ten bureaus within MOFA. Several positions of the Foreign Policy Coordinator were created in the Policy Coordination Division so that they could be involved in the policy-making processes more actively. The Policy Coordination Division was also designated to play the central role in shaping Japan's foreign policy. The

---

[xiv] This individual was arrested in March 2001, and received a guilty verdict in 2002 and was sentenced to over seven years in prison. See, for example, Ministry of Foreign Affairs of Japan, *Gaimu Daijin Danwa: Matsuo Moto-Youjin Gaikoku Homon Shien Shitsu-cho ni kakawaru Jiken ni Tsuite* (Foreign Minister's Statement: In Regards to the crime that the former VIP Foreign Visit Support Office Director Matsuo involved) 12 March, 2002, http://www.mofa.go.jp/mofaj/press/danwa/14/dkw_0312.html (accessed 16 April, 2008).

National Security Policy Division was selected as the "lead" division in shaping Japan's national security policy.[88]

Furthermore, in the attempt to grant the Foreign Policy Bureau the influence that corresponds with its intended stature within the ministry, MOFA made the institutional decision to raise the position of the Foreign Policy Bureau within its bureaucracy. Its decision was demonstrated mainly through the appointment of the senior personnel in the bureau. That is, by making it custom to appoint its best and brightest senior diplomat to the Foreign Policy Bureau Director-General position, MOFA sent a signal that the Foreign Policy Bureau has a higher stature within its bureaucracy.[xv]

To prove this point, MOFA assigned its most capable diplomats to the senior positions in the Foreign Policy Bureau. For instance, among those who served as the Director-Generals of the Foreign Policy Bureau since the Bureau's creation (Shunji Yanai, Yutaka Kawashima, Ryozo Kato, Yukio Takeuchi, Shotaro Yachi, Tsuneo Nishida, Masaharu Kono, and Chikao Kawai), four have risen up to assume the position of the administrative vice minister, the highest bureaucratic position within MOFA, so far.[xvi] Also, it is often said that Ryozo Kato would have succeeded Yanai as the vice minister, but was appointed to become the Ambassador to the United States instead, because of the turmoil within MOFA that included tension between then Foreign Minister Makiko Takana and the MOFA bureaucracy, and a scandal that involved Muneo Suzuki, a powerful Liberal Democratic Party politician that had a vested interest in Japan-Russia relations.[89] Even below the level of director-general, MOFA has made conscious personnel decisions to signal the seniority of the Foreign Policy Bureau over other regional and functional bureaus. For instance, while sharing the titles such as "deputy director-general," "director" and "deputy director," those who held these positions in the offices within the Foreign Policy Bureau are generally a few years senior to those who have the same job title in other bureaus.[xvii]

[xv] Seniority of the Director-General of the Foreign Policy Bureau is also illustrated by the fact that he/she is selected from those who are currently serving as the director-general of other bureaus. For instance, Shunji Yanai, the first Director-General of the Foreign Policy Bureau, served as the Director-General of the Treaty Bureau (today's International Law Bureau) prior to his appointment as the Foreign Policy Bureau's director-general. The current Director-General of the Foreign Policy Bureau Chikao Kawai served as the Director-General of North American Affair Bureau prior to his current position.

[xvi] Whether Masaharu Kono (recently appointed to be the Deputy Foreign Minister for Economic Affairs) and Chikao Kawai (appointed to be the Assistant Chief Cabinet Secretary) will be promoted to the vice minister is still unknown.

[xvii] For example, Nobukatsu Kanehara, the former director of the Policy Coordination Division of the Foreign Policy Bureau has already served as the director of the Japan–US Security Treaty Division and worked at the Embassy of Japan in Washington DC as the Political Minister before assuming the current position. Similarly, Kazuyoshi Umemoto, before being appointed to be the

Recent examples suggest that the Foreign Policy Bureau may have finally begun to function in the way it was originally intended—as the bureau that presides over the other bureaus' policymaking on specific issues, is involved in setting mid- and long-term policy priorities, and leading MOFA's effort in the area of Japan's national security policy. For instance, the National Security Policy Division played a central role in the process leading up to Japan's dispatch of JSDF vessels to the Indian Ocean in support of Operation Enduring Freedom (OEF) and its dispatch of JSDF ground troops to Iraq. It took the lead in coordinating with the Japan Defense Agency (JDA), while coordinating with the Japan-Security Treaty Division on Tokyo's relations with Washington, the Treaty Division on constructing the legal argument in support of authorizing such a dispatch, the Second Middle East Division on evaluating the situation on the ground, and the UN Policy Division on the coordination with the United Nations. Japan's recent efforts in deepening the security relationship with Australia and India are also led by the Foreign Policy Bureau.

The repeated attempts to raise the stature of the Foreign Policy Bureau suggest MOFA's effort in consolidating its policy-making capacity within the ministry as early as 1993. It demonstrates that MOFA recognizes the importance of having an office that can take into account different views within the ministry and weave them into a coherent set of policy principles and priorities. It also suggests that MOFA might have foreseen the situation in which MOFA input in Japan's national security policymaking cannot always come from the North American Affairs Bureau alone as Japan came to be expected to play a security role beyond the traditional framework of the US-Japan alliance. However, the evolution of the Foreign Policy Bureau—after all, it took almost ten years before it began to assume its intended role within MOFA—also illustrates the difficulty of changing the several-decade practice in which the North American Affairs Bureau has been the central player within MOFA when it comes to security policy issues.

National Police Agency: a bastion of internal security

If the Ministry of the Foreign Affairs is an old guard in managing Japan's national security policy vis-à-vis abroad, the National Policy Agency has dominated the area that can be categorized as the "homeland security" in today's term. Indeed, being the primary law enforcement agency, the National Policy Agency (NPA) has been responsible for maintaining Japan's internal security throughout Japan's postwar history. Because the Japan Defense Agency (JDA) (including the Japan Self-Defense Forces) is not statutorily authorized to play a

---

deputy director-general of the Foreign Policy Bureau, served as the deputy director-general of the North American Affairs Bureau.

tangible role in the day-to-day efforts to secure stability inside Japan (things continue to remain that way, despite JDA's elevation to the Ministry of Defense), the NPA served as a *de facto* leading national security agency in Japan.

The police organization in Japan is headed by the National Public Safety Commission, (NPSC) (*Kokka Koan Iinkai*), which belongs under the direct control of the prime minister. The chairman of the NPSC is a cabinet-level position, and the Commission has five members under the chairman (Chart 2-2-1).[xviii]

Chart 2-2-1. Relationship between the Prime Minister, the National Public Safety Commission, the NPA and other government agencies

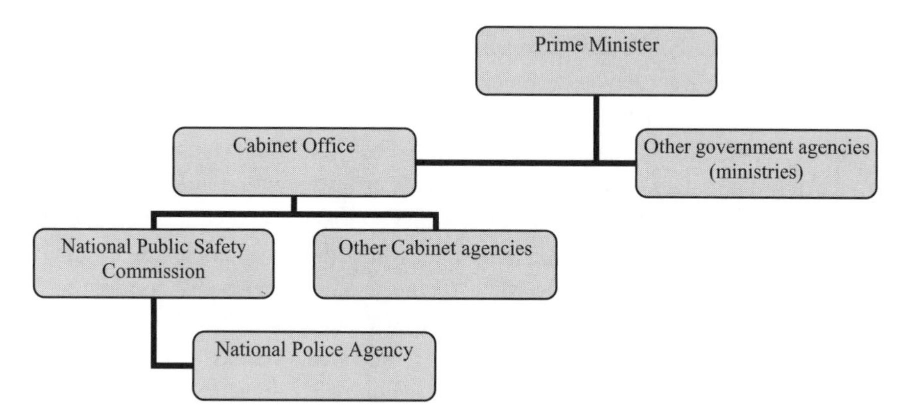

(Source: National Police Agency. http://www.npa.go.jp/english/kokusai/pdf/Poj2007-3.pdf (accessed 28 March 2008)).

The NPA is an institution that supports the NPSC in the day-to-day management of the national police organization (planning, budgeting and personnel), plays a major role when the Japanese government decides on the way to respond to situations that affect the nation's public safety (i.e., natural disaster, domestic disturbances), cooperates in international criminal investigations, and engages in law enforcement activities both inside and outside Japan that could affect lives, safety, and assets of the Japanese people. In addition, the NPA is also put in charge of maintaining its communication system, laboratories, personnel training facilities for its personnel, as well as activities of the Imperial Police.[90]

[xviii] As of April 2008, the commission is headed by the Honorable Shinya Izumi, a member of the House of Councillors. The current members are Yukio Sato (former Ambassador to the United Nations), Yoshiyuki Kasai (Chairman of Japan Central Railway Company), Mariko Hasegawa (Professor, Graduate Research Institute of Policy Studies), Nobuyuki Yoshida (Managing Director, Sankei Shimbun), and Kenjiro Tao (Judge, Hiroshima Superior Court), http://www.npsc.go.jp/detail/index.html (accessed 2 March 2008).

In case of an emergency (i.e. large-scale disasters, domestic disturbances) that requires the police mobilization to maintain public order, the prime minister, based on the recommendation from the NPSC, not the MOD, declares a "national emergency."[91] Once a "national emergency" is declared, the prime minister, not the NPSC chairman, directly commands the NPA.[92]

The Police Law (*Keisatsu-ho*) provides a basic legal foundation for Japan's national law enforcement structure. Police in Japan are given a mandate to "protect people's rights and freedom, and maintain public safety and order."[93] The NPA, as the institution that commands the national police structure, therefore is mandated in protecting Japan from any source of destabilization within Japan.

Furthermore, the Police Law also authorizes the NPA to engage in international activities in the areas beyond criminal investigation, albeit in the context of law enforcement. For instance, the NPA is authorized to engage in the situation outside Japan that "damages, or has the risk of damaging, Japanese people's lives, physical safety or assets, and/or Japan's critical national interests."[94] The Police Law also authorizes the NPA to engage in issues related to international emergency disaster relief.[95] In addition, while the law anticipates criminal activities in Japan (from the wording of the text, it appears that terrorist and hijacking activities are anticipated), the law also authorizes the NPA to respond to the situation in Japan that, if left unattended, "could gravely impact international relations and infringe on other countries' critical national interests" for law enforcement purposes.[96] Recently, as terrorism is increasingly recognized as a national security issue rather than a mere law enforcement issue, the NPA's activities in the area of counter-terrorism, including international investigative cooperation and intelligence-sharing, has increased its role in national security as a result.

Chart 2-2-2. Organizational Structure of the National Police Agency

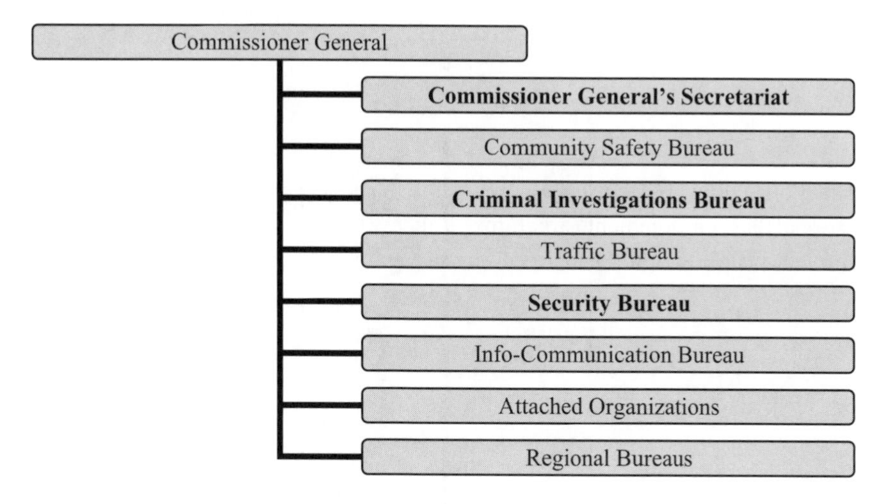

(Source: National Policy Agency. http://www.npa.go.jp/english/kokusai/pdf/Poj2007-5.pdf (accessed 25 March 2008)).

Out of the eight NPA bureaus, three bureaus should be highlighted in particular for their roles in Japan's homeland security. The Commissioner General's Secretariat (*Chokan Kanbo*) is in charge of providing directions for the protection of classified information within the NPA. It also houses the Office of the Executive Assistant to the NPSC Chairman, and serves as the communication window between the NPSC and the NPA.[97] The Secretariat also coordinates policies within the NPA, including its international activities (Chart 2-2-3).[98]

Chart 2-2-3. Organization of the Commissioner General' Secretariat

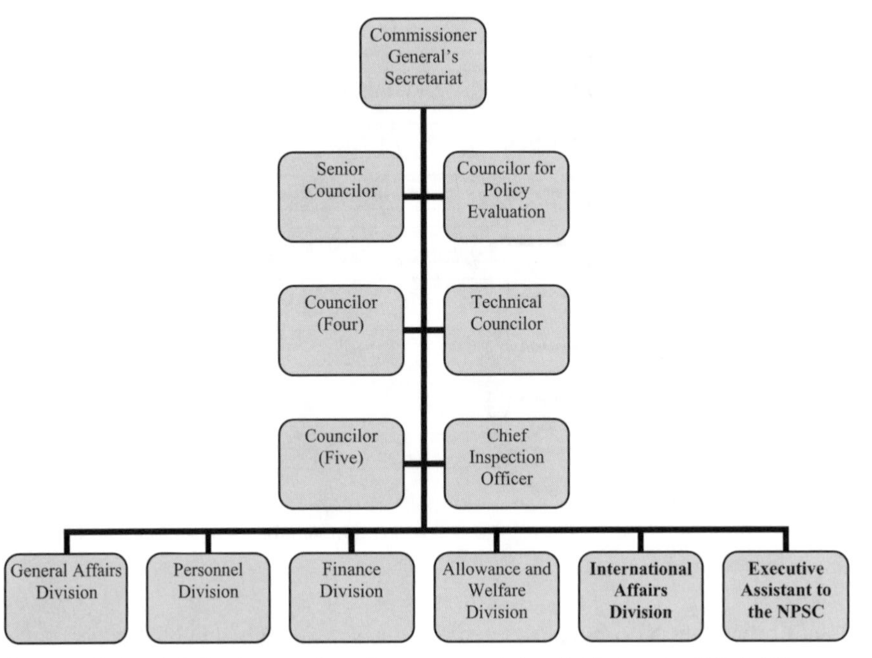

(Source: National Police Agency. http://www.npa.go.jp/english/kokusai/pdf/Poj2007-5.pdf (accessed 2 March 2008)).

Second is the Criminal Investigation Bureau (*Keiji-kyoku*). The bureau is in charge of criminal investigation in general, as well as forensics and crime rate statistics. The Organized Crime Department in the bureau is particularly important for the international aspect of its activities. The department is in charge of Japan's international criminal investigation, manages the NPA's relationship with International Commission of Police Organization (ICPO), addresses issues related to organized criminal groups in Japan and other types of organized crimes (unless other bureaus already claim the primary responsibility for them), controls firearms and drugs, and manages issues that arise with the NPA's cooperation in international criminal investigation.[99]

Finally, the Security Bureau (*Keibi-kyoku*) is in charge of public security (*koan*). It also is responsible for providing protective services to VIPs. It's Foreign Affairs and Intelligence Department functions as the window through which the NPA interacts with the law enforcement as well as intelligence organizations outside Japan (Chart 2-2-4.) The Security Bureau is also in charge of shaping and implementing the response plan in case the prime minister declares a "national emergency."[100]

Chart 2-2-4. Organization of the Security Bureau

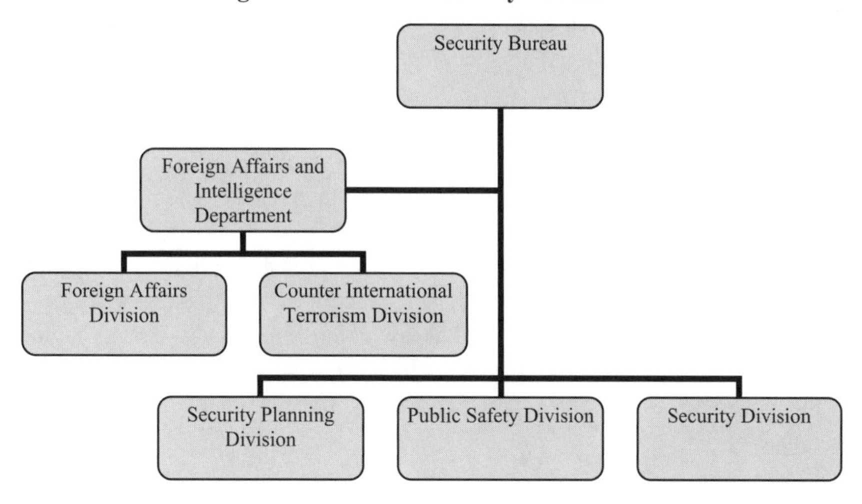

(Source: National Police Agency. http://www.npa.go.jp/english/kokusai/pdf/Poj2007-5.pdf (accessed 20 March 2008)).

Because of its mandate to maintain public order and safety, the Security Bureau plays a quiet yet critical role in collecting intelligence on groups and individuals (including ideologically extreme groups such as the Japan Red Army and Aum Shinrikyo) that are potentially threatening to Japan's internal security. In order to enhance its efforts in internal security, it also collects foreign intelligence on the movements of terrorists and their ties to the groups and individuals in Japan. This has made the Security Bureau the most influential bureau in the NPA throughout its history.

In addition to the statutory mandate given to the NPA for Japan's internal security, the NPA has also carefully built up a network of its personnel within the Japanese government in order to maintain its status and influence in homeland defense. For instance, similar to MOFA, one of the prime minister's official secretaries is customarily seconded from the NPA. Also, the NPA personnel have occupied key positions in other national security agencies in Japan. In addition to the routine inter-agency personnel exchanges, the NPA has maintained a director- and department chief-level position in defense intelligence within the MOD for its detailees. The director of the Cabinet Intelligence and Research Office (CIRO), along with several key positions in charge of foreign intelligence, is also filled by seconded senior NPA officials. Furthermore, the position of the Deputy Assistant Cabinet Secretary in charge of the National Security and Crisis Management (a key position in Japan's response to national emergencies, as discussed later in this chapter) is usually filled by retired NPA senior officials who have had a long career in public safety. The NPA also often assigns its officials to Japanese embassies abroad, where they function as the point of contact with the intelligence community in their host countries.[xix]

An unambiguous statutory designation of the NPA as the primary agency for internal security, the international aspects of its mandate and the ongoing practice of detailing its personnel to key national security positions across the Japanese government have made the NPA a key national security policy agency in Japan. The role of the NPA in Japan's security policymaking will likely enhance as what used to be recognized as law enforcement issues (smuggling of illegitimate materials, terrorism) come to be seen as national security problems in the post-9/11 world given the increasingly transnational nature of these challenges.

Ministry of Defense Internal Bureau: organization at a crossroad[xx]

In January 2007, based on the legislation enacted in December 2006, the Japan Defense Agency (JDA) was upgraded to the Ministry of Defense (MOD). While this raised the statutory status of this agency from "agency" to "ministry," its basic organizational structure of a civilian International Bureau (*naikyoku*) exercising oversight over the uniformed Self-Defense Forces (JSDF) remained unchanged.

In the organizational description of the MOD, the Internal Bureau (with approximately 22,000 personnel) is described as "one of the twelve organizations subordinate to the Minister of Defense."[101] However, this is misleading. In practice, the Internal Bureau manages the JSDF in its operation, planning, acquisition and personnel.[102] Furthermore, the Internal Bureau is tasked to manage the relations with US forces in Japan, including addressing the grievances raised by local communities that host US forces.[103]

The Internal Bureau is divided into six bureaus. Among the six bureaus, Defense Policy Bureau and Operational Policy Bureau are particularly important (Chart 2-3-2).

[xix] For instance, at the Embassy of Japan in the United States, Police Attaché is the official point of contact with the Central Intelligence Agency. The role of the NPA in the Japanese intelligence community will be further discussed in Chapter Four.

[xx] The Ministry of Defense can be divided between the Internal Bureau (*naikyoku*) that is predominantly civilian, and the Self-Defense Forces. This chapter focuses on the Internal Bureau as the "civilian" institution. The Self-Defense Forces will be examined in detail in Chapter Three.

Chart 2-3-2. Organization of the MOD Internal Bureau (simplified)

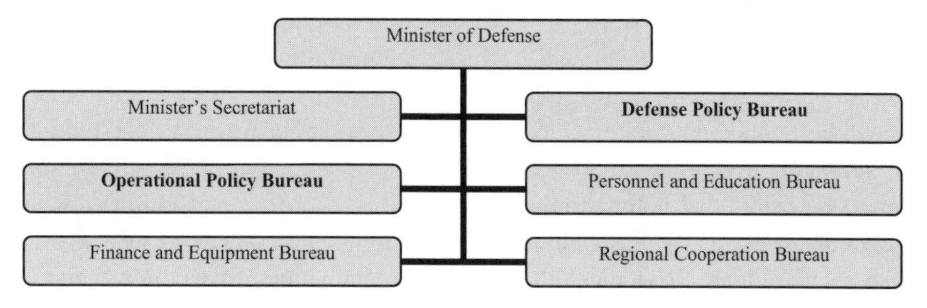

(Source: Ministry of Defense. http://www.mod.go.jp/j/defense/mod-sdf/sosikizu/inner/index.html (accessed 10 February 2008)).

The Defense Policy Bureau's primary task is to develop a defense strategy that takes into account Japan's broader national interest and national security policy goals.[104] Specifically, it is in charge of (1) shaping Japan's defense policy, (2) managing the MOD's defense exchanges, (3) planning the JSDF's organization and platforms, and (4) playing a central role in the MOD's efforts in collecting and analyzing intelligence.[105]

Chart 2-3-3. Organization of the Defense Policy Bureau

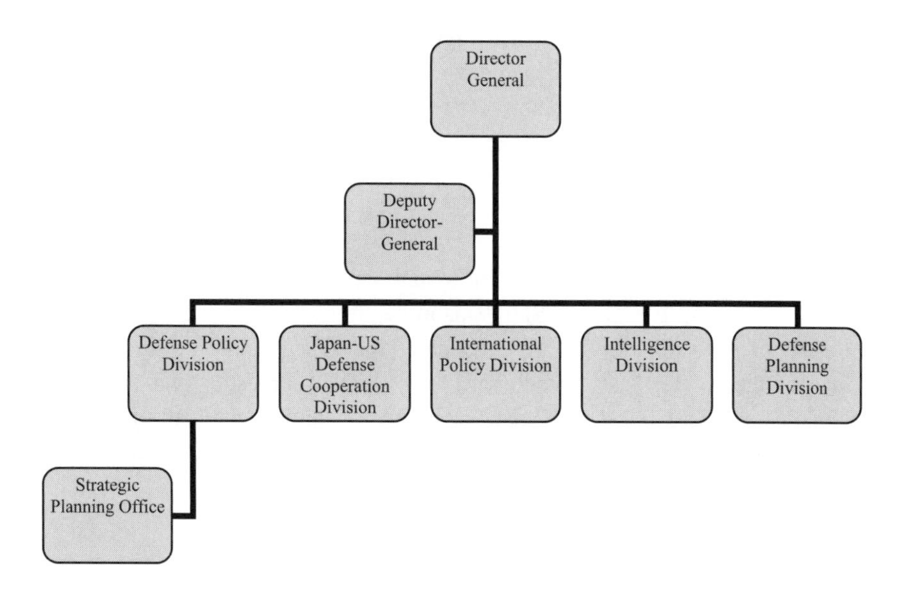

(Source: Ministry of Defense. http://www.mod.go.jp/j/defense/mod-sdf/sosikizu/inner/index.html (accessed 3 February 2008)).

The Defense Policy Division, as the division with the highest seniority within the Defense Policy Bureau, is in charge of a wide-range of issues in Japan's defense policy. The Japan–US Defense Cooperation Division specifically focuses on Japan's defense relations with the United States. This section used to be one of the units within the Defense Policy Division but was developed into a full division at the time of reorganization in September 2007, given the increasing amount of defense policy issues that Japan needs to coordinate with the United States. The International Policy Division is in charge of Japan's defense exchanges with the countries other than the United States. Intelligence Division manages the MOD's intelligence activities. Although the Defense Intelligence Headquarters (DIH) is an organization that is separate from the International Bureau, the Intelligence Division provides a basic oversight on the management of the DIH, and directs its intelligence collection and analyses effort. Finally, the Defense Planning Division, working with each JSDF service, establishes a priority for defense planning, particularly in the area of new acquisition and modification/upgrade of the existing platforms. In short, the Defense Policy Bureau is at the forefront of every aspect of Japan's defense policy.

The current division of responsibilities within the Defense Policy Bureau reflects how the Internal Bureau sees Japan's defense relations—defense policymaking in general, relationship with the United States, relationship with the rest of the world, and the defense procurement. At the same time, as the MOD tries to increase its engagement in the national security policymaking process in Japan, it also is beginning to recognize the necessity of an in-house policy planning capacity. The establishment of the Strategic Planning Office within the Defense Policy Division in September 2007 reflects such an internal thinking in the MOD.

The Operational Policy Bureau (*Unyo Seisaku Kyoku*) has the responsibility to ensure an effective use of the JSDF capabilities to secure and promote Japan's national interests.[106] Under this mandate, the Operational Policy Bureau manages the issues associated with the JSDF domestic and overseas deployments (Chart 2-3-4). It also is tasked to handle administrative work related to the information and communication within the MOD, including the JSDF.[107]

Chart 2-3-4. Organization of the Operational Policy Bureau

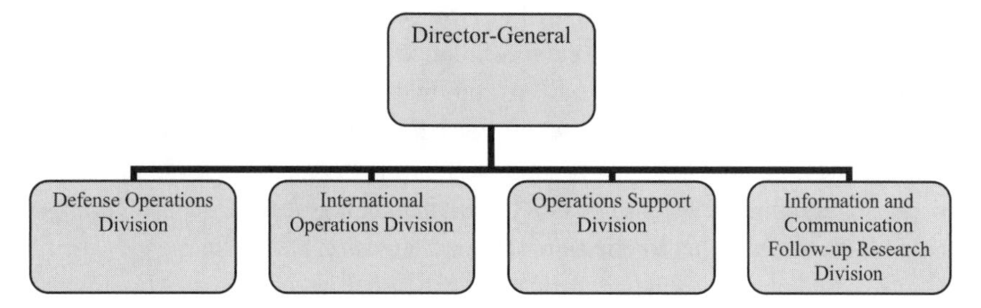

(Source: Ministry of Defense. http://www.mod.go.jp/j/defense/mod-sdf/sosikizu/inner/index.html (accessed 3 February 2008)).

With the above mandate, the Operational Policy Bureau manages all the issues that involve JSDF domestic and international operations. This bureau is also the first responder in case of JSDF-related accidents in Japan. For instance, when the Maritime Self-Defense Force (JMSDF) Aegis destroyer *Atago* collided with a fishing boat in March 2008, the Operational Policy Bureau, with the coordination with other divisions within the Internal Bureau as well as Maritime Staff Office, initially respond. As the result of the deliberation by the Advisory Council on the MOD Reform, however, the MOD decided to eliminate the Operational Policy Bureau and consolidate it with the Operation Directorate (J-3) of the Joint Staff Office.

For most of its history since its establishment in 1954, the JDA/MOD hardly played any role in shaping Japan's national security policy. Due to the lack of a full ministerial status within the government, the JDA was placed among the agencies subordinate to the Prime Minister's Office. Its role was confined to the management of the JSDF and coordination with the local governments that host US forces in Japan and the JSDF facilities on the issues arising from hosting these forces. With the tight limits on its military activity during the Cold War, the JDA/MOD was expected to play the role primarily of a "management agency" (*kanri kancho*) rather than a "policy agency" (*seisaku kancho*) and had functioned as such.

Changes came with the end of the Cold War as pressure began to mount on Japan to make more tangible contributions to the efforts to improve the international security environment. As such international demands rose, so too did expectations of a growing JDA role in Japan's national security policy. In particular, SDF participation in international activities including UN peacekeeping operations (PKO) obligated the JDA to play a greater role. Changing expectations of Japan in the evolving Post-Cold War security environment also resulted in a greater emphasis on the military aspect of the US-Japan alliance. Consequently, the US Department of Defense (DOD) became a lead figure on the US side in alliance consultations.[108] This, in turn, raised the role of the JDA as an institutional counterpart of the US-Japan alliance discussion. This trend, which was first noticed came when the two countries redefined the bilateral alliance in the mid-1990s, was further advanced by the developments in the post-9/11 environment—including the Defense Policy Review Initiative (DPRI) negotiations between 2002-2006.

The upgrade of the JDA to a ministry (and the change of its official name to the MOD) meant several things for the MOD. First and foremost, it meant that the MOD now enjoys certain procedural prerogatives—such as the right to directly negotiate its annual budget with the Ministry of Finance—that it had not had prior to becoming a ministry. Further, its ministerial status also positions the MOD as being equal to MOFA (which historically had taken a lead in shaping Japan's national security policy), and allows the MOD to demand, at minimum, equal involvement in shaping Japan's national security policy.[109]

In principle, the JDA's upgrade to the MOD was a positive step for Japanese security policy. However, the MOD still suffers from a number of challenges. First, despite the several in-house reorganization efforts since January 2007, the MOD still lacks a strong policy-planning capacity. While the MOD has invested in developing an institutional policy-planning capacity, it is far from sufficient. For instance, the MOD created the Strategic Planning Office at the time of the September 2007 reorganization. This office was intended to be an office that would focus on long-term strategy planning, such as drafting the National Defense Program Guideline, revising the overall policy for the MOD's defense exchange programs, assessing the future security threat, etc. In reality, however, the Strategic Planning Office has become a place where "the policy issues that involve more than one division within the MOD, both short- and long-term, are brought in" and consequently are "...hardly a place to focus on long-term issues.[110] The office's place within the MOD hierarchy—an office within the Defense Policy Division of the Defense Policy Bureau—does not grant the institutional clout that the office may need to fulfill its policy-planning responsibility. Its Chief, although holding the title of "director," is junior to the directors of not only the Defense Policy Division, but also other full divisions within the MOD. Considering the US Department of State's Policy Planning Staff reports directly to the Secretary of State, the bureaucratic stature of the MOD Strategic Planning Office is far from sufficient to be able to offer a long-term strategic view that wins the ears of senior officials within the MOD, let alone across the Japanese government.

Furthermore, the repeated MOD reorganizations—triggered by the scandals related to defense procurement, cases of intelligence leaks, and JSDF accidents—have created confusion within the MOD bureaucracy, spreading the missing sense of direction and lowering the morale of its officials. In particular, the initial reorganization proposal suggested by the Defense Minister Shigeru Ishiba of merging the Internal Bureau and the staff offices of three JSDF services and creating one staff office stocked with MOD personnel, both civilian and military.[111] The Advisory Council of the MOD Reform—established under the chairmanship of the Chief Cabinet Secretary in February in 2008—submitted its recommendation to the prime minister in June 2008.[xxi] In putting together the recommendations, some Advisory Council members were concerned that the original purpose of the council may be lost because the Council spends too much time on discussing how to change the "box (organization)" of the MOD rather than spending more time on what is inside the box. In fact, several Advisory Council members even warned that, while reorganization can be a useful tool in MOD reform, real change will not be brought to the MOD so long as the existing organizational culture and the mentality behind its business practices do not change.[112]

Still, the role of the Internal Bureau (*naikyoku*) indeed needs serious re-examination. As discussed earlier, the Internal Bureau historically has supervised and controlled all aspects of the SDF—from procurement to personnel—to keeping the SDF down" under the name of civilian control. The proponents of maintaining the Internal Bureau have argued in the past that the control of the JSDF by the Internal Bureau will prevent the SDF from returning to its militarist past. However, this is an anachronistic management model when the SDF is encouraged to expand the scope of its activities beyond Japan's borders. Now that Japan has a mature democracy, it is time to rethink the role the Internal Bureau played vis-à-vis the SDF, and consider a fundamental reorganization based on the principle that civilian officials and SDF officers work in partnership to shape a security policy for Japan, so that the MOD can proactively participate in the security policymaking process. The current status of the MOD reform discussion will be considered more carefully later in this chapter.

[xxi] Based on the Advisory Council's recommendation, the Ministry of Defense announced its reorganization plan in August 2008. See *Bouei-sho ni okeru Soshiki Kaikaku ni kansuru Kihon Houshin* (The Basic Principles for the MOD Organizational Reform), 27 August, 2008, http://www.mod.go.jp/j/news/kaikaku/20080827a.pdf (accessed 10 September 2008).

Cabinet Secretariat: increasing role, its effectiveness still in question

The Cabinet Secretariat (*naikaku kanbo*) is an organization that has seen its influence on national security policymaking in Japan steadily rise since the 1990s. As an organization that directly supports the prime minister, the Cabinet Secretariat is tasked with shaping the policies that are important for the prime minister and his/her cabinet and playing an intermediary role among the ministries as necessary. It also collects intelligence on the important policy issues.[113] The Cabinet Secretariat has 716 employees as of the FY 2008-09 (Chart 2-4-1).

Chart 2-4-1. Organizational Chart of the Cabinet Secretariat (simplified)

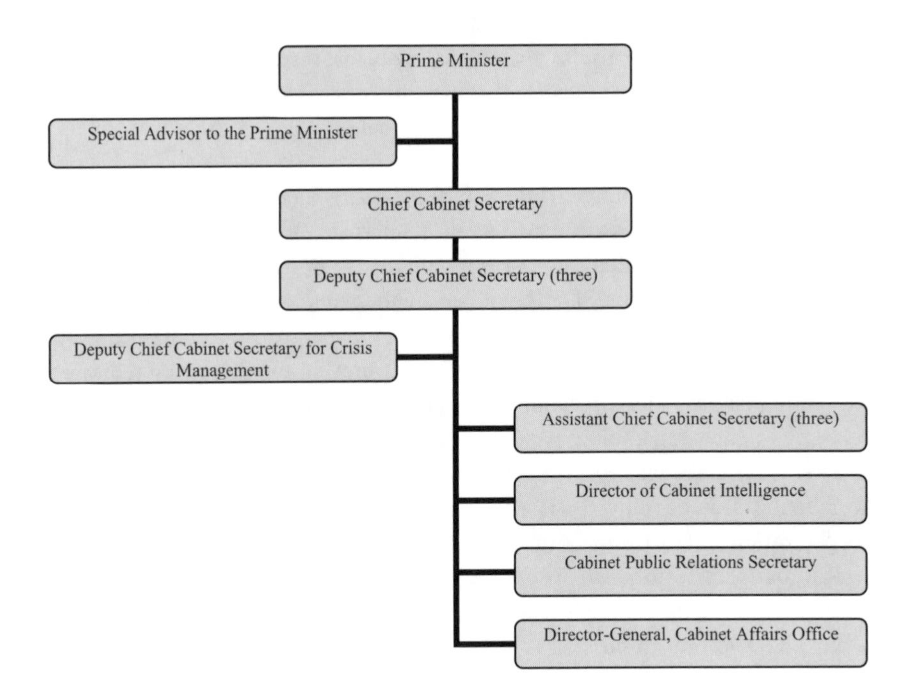

(Source: Cabinet Secretariat, *Soshiki-zu* (Organizational Chart). http://www.cas.go.jp/jp/gaiyou/sosiki/index.html (accessed 2 March 2008)).

Within the current organization of the Cabinet Secretariat, there are six positions that are relevant in Japan's national security policymaking. One is the Special Advisor to the Prime Minister. Out of five special advisors to the prime minister that are allowed under the Cabinet Law,[114] one is designated to be in charge of national security affairs. This position, however, has been vacant since Yuriko Koike, appointed by then Prime Minister Shinzo Abe in September 2006, left the position to become the defense minister in July 2007 (since then, Koike left the job of defense minister in August 2007 after a high-profile battle with Takemasa Moriya, then the vice minister of the Ministry of Defense). When Shinzo Abe launched the initiative to explore the establishment of an American National Security Council-style staff organization to support the Prime Minister and Chief Cabinet Secretary on providing greater guidance and input, as well as making decisions on Japan's national security policy, this position would have been critical in heading the envisioned organization.

Chief Cabinet Secretary is arguably the most important individual (next to the prime minister him/herself of course) in the Cabinet Secretariat when it comes to Japan's national security policymaking. The Chief Cabinet Secretary is mandated to provide oversight for all the works that the Cabinet Secretariat is involved.[115] Of all the senior staff in the Cabinet Secretariat, only the Chief Cabinet Secretary is granted the status of Minister of State, and therefore is authorized to participate in the cabinet meeting. This position is also the only position that has a pre-World War II tradition. Before 1947, the position had the title of the Executive Secretary of the Cabinet (*naikaku shokikan*-cho)—when the current Japanese constitution took effect in 1947, the position gained the current title of the Chief Cabinet Secretary. When describing the role of the Chief Cabinet Secretary using US terminology, some describe the position as "three positions in one"—that is, the Chief Cabinet Secretary of Japan assumes the role of (1) vice president, (2) national security advisor, and (3) chief of staff. In concrete terms, the Chief Cabinet Secretary plays a quiet but critical role in working with the government (all the ministries and agencies), and the Diet (both ruling and opposition parties) in order to implement his/her cabinet's policies. Also, it is often the Chief Cabinet Secretary, not Special Advisor to the Prime Minister for Public Relations or the Cabinet Press Relations Secretary, who holds press conferences on a regular basis—this effectively makes the Chief Cabinet Secretary a government's spokesman as well.[116]

As such, throughout the history of Japanese politics, the Chief Cabinet Secretary has had the highest confidence of the prime minister at the time. The position is often described as "*sori no nyobo-yaku* (the role of prime minister's wife))" or "*sori no futokoro gatana* (the prime minister's right hand man)," both referring to the critical nature of Chief Cabinet Secretary's support for the prime minister, as well as the position's influence in the government as someone who has the ears of the prime minister. Furthermore, the Chief Cabinet Secretary was designated to be the first-in-line to assume the position of acting prime minister should the prime minister be incapacitated due to illness or other emergency reasons in April 2000. This has made this position all the more important within the government, making him/her one of the key players in Japan's national security policymaking as well.

Deputy Chief Cabinet Secretary for administration is also a critical player in Japan's national security policymaking. Its bureaucratic status within Japanese bureaucracy, and the influence that the position brings to it, not the expertise in national security affairs required for the job, makes this position very important in Japan's national security policymaking. Simply put, Deputy Chief Cabinet Secretary sits at the top of the entire Japanese bureaucracy. Although there is no formal "requirement" to be appointed as the Deputy Chief Cabinet Secretary for administration, it is customary that a retired senior civil servant is appointed to serve in the position after having completed service as the administrative vice minister—the highest bureaucratic position in Japanese bureaucracy—at one of the ministries in the Japanese government.[xxii] This makes the Deputy Chief Cabinet Secretary for administration the highest-ranking bureaucrat in Japanese bureaucracy: this status alone allows the Deputy Chief Cabinet Secretary for administration to exert influence in inter-agency negotiation during policymaking.

The longevity of the tenure also makes the Deputy Chief Cabinet Secretary for administration important in Japan's policy/decision-making process. Deputy Chief Cabinet Secretary is not the Minister of State and therefore, he/she is not obligated to resign as the cabinet changes. While Parliamentary Deputy Chief Cabinet Secretary (two are appointed) rotates in and out with the cabinet changes, Deputy Chief Cabinet Secretary for administration tends to stay, providing the only sense of continuity at the senior level of the government. In case in point, Japan has had five prime ministers since 2000 whereas only three individuals have served as the Deputy Chief Cabinet Secretary for administration during the same period.

The critical role of the Deputy Chief Cabinet Secretary for administration was tested a number of times throughout the 1990s when Japan faced various crises. For instance, when the Hanshin-Awaji earthquake hit Japan in January 1995, it was Nobuo Ishihara, then Deputy Chief Cabinet Secretary for administration, that played a key role in the Cabinet Secretariat's efforts in collecting the information on the damage. When the first North Korean crises occurred in 1993 and the tension for potential military conflict on the Korean Peninsula rose, it was also Ishihara that orchestrated the Japanese government's effort to

---

[xxii] Usually, former vice ministers of the agencies that used to be a part of pre-World War II Interior Ministry (*naimu-sho*)—the Ministry of Home Affairs (*Jichi-sho*), the NPA, the Ministry of Health and Welfare (*kosei-sho*), and the Ministry of Labor (*rodo-sho*), for example—are appointed to serve in this position.

respond, putting together contingency plans, identifying the shortcomings in the existing legal frameworks along the way. Finally, it was also Ishihara that initially spearheaded the Japanese government's effort to improve its intelligence gathering and analyses capability.[117]

Supporting the Chief Cabinet Secretary and the Deputy Chief Cabinet Secretary, Deputy Chief Cabinet Secretary for Crisis Management is obviously an important player for its central role in coordinating the Japanese government's response to a national crisis. The position has a mandate to assist Chief Cabinet Secretary and Deputy Chief Cabinet Secretaries in the area of crisis management.[118] Since extensive knowledge in the workings of the domestic security system is required for this position, every individual that has served in this position (including the incumbent) up to the present are former senior NPA officials. Also, while most of the senior government positions rotate every 18-24 months, the Deputy Chief Cabinet Secretary for Crisis Management serves a longer term—the average period of service of the three former Deputy Chief Cabinet Secretary for Crisis Management is three years.[119]

Assistant Chief Cabinet Secretary for national security and crisis management is mandated to "assist the Chief Cabinet Secretary, Deputy Chief Cabinet Secretary, and Deputy Chief Cabinet Secretary for Crisis Management." The position is customarily filled by an official seconded either from the MOD or NPA (the incumbent is a seconded MOD official). While the Deputy Chief Cabinet Secretary for crisis management ultimately takes charge in Japanese government's efforts to respond to national emergencies, the Assistant Chief Cabinet Secretary plays a primary role within the Cabinet in shaping Japan's national security policy on a day-to-day basis.

The role of the Assistant Chief Cabinet Secretary for national security and crisis management and his team has been increasing in Japan's national security policymaking. Following the 9-11 terrorist attacks in 2001, for instance, they played a central role in drafting the Anti-Terror Special Measures Law, which enabled Japan to dispatch the JSDF for a refueling mission in the Indian Ocean. When then Prime Minister Junichiro Koizumi expressed his support for US war against Iraq in March 2003, then Chief Cabinet Secretary Yasuo Fukuda and then Assistant Chief Cabinet Secretary for national security and crisis management Keiji Ohmori initiated the decision to form an interagency team (comprised of the officials from MOFA, JDA and other agencies) to prepare the Iraq Reconstruction Special Measures Law.[xxiii] Further, this team played a

---

[xxiii] He is the fifth MOD "proper" to hold this position. Most of his predecessors all started their civil service career either at the NPA or the Ministry of Finance (MOF) and then were transferred to

central role in drafting the contingency legislation which was enacted in 2003, as well as the US force realignment implementation legislation. Furthermore, this position and its supporting staff played a leading role in the process of Japan revising the 2004 National Defense Program Guideline. Compared to 1995, the office of the Assistant Chief Cabinet Secretary for national security and crisis management was much more involved in the revision process, including the drafting.[120] As such, among the agencies that are traditionally identified as the national security policy agencies (NPA, MOD, and MOFA), there seems to be an acknowledgment that the Assistant Chief Cabinet Secretary and his office will likely expand their role in Japan's national policymaking.

Finally, the Director of Cabinet Intelligence (DCI, *Naikaku Joho Kan*) has an important role of collecting and providing the intelligence on high-priority policy issues for the cabinet in order to support the Prime Minister, the Chief Cabinet Secretary, and the Deputy Chief Cabinet Secretary for National Security and Crisis Management.[121] The DCI also heads the Cabinet Intelligence and Research Office (CIRO). The Cabinet Intelligence Satellite Center, established in 2001 following Japan's decision to introduce the multi-purpose information-gathering satellite, also reports to the DCI. With the most recent reorganization that took effect in May 2008, the Cabinet Intelligence Officer has five Senior Intelligence Analysts (*bunseki-kan*) directly reporting to him. The position of the Cabinet Intelligence Officer is customarily assumed by the senior officials seconded from the NPA, particularly those who developed their careers in the NPA in the field of public safety and security.[xxiv]

It took several organizational restructurings in the Cabinet Secretariat to become today's organizational structure. First began with then Prime Minister Yasuhiro Nakasone's decision to create six policy coordination offices in 1986; the ultimate goal behind the past reorganization efforts was to enhance the Cabinet Secretariat's capacity so that it could better assist the prime minister in policy- and decision-making processes. Restructuring of national security-related offices was a part of an overall effort to enhance the support for the prime minister within the Cabinet Secretariat.

During this process, the organizational structure for Japan's national security policymaking was streamlined, its authority steadily consolidated. When the process began in 1986, the Cabinet Office of National Security was established as one of the six cabinet offices, whose director was dual-hatted as the director

---

the MOD in mid-career; Shinoda, Tomohisa, "Japan's Top-Down Policy Process to Dispatch the SDF to Iraq" *Japanese Journal of Political Science* vol. 7 November (1) (2006) 75–76.

[xxiv] For instance, the incumbent served as the director of Foreign Affairs and Intelligence Department before assuming the current position.

of the Office of National Security in the Prime Minister's Office. However, this organizational arrangement was cumbersome even when the position of director of the two offices was effectively served by the same individual. The authority was divided between the Office of National Security in the Cabinet Secretariat and the Office of National Security in the Secretariat of the Prime Minster's Office, and the roles of the NPA and MOD (then JDA) were not clear.[xxv] The inefficacy of this system was revealed in the mid-1990s when Japan suffered from a series of natural and manmade disasters as well as national security crises. Each time, the Japanese government was criticized for the tardiness of its response as well as the lack of a sense of urgency. Inside the government, confusion over the flow of information as well as important information not being communicated to the prime minister due to bureaucratic stovepiping led to the prime minister's inability to respond timely and effectively.[122]

Further rationalization of national security-related positions within the Cabinet Secretariat in the 1990s took place in the context of how to better equip the prime minister with the institutional support necessary for crisis management. The position of the Deputy Chief Cabinet Secretary for Crisis Management was created in April 1998 as the central coordinator in the Japanese government's crisis management system. At this time, the Offices of National Security in the Cabinet Secretariat as well as the Prime Minister's Office were renamed as the Office of National Security Affairs and Crisis Management.[123]

When the comprehensive administrative reform took effect in January 2001, the Prime Minister's Office was abolished and reorganized, along with several other agencies, into the Cabinet Affairs Office (*Naikaku-fu*). At that time, the Office of National Security Affairs and Crisis Management in the Prime Minister's Office was abolished, and its function and authority was integrated into the Cabinet Secretariat. In turn, the Office of National Security Affairs and Crisis Management was reorganized as the organization under the Cabinet Counselor for Crisis Management (*kiki kanri tantou shingi-kan*) who reports to the Assistant Chief Cabinet Secretary for National Security and Crisis Management.[124] With the streamlining of the organization, the office of Assistant Chief Cabinet Secretary for national security and crisis management also began to assume a greater role in providing policy and legislative support for the Chief Cabinet Secretary and the Prime Minister in the area of national security. As previously examined, this office played a leading role in drafting the 2001 Anti-Terrorism Special Measures Law, the 2008 Replenishment

---

[xxv] The Office of National Security in the Cabinet Secretariat was in charge of addressing the issues that require cabinet-level attention, and the Office of National Security in the Prime Minister's Office was in charge of inter-agency coordination on day-to-day business.

Support Special Measures Law, and the 2003 Iraq Reconstruction Special Measure Law. The office also played a key role in enacting the contingency legislation in 2004.

The repeated reorganization of the Cabinet Secretariat, including the national security-related offices, suggests that the status of the Cabinet Secretariat is still evolving. One should note that the past reorganization efforts often focused on how to help political leadership better respond to national emergencies. The evolving role of the office of Assistant Chief Cabinet Secretary also suggests that the Cabinet Secretariat has been more actively engaging in interagency policy coordination process. However, despite the calls to improve the Cabinet Secretariat's policy-planning capacity existed as early as the 1980s, the efforts in this area are still at a nascent stage. The attempt by then Prime Minister Shinzo Abe to create an American-style National Security Council within the Cabinet Secretariat (discussed later in the chapter) was in fact the first serious effort in this regard. Thus, although the Cabinet Secretariat is better structured to handle national emergencies such as large-scale disasters, its policy-making capacity still has much room for development.

CHALLENGES AHEAD

The civilian institutions in Japan's national security policy infrastructure have evolved over time. The evolution of their organization accelerated after the end of the Cold War. Looking ahead, what are the anticipated challenges for these institutions in the years ahead if Japan is to have a sound institutional foundation for its national security policy?

The continually shifting dynamics concerning which agencies are in charge of shaping and executing Japan's national security policy is important to note. Aside from the challenges that each civilian institution faces, interagency coordination perhaps remains the greatest challenge in making Japan's security policy infrastructure function effectively.

Interagency coordination is not a new challenge for Japan's national security policy infrastructure. Even during the Cold War, the ideal goal for Japan was to have all the relevant government agencies—MOFA, JDA, NPA and the offices in the Cabinet Secretariat and the Prime Minister's Office in charge of national security and crisis management—to coordinate closely in shaping and executing Japan's national security policy. In reality, however, the interagency coordination was a serious challenge for these institutions. The NPA had the primary dominance in the issues that have to do with maintaining stability in Japan, and MOFA (North American Affairs Bureau, to be exact) had the primary responsibility in tending to Japan's alliance relations with the United States. The Cabinet Secretariat—what would have been the logical place within the Japanese bureaucracy to be in charge of shaping Japan's strategy and setting priorities for its national security policy—did not play a role much greater than that of coordinator for the agencies.[125] While the Office of National Security Affairs was established in 1986 with the intention of growing into an organization that would play a leading role in shaping Japan's national security policy, the effectiveness and the status of the office highly depended on the personal stature of its director and his/her personal relationship with the prime minister. This made it difficult to institutionalize the influence of this office in the policymaking process. Furthermore, during the Cold War, the global strategic environment was stable enough under the bipolar world order that Japan, while possessing the JSDF to defend itself from external aggression, did not ever have to actually consider using them. In such an environment, Japan's national security policy could be simply compartmentalized between external (countering threats from the Soviet Union) and internal (preserving domestic public order): MOFA's tending to Japan's relationship with the United States and the NPA's attention to domestic security sufficed. This provided little incentive for interagency coordination, allowing almost no role for the JDA within Japan's national security policymaking system.

Indeed, the Japanese government has ensured that the JDA stayed as a second-tier government agency through institutionalized bureaucratic customs in the past. For instance, until the 1990s, senior JDA positions were filled with officials that were seconded from the other leading national security policy institutions such as MOFA, Ministry of International Trade and Industry (MITI, was renamed as the Ministry of Economy, Trade and Industry (METI) in 2000), NPA and the Ministry of Finance (MOF). The senior positions within JDA that was in charge of JDA's external relations used to be filled by the officials that were seconded either from the NPA or MOFA.[xxvi] Senior JDA positions that are in charge of Japan's defense policy used to be filled with the officials seconded from the MOF or the NPA.[xxvii]

Circumstances changed drastically when the Cold War ended, which brought two major changes in Japan's security environment. First, as the bipolar global security structure gave way to the uncertain global security situation, Japan realized that it could no longer participate in world affairs only through

---

[xxvi] In fact, the tradition of placing senior MOFA officials in the position of the Councilor for International Affairs of the Internal Bureau still continues today and MOFA officials that are the rank of deputy director-general are seconded to the MOD to fill the position.

[xxvii] Prior to Takemasa Moriya assumed the position of the vice minister of defense in 2004, for example, there were only four others who spent their entire career as public servants at the JDA. Others were all seconded either from the NPA or MOF.

economic means. In other words, in order to assert itself as a responsible member of the international community, Japan now had to have its people, particularly the JSDF, take part in international efforts to maintain peace and stability. Even if the scope of what missions the JSDF could take part in were limited, it would be necessary for Japan to prove its willingness to share the burden of maintaining global peace and security.[126]

Secondly, questions about the validity of maintaining the US–Japan alliance in the post-Cold War era began to surface. In particular, the US–Japan alliance as a bulwark against communism and the Soviet threat had to be repositioned in a new strategic context if it were to survive after the collapse of the Soviet Union. As described later, such circumstances intensified the expectations that the United States held toward Japan. In the 1990s, the acknowledgement that the US–Japan alliance need to be redefined came in the form of the 1996 Tokyo Declaration for Security, which resulted in the revision of the US–Japan Guidelines for Defense Cooperation in 1997 and paved the way for Japan to enlarge its role in the US–Japan alliance. Given these changes, Japan entered a period in which it now had to start thinking about how to use the JSDF.[127]

The external changes triggered a shift in interagency dynamics in Japan's national security policy infrastructure. Namely, the increasing need for Japan to dispatch the JSDF abroad and the redefinition of the US–Japan alliance enhanced the JDA with its command of a 240,000-people-strong JSDF. While other agencies (i.e., MOFA and the NPA) were—and still are, to some extent—hesitant to accept the JDA's greater role, they almost had no choice, because only the JDA could command the JSDF.[128]

Today, compared to the early 1990s, the interagency coordination has improved a great deal. The MOD still accepts seconded officials from NPA, MOFA, MOF and MITI, but it also lends its officials to these agencies as well. For instance, the MOD began two-way personnel exchanges with the NPA, under which a director-level MOD official is placed in the NPA's Security Bureau. MOFA and the MOD have been exchanging their personnel among the offices related to nonproliferation, arms control, intelligence, regional security, and the US-Japan alliance for some time. Between the MOD and METI, as well, a deep cooperative relationship has been established between the two through personnel exchanges in the area of export control.[129]

In particular, improvement in the relationship between the MOD and the NPA in recent years is noteworthy. In 2000, the NPA and the MOD (then JDA) revised the basic cooperative agreement in case of JSDF mobilization to maintain public order in Japan. The original agreement which was put in place in 1954 only envisioned the scenario in which the JSDF and Japanese police would work together to qualm domestic disturbances such as a riot, and did not have unconventional scenarios (e.g., activities by North Korean agents in Japan) in mind. New agreements which spelled out specifics of the cooperation on the ground were signed in May 2002 between the SDF headquarters across Japan and the local police forces. In addition, the MOD (then JDA) and the NPA developed common response guidelines in case of incursion by armed foreign agents into Japan in September 2004. Regional JSDF headquarters and local police forces throughout Japan followed suit by also developing a common response manual in March 2005. Since then, the JSDF troops and local police forces have conducted a number of table top exercises as well as real joint exercises.[xxviii]

Interagency coordination still has much room for improvement, however. For instance, as much as the relationship has improved between the MOD and the NPA, many differences in culture remain—i.e. MOD, being a organization for national defense, focuses on deterring and stopping the adversary at all costs, whereas the NPA, primarily being a law enforcement agency, takes pains to ensure that its actions can be backed up with legal justification. While information-sharing has been much encouraged across the relevant national security agencies, a great deal of hesitancy remains, in particular, on the part of the MOD to share imagery data.[130] While the MOD and METI have increasingly had more discussions on cooperation in the area of export control, the discussion is often not open to other relevant government agencies such as MOFA.

Furthermore, as more agencies have assumed stakes in national security policy and Japan's national means to pursue its security, interagency coordination only increases in complexity. The Cabinet Secretariat-run Satellite Information Center is a good example of how the interagency coordination becomes more complicated as more agencies have day-to-day interactions with Japan's national security policy. The administrative staff and the analysts in the Cabinet Satellite Center, which was established in order to introduce indigenous information-gathering satellite (IGS), come from fifteen Japanese government ministries and agencies. While its imagery analysts are primarily seconded from the MOD, the satellite system is operated by the team that are by and large seconded officials from the Ministry of Land, Infrastructure and Transportation (MLIT) and *Somusho* (MEXT), neither of which has much exposure to national security

---

[xxviii] As of May 2008, JSDF regional headquarters have held the total of forty-two table top exercises with every single prefectural police headquarters. They also have conducted a total of fourteen real joint exercise with thirty prefectural police headquarters; Unclassified fact sheet provided to the author from the MOD: 8 May 2008.

issues.[131] This makes the interagency coordination within the Cabinet Satellite Information Center all the more important, but more complex as well.

Secondly, the development of the policy-planning capacity within the Cabinet Secretariat remains an important challenge. In fact, if Japan is to have an effective security policy infrastructure to support its political leadership, an enhanced Cabinet Secretariat at the top to support Japanese leadership would be a key necessity.

In this context, the debate over creating the Japanese-style National Security Council (J-NSC) while Shinzo Abe served as prime minister was interesting. Although expressing concerns in the beginning, the relevant national security policy agencies, including MOFA, MOD and NPA, eventually supported the idea.[132] While recognizing that the details of the J-NSC would take time to be finalized, these agencies all acknowledged the need for a national security office in the cabinet that functions like a policy planning staff for the prime minister and chief cabinet secretary.[133]

On the other hand, the officials in the Cabinet Secretariat, including those who have been seconded from other government agencies, turned out to be less supportive of the idea.[134] Typical concerns they raise include (1) that the current Japanese bureaucracy could use fewer layers of supervision, not more; and (2) that too much overlapping of the proposed functions of the J-NSC and the existing function of Cabinet Secretariat offices would exist. They also raise questions about whether qualified individuals can be found and recruited outside the Japanese government.[135] They usually argue that further expansion of the existing office in its staff size and authority would serve the prime minister and the chief cabinet secretary adequately for the time being.

Still, both proponents and opponents of the J-NSC idea agree that even the expansion and enhancement of the existing organization only provides temporary solutions. Consensus seems to exist throughout the Japanese government that the current policy- and decision-making processes in Japan's national security policy infrastructure inhibit the Japanese government from (1) conducting long-range strategic planning and providing strategic guidance to the government agencies, (2) executing national security policies that require a complex web of interagency coordination to succeed, and (3) assisting the prime minister and chief cabinet secretary's decision-making based on policy analyses and proposals using information acquired independently from the bureaucracy. They recognize that the Chief Cabinet Secretary carries too big a political and policy portfolio, so that appointing the Chief Cabinet Secretary for National

Security Affairs, for instance, and having him/her head the J-NSC is a reasonable proposition.[136]

In this context, both proponents and opponents of the J-NSC concept lament that the J-NSC debate was overly politicized by having two politicians with strong egos at the time (Yuriko Koike and Yasuhisa Shiozaki, respectively serving as the Special Advisor to the Prime Minister in charge of national security and Chief Cabinet Secretary at the time) closely involved in the debate. As a result, the discussion always had an overlay of "proxy war" between Koike and Shiozaki over who was closer to Abe, who had his ears, and who would be the prime minister's national security advisor. They point out that the real discussion on how to institutionalize stronger support for the prime minister's policy and decision-making process should be independent from the bureaucracy on one hand, while maintaining political non-partisanship on the other was lost in the debate.[137]

Almost twenty years since the Cold War ended, civilian institutions in Japan's national security policy infrastructure have evolved in the direction of greater interagency coordination and enhancement of the Cabinet Secretariat. Substantial progress has been made in improving the tension that had existed between the MOD and other agencies that used to restrict the MOD's scope of activities. However, Japan still has much to go in further overcoming the tension and the rivalry among these agencies. While the interagency coordination among national security institutions have improved, Japan still lacks the institution in the government that support the prime minister's policy- and decision-making capacity in the policymaking processes. The Cabinet Secretariat, albeit having made considerable progress in placing itself in a more effective position, still needs to have its authority further enhanced by appropriate political and bureaucratic stature within the Japanese bureaucracy in order to perform that function. This will continue to keep Japan's national security policymaking process essentially decentralized, inhibiting the prime minister from having his/her policy priorities better reflected and making decisions with greater agility.

—3—
UNIFORM INSTITUTIONS

The civilian agencies that are examined in the previous chapter are expected to provide strategic direction and set priorities in Japan's national security policy. When prioritized policies require manpower to execute them, other parts of Japan's security policy infrastructure shoulder that task. Most commonly, such tasks are implemented through the activities by the Japan Self-Defense Forces (JSDF), Japan Coast Guard (JCG) and, in case of emergency situations inside Japan, local police forces and other responders (i.e., fire departments, medical facilities). In this chapter, the three organizations—JSDF, JCG and local police forces—that play primary roles in the Japanese government's efforts in response to national security crises will be examined on their organizational structure, the evolution of their roles in Japan's national security policy since the end of the Cold War, and the future challenges they face as organizations.

THE JAPAN SELF-DEFENSE FORCES

The Japan Self-Defense Forces (JSDF) originates in the National Police Reserve (*Keisatsu Yobi-tai*) that was established in 1950. After first being renamed as a Security Force (*Hoantai*) in 1952, the SDF (*Jiei-tai*) was officially inaugurated with its current name in 1954 when the Japanese Diet passed legislation that established the Japan Defense Agency (JDA)[138] and the SDF.[xxix][139] In the first five decades of its history, the core mission of the JSDF was defined as defending Japanese territory. Since the 1990s, however, as anticipation rose for JSDF's participation in peacekeeping and other international operations by multinational forces, calls for placing greater emphasis on international operations steadily grew. Consequently, when the Self-Defense Forces Law—the law that defines the SDF organizational structure and responsibilities—was revised alongside the Japan Defense Agency (JDA)'s upgrade to the Ministry of Defense (MOD) in 2006, the core mission of the JSDF was redefined as (1) defense of Japan, and (2) engagement in the international activities that are deemed to contribute to a stable and secure international security environment.[140]

[xxix] For a detailed discussion of the evolution of JSDF missions, see Tatsumi, Yuki. "Self-Defense Forces Today—Beyond an Exclusively Defense-Oriented Posture?" in Tatsumi, Yuki and Andrew L. Oros eds.. *Japan's New Defense Establishment: Institutions, Capabilities and Implications* (Washington: The Henry L. Stimson Center 2007) 25-32.

For most of its five-decade-long history, the JSDF has suffered from the fundamental problem as an institution—the constitutionality of its existence itself had been questioned. Article Nine of the Japanese constitution reads as follows:

Aspiring sincerely to an international peace based on justice and order, the Japanese people forever renounce war as a sovereign right of the nation and the threat or use of force as means of settling international disputes. 2) In order to accomplish the aim of the preceding paragraph, land, sea, and air forces, as well as other war potential, will never be maintained. The right of belligerency of the state will not be recognized.[141]

A logical reading of this sentence poses a question why, under a constitution that explicitly outlaws Japan to possess military, the JSDF was able to come into being in the first place. A short answer to this question would be because the JSDF was originally *not* established as a military force but rather created as a constabulary force. Further, because the National Police Reserve was established through a General Headquarters (GHQ) ordnance, a normal legislative process was effectively skipped over.[142] During the debate that led to the reorganization of the NPR into the JSDF, the Japanese government explained that the creation of the JSDF would not violate the constitution because "war potential refers to a force with the equipment and organization capable of conducting modern warfare… it is neither unconstitutional to maintain capabilities that fall short of war potential nor …to utilize these capabilities to defend the nation from direct invasion."[143] This original characterization of the JSDF continues to handicap it today.

The JSDF consists of three services—Ground Self-Defense Force (GSDF), Air Self-Defense Force (ASDF) and Maritime Self-Defense Force (MSDF). As of the end of the fiscal year (FY) 2007, the JSDF's personnel numbers totaled 236,028.[144] Its FY 2007 budget is approximately $41.14 billion.[145] Each service is led by the Chief of Staff (*bakuryocho*) who, with the support from the officers in the Staff Offices (*bakuryo kanbu*), oversees the day-to-day operation of each JSDF service and also serves as the highest-ranking military advisor to the defense minister.[146] The SDF Law designates the prime minister as the supreme commander of the JSDF. The minister of defense, supported by each service chief as well as the Chairman of Joint Staff, commands the JSDF.[147]

Air Self-Defense Force

JASDF is the newest service that was established after World War II. With approximately 44,717 active duty personnel and 800 in reserve (as of FY 2007),[148] the JASDF has three core missions: defense of Japan's airspace, response to large-scale disasters and other emergencies, and contribution to international efforts for peace and security.

The primary mission of the JASDF is to defend Japan's airspace. During peacetime, JASDF aircraft and surveillance radars are put on alert to (1) detect unidentified aircrafts that enter Japanese airspace, (2) identify whether such aircrafts are friends or foes, and (3) in case of suspicious aircrafts, counter them and ensure that they exit Japanese airspace as soon as possible. In time of conflict, JASDF would destroy, if necessary, enemy aircraft that invades Japan's airspace. In 2003, its primary responsibility in the defense of Japan's airspace made the JASDF the service responsible for the operation of Japan's ballistic missile defense system.[149]

Secondly, the JASDF supports local authorities in Japan in case of large-scale disasters (natural or manmade) by providing aerial reconnaissance and transporting aid materials and personnel. The dispatches are made based on the requests from local authorities, usually by the prefectural governments. In order to respond to such requests in a more effective and timely manner, the JASDF established a set of guidelines that defines (1) the general principles for response, (2) anticipated damages, and (3) anticipated nature of the requests under four geographical environments—urban areas, rural areas (mountains), distant islands, and special circumstances (i.e., emergencies that involve weapons of mass destruction (WMD), terrorist incidents). In each situation, the JASDF is primarily expected to provide initial surveillance capability, and transportation including the evacuation of the residents in the affected area.[150]

Finally, since the end of the Cold War the JASDF has been increasingly asked to utilize its domestic disaster relief capabilities—its transport capability, in particular—for international disaster relief and other multinational activities.[151] Since 1992, the JASDF has participated in UN peacekeeping efforts in Cambodia, East Timor, and the Golan Heights, as well as in international disaster and humanitarian relief activities in Rwanda, Afghanistan and Indonesia. The JASDF has also conducted transport missions out of Kuwait in support of the reconstruction efforts in Iraq since 2003.[152]

The JASDF is managed through five functional commands (Chart 3-1-1).

Chart 3-1-1. Organization of the JASDF[xxx]

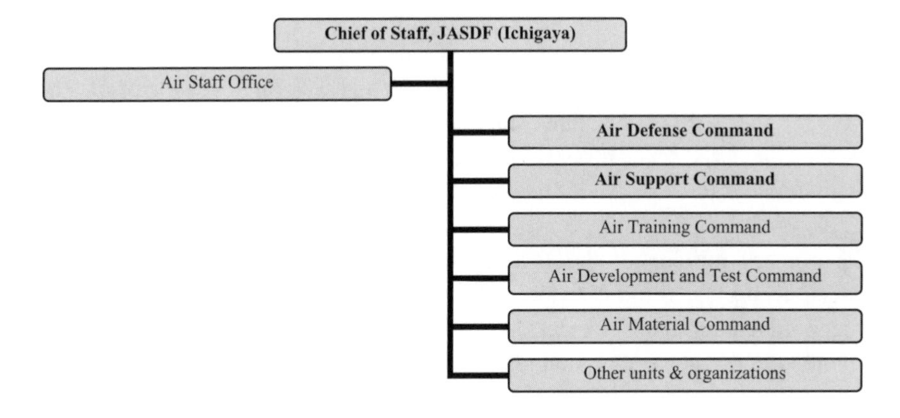

(Source: Ministry of Defense. http://www.mod.go.jp/asdf/english/formation/index.html (accessed 5 March 2008)).

Two commands are critical to JASDF's operations. First, the Air Defense Command (*Koku Sotai*) is the biggest JASDF command and oversees JASDF's air defense operations. It is also the first group that will be given air combat missions. Four regional air forces (Northern Air Defense Force, Center Air Defense Force, Western Air Defense Force, and Southwestern Air Composition Division), a tactical air reconnaissance group, an airborne early warning group, a headquarters flight group, and a tactical fighter training group are placed under this command, and is commanded by a three-star general.[153] After Japan decided to introduce ballistic missile defense, the Air Defense Command also took on the responsibility of operating Japan's ballistic missile defense system. With the establishment of the Bilateral Joint Operation Center for ballistic missile defense at Yokota Air Force Base (AFB), the Air Defense Command and the units relevant for the operation of ballistic missile defense will co-locate with US Fifth Air Force Headquarters at Yokota AFB to enable better bilateral coordination.[154]

Secondly, the Air Support Command, headquartered in Fuchu, coordinates and oversees JASDF's transportation missions, both domestic and international. It also supports the combat missions carried out by the troops under the Air Defense Command by providing necessary support, such as air traffic control and providing weather information. An air rescue wing, three tactical airlift wings, an air traffic control service group, an air weather service group, a flight

---

[xxx] "Other organizations" in the chart include Air Staff College, Central Air Band, Central Air Base Group, Air Communications and Systems Wing, Aero-safety Service Group, SDF hospitals and other facilities throughout Japan.

check squadron, and a special airlift group belong to this command. As the command that oversees the JASDF transportation mission, the role of this command has grown along with JASDF's increased participation in international missions. For instance, JASDF's ongoing missions in Iraq, and its participation in relief operations after the 2004 tsunami in Southeast Asia are both activities that have taken place under this command.

For most of its organizational history, response to incursions into Japanese airspace was the primary mission for the JASDF. Its force structure has emphasized air reconnaissance and defense missions. Rules of engagement for these missions are extremely strict, with shooting down suspicious planes allowed only when Japan is under imminent danger. Since the 1990s, responding to the diversification of its mission, the JASDF force structure has begun to shift away from its almost exclusive focus on air-to-air defense. In particular, as Japan decided to introduce a ballistic missile defense (BMD) system in response to the missile threat primarily posed by North Korea, the JASDF was designated as the lead JSDF service in Japan's efforts in acquiring BMD capabilities. Further, as JASDF's transportation capability turned into an asset that Japan could utilize for participating in various multinational military activities overseas, officials recognized the need to enhance the range and capability of its transport squadron.

Today, the JASDF force structure is in transition from the Cold War-era force structure that heavily emphasized fighter squadrons geared toward air-to-air defense operations to a structure that strikes better balance among the capabilities for air-to-air operations, ballistic missile defense, and transport. In particular, in response to the increasing need for the JASDF's transport capability in international disaster relief and other multinational operations, the JASDF began the process of overhauling its cargo fleet. In addition, the JASDF began to acquire mid-air refueling capability, recognizing that the lack thereof has restricted the agility in transport operations overseas.

The JASDF arguably is one of the most advanced air forces in the world. Despite its effort to consolidate and downsize, it continues to possess a sizable fighter fleet: as of FY 2007, it owns 280 combat capable aircrafts, out of which 260 are fighters.[155] When measured by the number of fighter aircraft and the supporting air control and warning systems, Japan trails only after the United States, England and France. This already makes the JASDF the world's fourth most powerful air force.[156]

As the lead service in BMD operations, a great deal of investment has been made in purchasing Standard Missile (SM)-3s, upgrading the radar systems of the JASDF surveillance aircraft as well as command and control systems that ensure that the JASDF BMD-related assets can function seamlessly with the assets operated by the Maritime Self-Defense Force (JMSDF). As of 2007, the JASDF commands six surface-to-air missile (SAM) groups which include eighteen batteries of PAC-3 (sixteen of them have been operational since 2006).[157] Given that US bilateral cooperation in BMD is most advanced with Japan, one can argue that JASDF's capability in BMD, with its current as well as to-be-acquired capability, is also one of the most advanced.

Looking into the near- and medium-term future, however, the JASDF faces considerable challenges. First is the future of its fighter fleet. The JASDF's most prominent asset for air defense has been its fighter. As its existing fighter fleet (consisted of F-2, F-15 and F-4) is aging, the modernization of its fighter is a major concern for the JASDF. On the one hand, with rapid modernization of China's People's Liberation Army Air Force (PLAAF), JASDF's capability advantage vis-à-vis PLAAF has been quickly shrinking for the last several years.[158] This has convinced the JASDF that, as it looks at the replacement aircraft for F-4s, the acquisition of fifth-generation fighters is key to maintaining the capability advantage against the PLAAF. On the other hand, given the JASDF's preference to acquire the equipment that already has proven capability, this only leaves the F-22 as JASDF's preferred choice to replace the F-4. However, under the Obey Amendment inserted in the FY 1998 Defense Appropriations Act, US law prohibits the foreign transfer of F-22s, making it highly uncertain when, if at all, F-22s can be released to Japan.[159] So far, the JASDF decided to wait to better gauge the releasability of the F-22 by accelerating the pace of upgrading the F-15 to lengthen its operational life.[xxxi] However, this can only serve as a temporary solution, and the JASDF will have to make its fighter acquisition decision in the next two to three years.[160]

Future of JASDF's transport capability is also in question. In response to the increasing needs, the JASDF has continued its effort to enhance its transport capability. In order to complement the existing transport capability the JASDF has been investing in the indigenous research and development of next-generation medium-range cargo aircraft (C-X). While considerable debate remains in and outside Japan regarding the wisdom of the JASDF attempting to indigenously develop the C-X (primarily driven by fiscal concerns), the JASDF originally projected to start acquiring new generation cargo by the end of FY

[xxxi] It is worth noting that the upgrading of the F-15 that was anticipated under the Mid-Term Defense Program FY 2005-2009 will be completed a year earlier than schedule by the end of FY 2008; Yasunori Nishida, "*Heisei20-nendo Bouei Kankeihi ni Tsuite* (FY 2008 Defense Budget)." *Finance* March 2008, 22.

2009. However, due to delays in testing, its introduction will be postponed at least until 2010.

Ultimately, the question that the JASDF faces is the vision for its force structure in the post-Cold War, post-9/11 world. Will the JASDF maintain its predominant focus on its air defense capability with its fighter, or will it aim to have a force that has a better balance between fighter, and transport and other logistic capability? How will it integrate the BMD system in its operational concept? Lack of clear answers to these questions will continue to complicate JASDF's modernization effort.

Ground Self-Defense Force

The Ground Self-Defense Force (JGSDF) holds the largest number of active-duty as well as reserve personnel of the three JSDF services. At the end of FY 2007, it had 144,994 personnel, 46,000 reserves, and 3,920 assistant reserves.[161] The primary mission of the JGSDF when it was established after the war was to "deter attack, repulse a small invasion, or provide a holding action until reinforced by the United States armed forces."[162] With the changes in the security environment surrounding Japan, the JGSDF missions have evolved. Today, the JGSDF describes its mission in the context of three areas of activities—responses to new threats, preparation for invasion, and efforts that contribute to improving the international security environment.[163] In concrete terms, its missions are threefold: homeland defense (both from conventional and unconventional threats), domestic disaster/humanitarian relief, and international activities (including participation in UN peacekeeping operations, international disaster/humanitarian relief efforts and participation in other types of activities conducted by multinational forces).

Homeland defense remains JGSDF's top-priority mission. While hardly recognized during peacetime, the JGSDF is indeed the first line of national defense in conventional warfare. From evacuation of citizens to consequence management, the JGSDF, working with the local authorities, will also command the on-the-ground operations in times of national emergency. However, in recent years, the JGSDF has begun to attract greater attention for its contribution in its other two missions—disaster relief and international activities.

JGSDF's role in domestic disaster relief activities first became known nationwide at the time of Mount Unzen Fugen's volcanic eruption in 1991. Because the JGSDF was the only organization that had the capability to operate near the eruption site, it ran around-the-clock surveillance of the volcanic activities, providing information to interested parties including evacuated residents, thus providing invaluable information and moral support. Its disaster relief operation in conjunction with the eruption continued until December 1995, which is the longest disaster relief deployment in the JGSDF's history.[164] Its large-scale disaster relief and support activities at the 1995 Hanshin-Awaji earthquake, along with its decontamination work and medical advice of JGSDF doctors and nurses at civilian hospitals at the time of the 1995 Sarin Gas attacks in the Tokyo subway, greatly contributed to improving the public image of the JSDF.[165] Since the end of the Cold War, the JGSDF has been dispatched to various parts of Japan for disaster relief operations, including the 2004 and 2007 earthquakes in Niigata, flooding in Kagoshima in 2006, and most recently in the aftermath of the earthquake in Iwate and Miyagi in June 2008.[166]

The JGSDF also has a long history of participating in international peacekeeping and other non-combatant operations. It first dispatched the engineering battalion in support of the UN Peacekeeping Operation in Cambodia in 1992. Since then, it has dispatched troops (mostly engineering and medical units) to the UN peacekeeping missions in Mozambique (1993), Golan Heights (began in 1996 and ongoing), East Timor (2002), and Nepal (2007). It also has dispatched troops to international disaster and humanitarian relief operations in Rwanda (1994), Honduras (1998), India (2001), Sumatra (2004), Pakistan (2005), and Indonesia (2006).[167] Furthermore, its participation in the reconstruction operation in Iraq in support of Operation Iraqi Freedom was a critical part of Japan's overall support of US-led coalition forces stabilizing post-conflict Iraq.

The JGSDF is divided into five regional armies, other specialized forces (including the Central Readiness Force) and six organizations (education and training institutions, Research and Development Headquarters, hospitals, logistics headquarters and the Regional Cooperation Headquarters). Out of these organizations, *Chiho Kyoryoku Honbu* (Regional Cooperation Headquarters) is a joint organization to facilitate the coordination between JSDF troops of all three services and local authorities throughout Japan (Chart 3-1-2).[xxxii]

[xxxii] Regional Cooperation Headquarters will be discussed later in this chapter.

Chart 3-1-2. Organizational Chart of the JGSDF (Simplified)

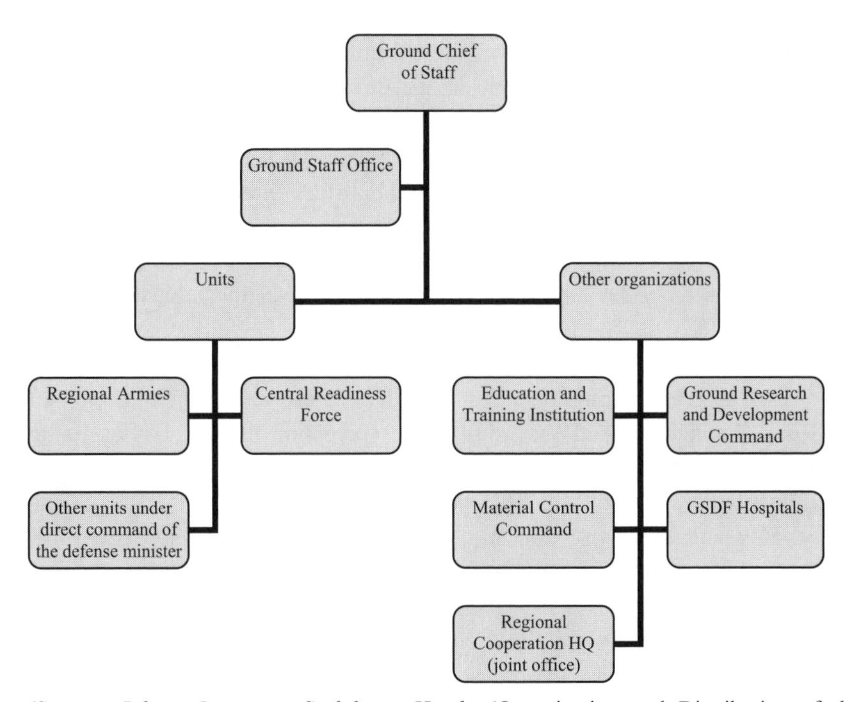

(Source: *Rikujo Jieitai no Soshiki to Haichi* (Organization and Distribution of the JGSDF). http://www.mod.go.jp/gsdf/about/chutonchi/index.html (accessed 6 March 2008)).

The JGSDF positions eight divisions and six brigades throughout Japan among five regional armies (northern, northeastern, eastern, central, and western). The Central Readiness Force (CRF), which was established in March 2007 and headquarters in Nerima, is a rapid-deployment force. It can respond quickly either to domestic emergencies or overseas missions.[168] Specialized units such as a WMD defense unit, special operations unit, and airborne unit belong to the CRF. The CRF also sends its personnel to participate in peacekeeping operations, to operate as an advanced party that conducts groundwork for follow-on JSDF deployments that are much larger in personnel size, as well as to train other countries' armed forces.[169]

The JGSDF has a number of training, research and educational institutions for its personnel. One institution that deserves particular attention is the Ground Research and Development Command (GRDC), also headquartered in Nerima, Tokyo. Led by a three-star general, the GRDC is mandated to conduct research on GSDF operational concepts, force structure, equipment, education and training, and develop new concepts in these areas. It also conducts analyses on its past operations, and puts together "lessons learned" from past JGSDF deployments. These "lessons learned" are collected, compiled, examined and analyzed, and eventually utilized for future training and education of the GSDF officers and soldiers. Most recently, at the time of the JGSDF deployment to Iraq, the materials compiled in GRDC's Center for GSDF Lessons Learned were used to prepare the troops that were to be deployed. Then, when its mission was completed in June 2007, researchers (all JGSDF officers) interviewed those who were deployed to Iraq. The results of these interviews were compiled and housed back in the Center for GSDF Lessons Learned. The JGSDF is also the only service in the JSDF that has a high school-equivalent youth educational institution.[170]

The JGSDF's primary mission is to defend Japanese territory from external invasion. During the Cold War, due to the perception that the Soviet Union posed the greatest security threat to Japan in those days, the JGSDF had to be ready to counter and repel Soviet large-scale invasion attempts that would use heavy tanks and artilleries. Because of the geography, Hokkaido (the most northern island in the Japanese archipelago) was envisioned to be the first logical target for the Soviets. Therefore, during the Cold War, the JGSDF concentrated its heaviest tanks and artilleries to the Northern Regional Army headquartered in Hokkaido. Also, since the JGSDF was not expected to operate overseas during the Cold War, the logistics support capability, including transport capability, was not given high priority. Rather, priority was placed on building a force that could fight conventional warfare in Japanese territory. Therefore, throughout the Cold War, the JGSDF invested its resources in acquiring heavy tanks, artilleries, surface-to-air missiles, and other heavy platform.

The end of the Cold War and the resulting changes in the international security environment mandated that the JGSDF reorganize. In particular, the JGSDF faced an urgent need to alter its force structure. The changing nature of the international system and security threats suggested that preparing only for a Soviet invasion was simply not sufficient to defend Japanese territory. Internally, the threat from large-scale invasion was replaced by the growing threat of domestic disruption caused by state and non-state actors employing unconventional methods. Further, the disappearance of the overarching Soviet threat has increased the risk that a clash over smaller-scale disputes (such as territorial claims) in East Asia would escalate into armed conflict. Externally, a growing need to participate in various non-combat peacekeeping operations and international disaster relief activities meant that the JGSDF became increasingly expected to handle long-distance deployment over a longer period of time. In short, the JGSDF has found itself in need of transitioning into a more mobile and agile yet lethal force that can respond to a broader set of threats.

The increasing awareness of new challenges has been driving the JGSDF's transformation efforts since the 1990s. Most visibly, the JGSDF has begun acquiring equipment that allows greater agility and mobility, including helicopters (combat, transport and multipurpose) and light armored vehicles. As insistent as it may be on maintaining a certain level of tanks and heavy artillery capability, the JGSDF has been reducing their numbers. For instance, the 2004 National Defense Program Guideline set the goal of reducing the JGDSF tanks by thirty percent. While short of achieving that goal, the JGSDF will have reduced its tanks by twelve percent by the time the current Mid-Term Defense Program is completed in FY 2009. Compared to the build-up level of tanks under the original 1976 National Defense Program Outline, this is a reduction by almost thirty-four percent.[171]

The JGSDF's transformation effort is also reflected in the changes in the deployment patterns of its forces. During the Cold War, the force structure of all the Regional Armies was more or less the same, with tanks and heavy artillery playing a central role. Under the 2004 NDPG, the JGSDF has set out to break this Cold War-era tradition. Today, the JGSDF deploys two types of divisions and brigades. One is readiness modernized divisions/brigades (*sokuo kindai-ka shidan/ryodan*). Deployed throughout Japan except for Hokkaido, their force build-up is geared toward responding to situations in which agility and flexibility of the force is essential.[172] The other, comprehensive modernized divisions/brigades (*sougou kindai-ka shidan/ryodan*), has a more traditional force structure that is deployed only in Hokkaido, with the assumption that Hokkaido is still the place that Japan faces a conventional threat.[173] Furthermore, the creation of the Central Readiness Force (CRF) demonstrates the JGSDF's interest in having a force that can be multi-tasked and deployed quickly to a broader range of threats more effectively.[174]

Today, the transformation of the JGSDF continues. Looking ahead, however, the JGSDF has several major challenges to overcome in order to evolve into a force that can meet the needs and expectations for it.

First, the necessity of a deeper reduction in JGSDF's tanks and heavy artillery needs to be debated more seriously. Heavy tanks and artillery are often subject to outside criticism as illustrative of the persisting Cold War-era mentality within the JGSDF. Only one-third of the tanks owned by the JGSDF today are capable of fighting in modern warfare. Moreover, the survivability of those that do have modern-warfare capability has long been in question due to the lack of self-protective armor. Further, the physical size of tanks severely restricts their maneuverability, making them only useful in Hokkaido.[175] The JGSDF may insist that it needs tanks for its homeland defense mission. It may also argue that now that the JGSDF is more likely to be asked to participate in overseas missions when security situations on the ground are unstable, retention of heavy equipment is justified. Even if the JGSDF's argument for retaining its tanks and heavy artilleries merits consideration, however, earnest questions still need to be asked. Whether holding onto tanks that are either obsolete or essentially not maneuverable in mainland Japan, or replace them with smaller and more maneuverable tanks is a key acquisition issue. At minimum, the present decision to maintain the current inventory of tanks should not be accepted at face value.

Secondly, not enough attention has been paid to the JGSDF's logistics. Up to present, the JGSDF has not invested much in the capability of its logistics. Because the JGSDF was not expected to conduct its operations outside Japanese territory, there was little perceived need for the JGSDF to develop capabilities in logistics. However, as the JGSDF's participation in overseas mission continues, it is also becoming critical that the JGSDF's logistical capability be developed accordingly in order to support the operations of the deployed JGSDF troops. Further, as the security threat against Japanese territory becomes diversified, it may allow the JGSDF little time before its troops are expected to conduct necessary operations. This makes the necessity for an enhanced logistical capability even more critical.[176]

Finally, as the JGSDF gains more experience in overseas operations, it is important that the "lessons learned" from such experiences are discussed openly to the greatest extent possible. Since its first participation in peacekeeping operations in Cambodia in 1993, the JGSDF has built fifteen years of experience in overseas operations. It has also gained valuable experiences through disaster relief operations in Japan. The "lessons learned" from these experiences are crucial as the JGSDF continues to evolve its force to be responsive and able to fulfill the role that is expected in today's security environment. In this context, the establishment of the Center for GSDF Lessons Learned in the Ground Research and Development Command in 2003 was epoch-making. Looking ahead, establishing a system in which "lessons learned" are collected, analyzed, and shared (as appropriate) will be a valuable process in JGSDF transformation.

Maritime Self-Defense Forces

At the end of FY 2007-2008, the JMSDF has 43,388 active duty personnel, with an additional 1,100 in reserve, making the JMSDF the service with the smallest personnel size.[177] With such a limited number of personnel, the JMSDF is tasked with three main missions. First, it defends Japan in the maritime domain. This includes the operation of sea-based components of the ballistic missile defense system, supporting defensive operations through conducting aerial reconnaissance and surveillance, and utilizing its submarines, surface combatants and transport vessels.[178]

In particular, surveillance and reconnaissance has long been a key JMSDF capability that directly contributes not only to the defense of Japan, but also to the maritime security of East Asia. The JMSDF surveillance aircrafts and helicopters perform missions regularly to identify any suspicious maritime activities around the Japanese territorial waters. During the Cold War, although hardly known to the broader public, this JMSDF capability functioned as an effective deterrent against Soviet submarines that operated in the Far East.[179] After the Cold War, JMSDF's surveillance, reconnaissance and patrol operations began to attract public attention as the media reported increased occurrences of suspicious maritime activities by foreign ships. In particular, the maritime patrol operations against a North Korean spy ship in March 1999 and against a Chinese submarine in November 2004 reiterated the significance of JMSDF's surveillance, reconnaissance and patrol capability for the defense of Japan.[180] In the last decade, the JMSDF was mobilized twice after its P3C aircraft identified such activities. In March 1999, the JMSDF was ordered to conduct maritime policing operations (*kaijo keibi kodo*) for the first time in its history when a North Korean spy ship entered the Japanese territory.

Secondly, the JMSDF engages in variety of overseas operations. In fact, the JMSDF is a forerunner to JSDF's participation in overseas operations—six JMSDF minesweepers engaged in a minesweeping mission in the Persian Gulf in 1992 after the 1990-91 Gulf War, marking the first-ever JSDF overseas deployment.[xxxiii] The JMSDF have also participated in international emergency disaster relief operations to provide medical and other support to the victims in the affected area. Further, it has engaged in salvaging a Russian submarine that had an underwater accident. Most recently, the JMSDF has supported the US-led multinational operation in Afghanistan to fight against terrorism by providing refueling support since 2001. Although suspended for several months at the end of 2007, the mission resumed in February 2008.[181] [xxxiv]

[xxxiii] See Ikari, Yoshiro, *Perusha-wan no Gunkan-ki—Kaijo Jieitai Soukai Butai no Kiroku* (Battleship Flag in the Persian Gulf: Record of JMSDF Minesweeping Flotilla) (Tokyo: Kojin-sha, 2007) for the accounts of those who were involved in the mission.

[xxxiv] Political turmoil in Japan, however, has created a great deal of uncertainty around the sustainability of the operation beyond January 2009.

Finally, in times of maritime accidents, the JMSDF responds to calls for search and rescue within Japanese territorial water. It also transports those who are afflicted by accidents to hospitals, as well as provides them with emergency relief materials. During natural disasters, it offers various supports at the request of prefectural governments and local communities.[182]

The JMSDF has four destroyer flotillas, five destroyer divisions, four submarine divisions, one minesweeper flotillas, and nine flight squadrons. They are organized into one fleet, five regional districts, an air training command and one training squadron. Each regional district is responsible for the defense of maritime areas which are divided into five regions: from Hokkaido to the northern tip of mainland Japan (jurisdiction of Ohminato District), the northeast to eastern part of Japan facing the Pacific Ocean (jurisdiction of Yokosuka District), the northeast to central west part of Japan facing the Sea of Japan (jurisdiction of Maizuru District), the southeastern part of Japan (Kure District) and the southern part of Japan (jurisdiction under Sasebo District). In addition, the JMSDF has communication command, material command, and six training schools for its officers and sailors (Chart 3-1-3).

Chart 3-1-3. Organizational Chart, JMSDF

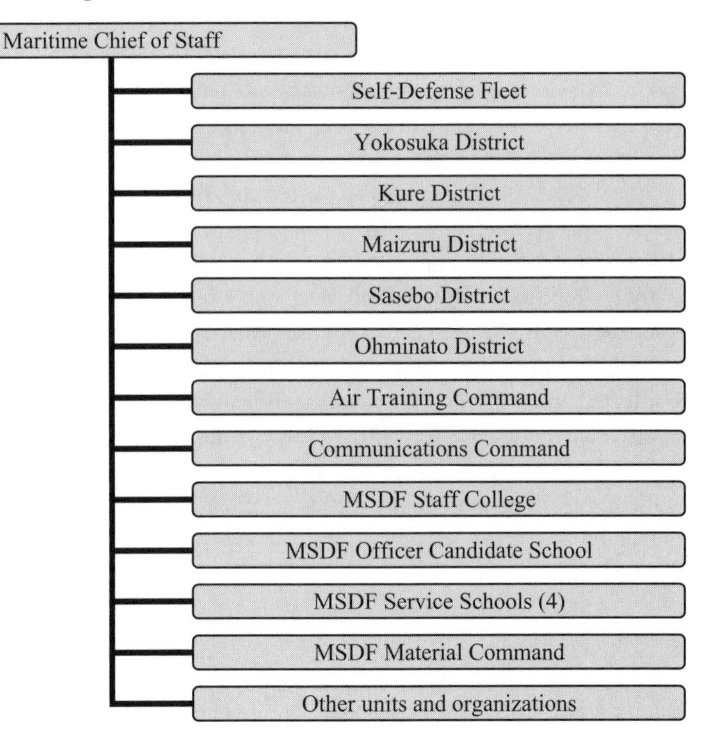

(Source: JMSDF, "*Kaijo Jieitai no Hensei* (JMSDF Organization)." http://www.mod.go.jp/msdf/formal/about/org/index.html (accessed 5 April 2008)).

With the reorganization implemented in March 2008, the JMSDF changed its operational structure. First, it altered the way it has organized destroyer units for mobile operations, re-organizing them into: (1) units that focus on the operation of helicopters, centered on the DDH that loads helicopters; and (2) units that focus on air defense, including the operation of ballistic missile defense, centered on the Aegis destroyers (DDG).[183] Further, instead of each district and the Self Defense Fleet separately commanding the units under their own jurisdiction, the Self-Defense Fleet essentially functions as a force provider. While certain basic functions (i.e., force protection) continue to stay with the regional districts and vessels, submarines, aircraft and helicopters continue to be stationed in one of the regional districts, the commander of the Self Defense Fleet now holds authority to decide the composition of vessels that will be used in each deployment. Commanders of each regional district, as force users, then command operations using the vessels assigned by the Self-Defense Fleet.[184]

When thinking about the force structure of the JMSDF, it is important to consider JMSDF's long cooperative relationship with the US Navy. Indeed, the relationship between the JMSDF and the US Navy is often said to be much closer than those between the JASDF and the US Air Force or the JGSDF and the US Army—so close that the JMSDF is sometimes called a part of the US Navy's Seventh Fleet by detractors. As such, from its earliest years, the history of the development of the JMSDF's force structure is closely related to the divisions of roles and their evolution between the JMSDF and the US Navy.

The divisions of roles between the US military and the JSDF are often described as "the spear (US military)" and "the shield (JSDF)." The relationship between the JMSDF and US Navy is no exception. In the context of such a basic division of roles, the JMSDF has organized its force structure around its primary mission of maritime defense of the homeland, focusing its force build-up efforts on three areas in particular—minesweeping, anti-submarine capabilities, and surveillance.[185] Because of the strategic environment in East Asia during the Cold War, the JMSDF build-up efforts for homeland defense also complemented the US Navy's deterrence capability in East Asia. In fact, those in the US Navy often point to how the anti-submarine and surveillance capabilities of the JMSDF contributed to deter the activities by the Soviet navy.[186]

The JMSDF's Cold War-era force structure and its force distribution reflected this reality. Having homeland defense of the maritime domain as its primary mission, the JMSDF focused on developing and acquiring assets for maritime defense (destroyers, frigates, and patrol/coastal combatants.) Due to the naval activities by the Soviet Union (particularly its submarines), the JMSDF had to develop the anti-submarine warfare (ASW) capability—submarines, patrol aircraft/combatant. Furthermore, because ensuring the freedom of navigation was deemed to be one of Japan's critical defense needs, mine warfare capabilities has also become critical. Anticipating that the threats against Japan will be conventional in nature and nation state-based, the JMSDF took a "zone defense" approach in distribution of these assets: while the JMSDF has secured mobile operation flotillas under the command of Defense Fleet, its assets were also distributed to five regional districts.

Today, the JMSDF has the extremely difficult task in conceptualizing its future force structure. On the one hand, the capabilities that were prioritized during the Cold War—homeland defense, mine warfare, and ASW—continue to be the JMSDF's core priority. On the other hand, the demand for JMSDF capabilities has been on the rise across the spectrum. Its capabilities in surveillance, anti-submarine operation, and minesweeping remain high. Particularly, with the emergence of a missile threat and the development of anti-access capabilities by China's People's Liberation Army Navy (PLAN), sustaining the JMSDF capability in these areas has become more important than ever. As the JMSDF is dispatched overseas with greater frequency, the demand for logistical support capabilities also has increased. In addition, since the 2003 decision by the Japanese government to introduce a ballistic missile defense (BMD) system, development of the BMD capability has been added to JMSDF's list of priorities.[187] Simply put, the JMSDF now finds itself having to enhance the capability of new areas while sustaining—or even strengthening—the capabilities that were its strength during the Cold War.

The recent acquisition decision by the JMSDF illustrates its effort to tackle this task. In responding to the demand for a greater JMSDF replenishment capacity, it introduced two AOE *Mashu* Class oilers in 2004 and 2005. Since they became operational, both vessels have replaced their predecessor AOE *Towada* Class oilers and have been engaging in the refueling mission in the Indian Ocean. Since there are only two vessels of this type, their operational tempo has been stretched to its maximum, with its crews experiencing several deployments to the Indian Ocean.

The acquisition of a new DDH *Hyuga* Class also signals the JMSDF's determination to maintain a balance between homeland defense capability and new operational areas. Built to be roughly the same size as the AOE *Mashu* Class, it is one of the JMSDF's largest vessels. Two DDH *Hyuga* Class destroyers—one will become operational in 2009 and the other in 2011—will replace DDH *Haruna* and *Hiei*. With an advanced command and control system, storage space that is big enough for either eight SH-60K surveillance helicopters or four MCH-101 transport helicopters, and the upgraded sonar system, it offers an enhancement of JMSDF's capability in the variety of areas. In case of a national emergency, the DDH *Hyuga* Class, as a wartime flagship, would serve as a command-and-control platform, coordinating the activities of other units while its organic helicopters conduct anti-submarine warfare operations. During peacetime, it would join the LST *Osumi* Class for peacekeeping and relief operations, as well as the other situations that are short of armed conflict that Japan foresees confronting on the high seas.[188]

Challenges for the JSDF

In addition to the service-specific challenges, the JSDF still faces three major challenges as an institution. While it is critical that both of the two challenges be addressed in enabling the JSDF to better support Japan to achieve its national security policy goals, both need long-term solutions and may need to overcome political and legal challenges.

First, how the JSDF can improve its performance as a joint force will continue to present the biggest challenge for the JSDF for the foreseeable future. The JSDF transitioned to a joint operation structure in March 2006. Today, the Chairman of the Joint Staff is granted the authority to (1) supervise the operations of the three JSDF services, (2) support the Minister of Defense on issues that involve the JSDF operations as his/her top military advisor, (3) execute the orders issued by the Minister of Defense regarding the JSDF operations, and (4) manage the administrative work of the Joint Staff.[189] Under the current structure, each service maintains responsibility for equipping and training its officers and soldiers as "force providers." But the Chairman of the Joint Chief and his staff, now as a "force user," has the jurisdiction over planning and executing joint operational plans. For the purpose of more effective and smoother joint operation, the Joint Staff Office also engages in planning joint training and other administrative tasks as necessary.[190]

There are signs that progress has been made. For instance, there has been greater communication efforts among the local units of the three SDF services at the Provincial Cooperation Office (PCO, *Chiho Kyoryoku Honbu*) that has been established in every prefectural capital throughout Japan (there are an additional three offices in Hokkaido). Renamed from Provincial Liaison Office (PLO,

Chiho Renraku-bu) in July 2006, it handles recruitment, public relations with local communities, and liaises with local governments to improve the relationship between the local community and the JSDF. The JSDF officers who have worked in the PCOs argue that after the March 2006 transition to a joint operation system, communication among the JSDF services at the PCO has significantly improved. Some also point out that the increasing frequency of JSDF overseas deployment has been an important driver in facilitating the inter-service cooperation at the PCO level.[191]

However, the JSDF has much room to improve in the assignment and training of its personnel for a joint force. On personnel management, it is questionable whether each JSDF service is motivated to assign its capable officers to the "joint" assignments. Prior to the March 2006 transition, there was a debate within the JSDF on whether an internal regulation should be created so that promotion beyond a certain rank will require experience in "joint" assignments: it was hoped that such a personnel management system would incentivize each JSDF service to assign its first-class officers to the positions in the Joint Staff Office. However, no clear guideline has been established, and it is unclear whether each service can really be persuaded to assign its capable staff outside its service. Further, JSDF officers and soldiers continue to be trained and educated by each service. As the JSDF is expected to operate in a joint environment more frequently (especially so in overseas missions), it is particularly crucial that the officers who command joint operations have knowledge, understanding and appreciation of such operations, as well as how to command them. Since the March 2006 transition, the curriculum at the Air, Ground, and Maritime Staff College, as well as the Joint Staff College began to put greater emphasis in joint education. The inter-service personnel exchanges that predate the transition (e.g., exchanges between students at the Staff Colleges had existed long before the March 2006 transition) has been enhanced. But because it has only been two years after the institutional efforts began in the JSDF for joint education, it will take a few more years before any tangible result can be achieved from these changes.

Second, although the Joint Staff Office is now in charge of matters related to JSDF operations, planning and programming responsibilities remain with each JSDF service. In other words, the Chairman of Joint Chiefs and his staff, while being a "force user," currently has no system through which their opinions can be considered in the force planning and programming process. Although the current programming and acquisition system may go through a drastic change due to the recommendations made by the Advisory Council on the MOD Reform as discussed in Chanter Two, a great deal of uncertainty remains on how each JSDF service can be incentivized to give up the plans and programming authority.

Finally, fiscal pressure will continue to constrain JSDF's efforts in modernizing their forces and adjust them to the evolving security environment. Although Japan is among the top five defense spenders, it spends less than 1 % of its Gross Domestic Product (GDP) on defense. In fact, since 2003, Japan's defense spending has been steadily decreasing by 0.9-1 percent.[192] Each JSDF service is going to need a considerable amount of resources in modernizing its assets and adjusting its structure to better meet today's security environment and capability requirements. The recent downward trend in defense budget, however, makes it clear that the resources available for the JSDF continue to be limited. In order to ensure that the JSDF can meet the 21st century security challenges, the availability of the resources will be a critical question.[193]

LAW ENFORCEMENT: JAPAN COAST GUARD AND LOCAL POLICE

In Japan, law enforcement agencies play important roles in national security policy. In particular, in case of emergencies inside Japan, law enforcement agencies are expected to bare primary responsibility in responding to the situation: the JSDF cannot be mobilized without their explicit consent and request. Even after the JSDF is mobilized, the cooperation between the JSDF and the law enforcement agencies are critical in successfully addressing national security concerns while maintaining public order.

Furthermore, in the post-9/11 security environment, what had traditionally been considered law enforcement matters are increasingly recognized as national security concerns. Terrorism and cyber crimes are a typical example of such concerns. Further, as the notion of maritime security and its significance to the country's national security is recognized more widely, piracy and other illegal activities that take place in the maritime domain are also being acknowledged more as potential national security threats. In Japan's case, in particular, its island geography makes maritime security one of its critical national security interests. As such, the law enforcement agencies are increasingly expected to cooperate with military and other elements of the country's national security policy community so that the security concerns are addressed both from law enforcement as well as national security perspectives.

In this context, the Japan Coast Guard (JCG) and Japanese police organization are both important components of Japan's national security policy infrastructure. This section examines these two organizations and discusses the recent efforts that they have been undertaking to respond to the changing environment surrounding their activities.

Japan Coast Guard (JCG)

The Japan Coast Guard (JCG), formerly named the Maritime Safety Agency (MSA), was established in 1948 as an agency under the Ministry of Transportation (today's Ministry of Land, Infrastructure and Transport and Tourism (MLIT)). It was established as a law enforcement agency that protects lives and prevents, investigates and stops illegal activities in the maritime domain.[194] Based on this mandate, the JCG has the mission of ensuring safety and security at sea by engaging in the following activities:[195]

- Enforcement of maritime laws and regulations;
- Maritime search and rescue;
- Prevention of maritime pollution;
- Prevention and suppression of criminal activities at sea;
- Criminal investigation and arrest at sea;
- Maritime regulation on ship navigation; and
- Business on waterways and navigation signs.

In the context of Japan's national security policy, it is important to note the JCG's primary responsibility is patrolling Japan's coastal areas, responding to violent activities at sea, engaging in criminal investigations and arrests at sea, detaining of suspects, participating in international investigative cooperation, and cooperating with other agencies including the police.[196] The JCG Law also authorizes the JCG to participate in international peacekeeping operations as long as it does not interfere with JCG's core mission.[197]

The Japan Coast Guard consists of two major components—central organization and regional coastal headquarters. (Chart 3-2-1.)

Chart 3-2-1. JCG Organization

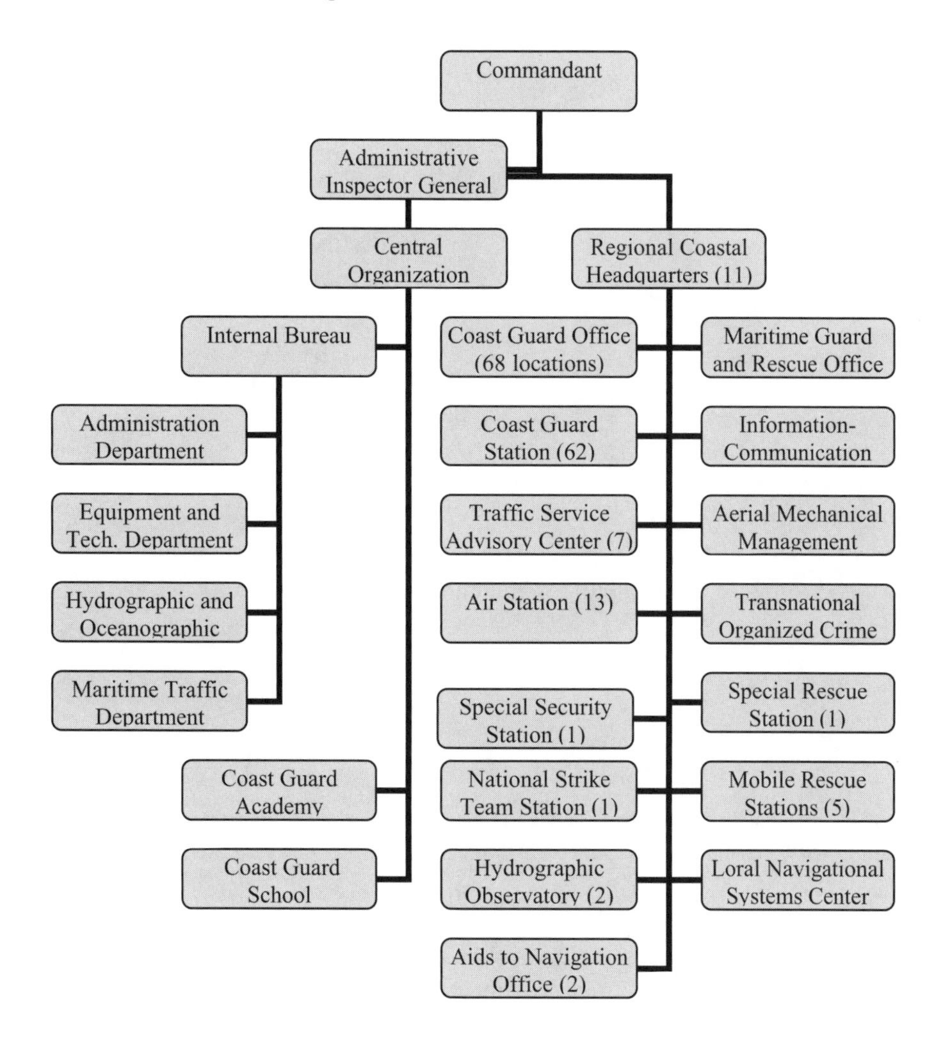

(Source: Japan Coast Guard "Organization," The Japan Coast Guard, *Kaijo Hoan Report 2007 nen-ban* (Maritime Security Report 2007). http://www.kaiho.mlit.go.jp/info/books/report2007/kakudai/p039_kakudai01.html (accessed 1 March 2008)).

The JCG with a staff of 12,321 (as of the end of FY-2006-2007) is much smaller compared to the JMSDF with its approximately 43,000 personnel.[198] Out of 12,324 personnel, those who are assigned to the central organization only amount to approximately nine percent (1,057). The vast majority—approximately 82.3 percent (10,738 personnel)—are assigned to eleven Regional Coastal Headquarters and engage in activities that ensure maritime safety in Japan's territorial waters and exclusive economic zones (EEZs) (Chart 3-2-2).[199]

Chart 3-2-2. JCG Regional Coastal Headquarters Areas of Responsibilities

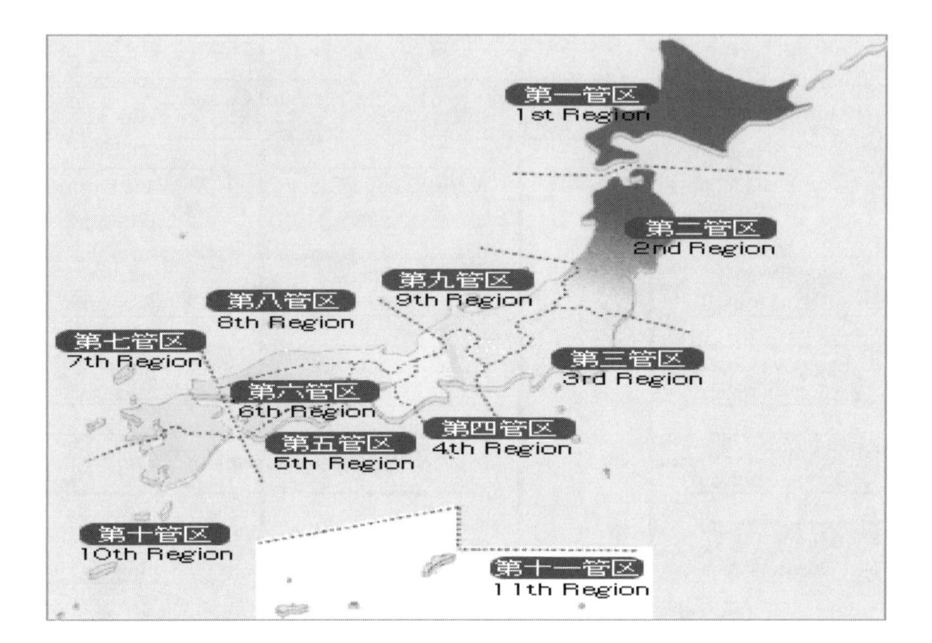

(Source: Japan Coast Guard, "Regional Headquarters Location." http://www.kaiho.mlit.go.jp/e/shigoto/soshiki/kanku/index_e.htm (accessed 1 March 2008)).

During the Cold War, the JCG, while being the agency that has primary oversight of issues of maritime security and safety in Japanese territorial waters, has maintained a relatively low profile in the area of national security policy. Since the end of the Cold War, however, its role in maritime security, particularly in the area that impacts Japan's national security interests, has been steadily expanding.

Japan's joining in the UN Convention on the Law of the Sea (UNCLOS) in 1996 was the initial factor that drove the JCG (then called itself the Maritime Safety Agency (MSA)) to strengthen and expand its role in maritime security. In its attempt to respond to the expansion of the sea surveillance area management after the enactment of UNCLOS, the JCG began its efforts to modernize and enhance its surveillance capability. A series of major maritime incidents that the JCG faced during the 1990s—the incursion of North Korean spy ships and the rising tensions in areas where Japan has territorial disputes (e.g., Takeshima/Tokdo Island, Senkaku/Daoyutai Islands)—further drove the JCG's effort to enhance its capability in surveillance, patrolling, and policing.[200] In particular, a sharp difference in the emphasis of the JCG's annual report can be identified between those that were published before 1998 and those that were published in 1998 and thereafter. In pre-1998 annual reports, the JCG's annual report emphasized its efforts in enhancing its capacity to respond to maritime accidents such as oil spills caused by wreckage of the tankers, and containing potential environmental damage created by such incidents.[201] After 1998, however, its annual reports have been putting more emphasis on discussing its efforts to address threats against the security of territorial waters, identifying an increasing number of weapons, drug and human smuggling cases, piracy, and other suspicious activities as the prime concerns. The JCG's efforts in policing the areas subject to territorial disputes between Japan and its neighbors have also been discussed with greater emphasis since 1998.[202]

After renaming itself to its current name in 2000, the JCG has expanded efforts to raise its profile as the "go-to" agency for Japan's maritime security policy. In April 2001, the JCG issued the *Maritime Safety Task Implementation Plan* (*Kaijo Hoan Gyomu Suiko Keikaku*) for the first time. This plan—described as a "medium- to long-term management plan in the private sector"[203]—identified its strategic goals and specific program objectives for the next five years.[204] After the plan was revised in 2004, the JCG issued *The Second Maritime Safety Task Implementation Plan* (*Dai Ni-ji Kaijo Hoan Gyomu Suiko Keikaku*) in April 2006. Between the two plans, the strategic objectives of the JCG have evolved into the ones in which the JCG is more self-aware of its role in the maritime security (Table 3-2-1):

Table 3-2-1. Comparison of the Strategic Objectives in JCG's Maritime Safety Task Implementation Plans

The 2001 Plan	The 2006 Plan
Maintenance of safety	Maintenance of maritime order
Securing the safety of maritime traffic	Maritime accident rescue
Maritime accident rescue	Maritime disaster prevention and preservation of maritime environment
Maritime disaster prevention and preservation of maritime environment	Securing the safety of maritime traffic
Collaboration and cooperation with foreign organizations	Collaboration and cooperation with foreign organizations

(Source: The JCG. *Kaijo Hoan Gyomu Suiko Keikaku* (*Maritime Safety Task Implementation Plan*), April 2001, http://www.kaiho.mlit.go.jp/seisakuhyoka/h16.4.8/keikaku.pdf (accessed 20 February 2008; The JCG, *Dai Ni-ji Kaijo Hoan Gyomu Suiko Keikaku* (Second Maritime Safety Task Implementation Plan), April 2006, http://www.kaiho.mlit.go.jp/seisakuhyoka/no2keikaku.pdf (accessed 20 February 2008)).

As Table 3-2-1 indicates, the language used in the 2006 plan—the term "maritime order," in particular—suggests that the JCG identifies its role in maintaining the safety and security of Japanese territorial waters in a broader context than strictly law enforcement perspectives. It suggests that the JCG now considers that its tasks include not only the conventional law enforcement activities of investigating the accidents and solving crimes but also activities that support creating a secure maritime order in which law enforcement is only one factor.

As the JCG's self-perception of its own mission evolves, so has its equipment. In particular, the spy ship incident in 1999 reminded the JCG to enhance its capability to patrol and, if necessary, capture such ships with close cooperation with the JMSDF. In both 2001 and 2006 Maritime Safety Task Implementation Plans, the enhancement of the JCG's surveillance and policing capabilities by modernizing its patrol ships and surveillance aircrafts are identified as one of the top priorities for the JCG.[205] The introduction of high-speed small patrol ships, acquisition of the patrol ships that can carry surveillance helicopters, and overall improvement in surveillance capability near and within Japanese territorial waters point to the JCG evolving into an enforcement organization that is faster, more agile, and has greater enforcement capability.[206]

In addition to the efforts to strengthen its capability, the JCG has been intensifying its efforts in the international arena. For instance, the JCG launched the Northwestern Pacific Maritime Security Conference, hosting its first meeting in Tokyo in December 2000. This annual meeting began as the venue where the heads of the agencies in charge of maritime security from Japan, the Republic of Korea (ROK), Russia and the United States gather, now includes China and Canada. Further, to expand on the efforts at the head-of-the-agency level, the meeting has been reorganized into the North Pacific Maritime Security Forum in 2005 at the time of its fifth annual meeting in Kobe, Japan. With the reorganization, the forum now has a two-tier structure with the North Pacific Maritime Security Expert Meeting and the North Pacific Maritime Security Summit.[207] The JCG has also been actively engaging in supporting efforts by Southeast Asian countries to develop their own maritime security institutions by providing assistance in education and technical training.[208]

With the JCG's heightened level of activities since 2000, there is an emerging view that considers the JCG as the "de facto fourth branch of the Japanese military."[209] To be sure, the JCG has been enhancing its capability. As of March 2006, the JCG commands 356 patrol and coastal combatants, 76 logistics and support ships, 46 maritime research and other technical support ships, and 72 aircrafts (including helicopters).[210] Further, the JCG has been accelerating the modernization of its vessels. Its 2005 annual report discusses at length its aging fleet and aircraft, and stresses the importance of implementing appropriate upgrading and modernization of its equipment so that it can continue to perform its missions in maritime security.[211] Further, with the revision of the JCG Law in 2002 concerning the rules of engagement, JCG inspectors can now use firearms and other weapons in order to force fleeing suspicious ships to stop for ship inspections. Even if the shooting ends up creating casualties, the shooting is deemed legitimate as long as the JCG Commandant agrees that the circumstances called for such an action.[212] Taking these changes together, it is fair to say that, compared to when it started with a mere 200 ships and 3 helicopters in 1948, the JCG today is a much stronger and dynamic organization.

However, it may be a stretch to treat the JCG as the "de facto fourth branch of the Japanese military" at present. First and foremost, it is still a law enforcement agency within the MLIT—it is not even a full-fledged police force in the sense that it is not placed under the supervision of the National Public Safety Commission (NPSC) in the way that the National Policy Agency (NPA) is. Even though the JCG is assuming an increasingly high-profile role in Japan's efforts to guard its maritime interests, its activities are fundamentally law enforcement-oriented. In other words, no matter how much stronger JCG's capability grows, its ultimate goal is to investigate incidents, make arrests, and persecute those who are responsible whenever possible.

Furthermore, even with the recent enhancements, the JCG is a far smaller—both its personnel size and budget—organization compared to the JMSDF. In 2004, for instance, the JCG has 12,297 personnel, and it had the annual budget of 169.6 billion yen. In the same year, the JMSDF had approximately 44,000 personnel and had the budget of 1.15 *trillion* yen. Even under the FY 2008-2009 in which the Ministry of Defense as a whole suffered significantly (for instance, no new program was funded), it still has 43,388 personnel and the budget of approximately 1.07 trillion yen.[213] Although recent JCG modernization has certainly been impressive, it is misleading to include its capability when discussing Japan's military capability to, for example, engage in overseas missions.

Local Police Forces in Japan

Chapter Two examined the National Police Agency (NPA) as one of the key civilian institutions in Japan's national security policy infrastructure that has the primary responsibility in maintaining public order and public security in Japan. As discussed in the next chapter, the NPA also is an important player in Japan's intelligence community. The NPA's supervising role to prefectural police throughout Japan is another way in which the NPA is involved in Japan's national security policy.

Japan has a centralized police organization under which the National Police Agency receives oversight from the National Public Safety Commission (NPSC). While focusing mostly on the day-to-day operations in police organization, the NPA is also the organization that makes key decisions on issues that have law enforcement implications at the national level. The NPA places seven Regional Police Bureaus (RPBs) throughout Japan. In addition to its function as the inspector of the overall administration of prefectural police, these RPBs provide the assistance to prefectural police in the following areas:[214]

- Facilitating cooperation among local prefectures in criminal investigations that involve several prefecutural police jurisdictions;

- Ensuring that the crisis management capability of the national government is fully maximized in response to large-scale disasters;

- Providing police organization-wide communication network so that police can effectively respond to national emergencies

- Supporting the investigations of cyber crimes; and

- Providing education and training of the senior staff of prefectural police.

As such, the relationship between the NPA and prefectural police can be best described by the analogy of the human body—the NPA is "the brain" and the prefectural polices are "the body." Once a national emergency occurs, therefore, it is prefectural police that will move as arms and legs of the police organization to actually bear the primary responsibility to protect lives, property and safety of the people and to maintain public order within their prefectural jurisdictions.[215] The personnel distribution vividly illustrates such a relationship between the NPA and local police organization. In 2007, the police organization as a whole (both the NPA and prefectural police included) had approximately 290,000 personnel. Among them, only 2.6 percent work in the NPA structure. The remaining 97.4 percent work for the prefectural police throughout Japan.[216]

Japan places local police organization in all of its forty-seven prefectures. The Public Safety Commissions in each prefecture exercise administrative oversight over prefectural police with the governors' supervision. This makes the prefectural governors commanders of the local police forces. (Chart 3-2-2).

Chart 3-2-3. Oversight structure of local police in Japan

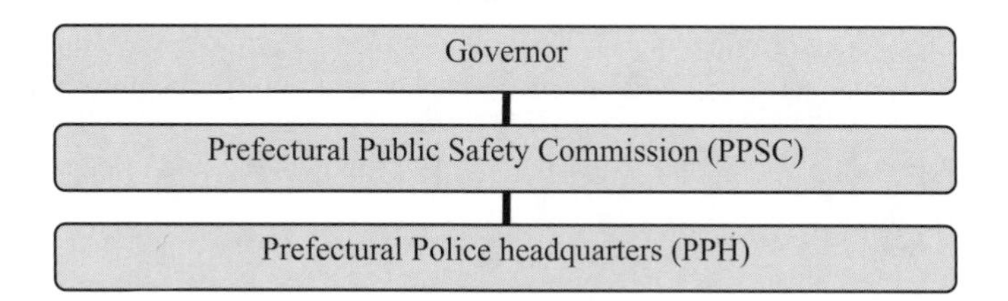

(Source: The National Police Agency (NPA) "Police of Japan: Organization." http://www.npa.go.jp/english/kokusai/pdf/Poj2007-3.pdf (accessed 2 February 2008)).

The prefectural police are headed by the chief of prefectural police headquarters (PPH) who answers to the Prefectural Public Safety Commission (PPSC). Under the PPH, police stations are distributed throughout the prefecture that handles day-to-day operations within their jurisdiction. With the exception of

Tokyo Metropolitan Police Department (TMPD) (because of the greater role it plays in the public security-related NPA activities), each PPH generally organizes in the following way (Chart 3-2-4):[217]

Chart 3-2-4. Typical Organizational Chart of the PPH

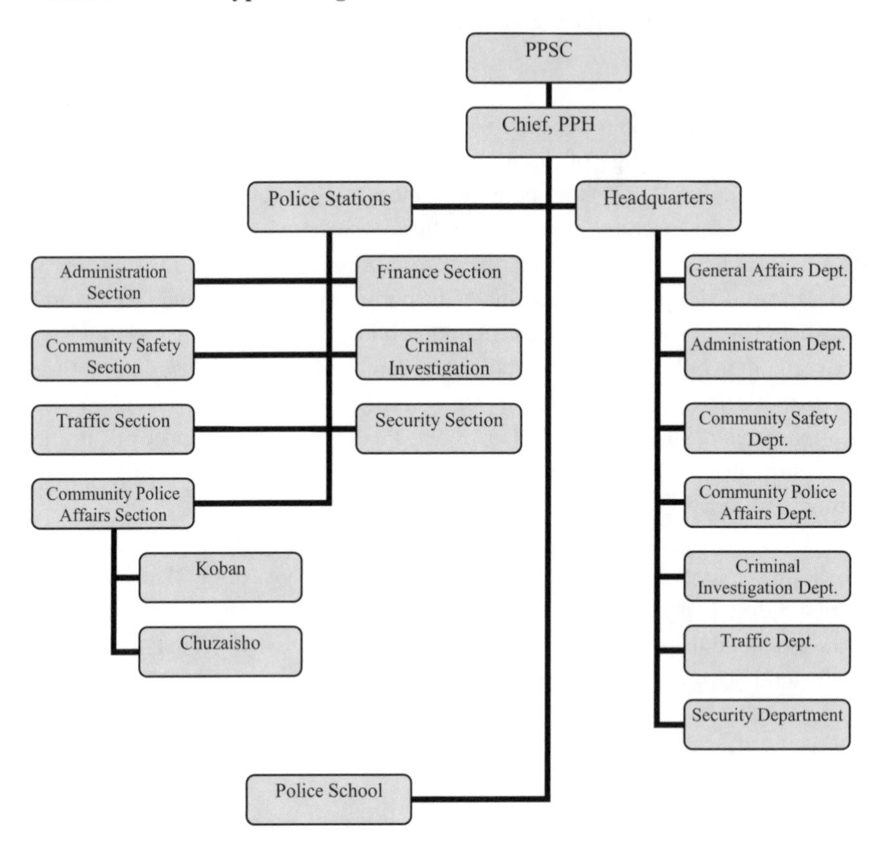

(Source: The National Police Agency, *Heisei 19 nen-ban Keisatsu Hakusho* (2007 Police White Paper). http://www.npa.go.jp/hakusyo/h19/honbun/index.html (accessed 3 February 2008)).

Japan's total size of its local police force is slightly bigger than that of the JSDF. In 2007, 282,313 people worked in the prefectural police organizations. Out of these personnel, about ten percent is the administrative staff. The remaining 90 percent—253,505 in actual numbers—are the policemen.[218] This figure includes those who are assigned to *kidotai* (riot police). *Kidotai* is a police force that is established specifically for responding to various emergencies. Each prefectural police typically has three types of *kidotai* units: permanent units, region-wide units (*kanku kidotai*) and the secondary units (*dai-ni kidotai*). The mission of each unit is as follows (Table 3-2-1):[219]

Table 3-2-1. Missions of three types of riot police

Kidotai type	Mission
Permanent units	Rapid response to emergencies. Organized along the specific functions including: Explosives Firearms Rescue for water accidents Rescue Nuclear, biological and chemical (NBC) terrorism
Region-wide units	Engagement in local policing activities in peacetime, but will be mobilized to function as the riot police units that can be dispatched beyond prefectural jurisdictions in emergencies.
Secondary units	Back-up for permanent units in various public security tasks.

(Source: The National Police Agency, *Heisei 19 nen-ban Keisatsu Hakusho* (2007 Police White Paper). http://www.npa.go.jp/hakusyo/h19/honbun/index.html (accessed 3 February 2008)).

In case of emergencies, based on the judgment of the governor, these police forces will be mobilized to maintain public order while responding to the situation through various tasks, including search-and-rescue and maintaining public order, to ensure the safety of its citizens. Particularly in recent years, the local police organizations in Japan are investing in acquiring the ability to mobilize assets beyond the prefectural jurisdictions in order to respond to large-scale disasters and other emergencies more effectively. For example, based on the lessons learned from the 1995 Hanshin-Awaji earthquake, Wider-Region Emergency Support Unit (*koiki kinkyu enjo-tai*) was established in each prefectural police in 1999. Consisting of a total of 4,700 personnel primarily designated among the policemen assigned to riot police across Japan, these units support prefectural police in collecting the information on damage, conducting emergency search-and-rescue, communicating the situation to the citizens, and securing safe passage out of the damage area. In the last few years, the capacity of these units have been further enhanced by acquiring units that are capable of conducting highly complicated rescue missions (Police Team of Rescue Units, P-REX), and units that can conduct identification and autopsy of victims in a timely manner.[220]

CHALLENGES

The previous sections have examined the organization and capabilities of the uniformed institutions that play key roles in Japan's response to national security and other emergencies. In aggregate, these institutions offer formidable capability. There are challenges, however, in facilitating the intra-institution cooperation to maximize their capabilities.

There have been efforts to establish frameworks for cooperation and specification of procedures. Following the 2001 agreement between the MOD (then JDA) and NPA on the inter-agency coordination of the JSDF's Public Security Mobilization, the designated JSDF regional headquarters and the Prefectural Police Headquarters (PPHs) signed an agreement that, among other cooperative measures, defined the division of roles between the JSDF and local police, designated points of contacts for communication, established coordination meetings to plan and conduct joint trainings in 2002. Further, in 2005, the designated JSDF regional headquarters and the PPHs created the guidelines for joint response against activities by armed hostile agents inside Japan. Based on these agreements, numerous joint table top exercises and joint training have been conducted between the JSDF units and police forces.

Similar efforts have been made by the JCG and the JMSDF to improve their cooperation in response to incursions by suspicious boats and ships. Following the first spy boat incident in 1999, the Japanese government released the list of "lessons learned" from the event.[221] The two institutions established procedures for joint response to such scenarios in the same year and have conducted joint training and exercises since. Indeed, thanks to government-wide efforts to improve the Japanese government's capability to respond to and manage crises, the cooperation and coordination between the JSDF and local police has greatly improved. Particularly in their response to large-scale natural disasters within Japan, collaboration not only between the JSDF and the local police force but also with local fire departments and hospitals has greatly improved.[222]

Still, there is much room for improvement in cooperation between the JSDF and local police, as well as between the JCG and the JMSDF. While the cooperation among these institutions has much improved in cases of natural disasters, it will take more joint training and joint exercises to ensure that they can cooperate just as well in the case of Japan being exposed to foreign threats. In particular, the relationship between the JCG and the JMSDF, while having grown more cooperative in recent years, has much to improve. For instance, in Japan's participation in the US-led Proliferation Security Initiative (PSI), the JCG has initially resisted JMSDF participation in PSI exercises, arguing that the activities involved are primarily law enforcement in their nature. In 2004, however, the JCG and the JMSDF also participated in *Team Samurai*, the multinational exercise under the Proliferation Security Initiative (PSI) that Japan hosted in 2004. This marked the first time that both the JCG and the JMSDF participated in a PSI exercise. But now that the JCG is moving toward acquiring greater firepower and greater mobility in countering smuggling, piracy, incursion of spy ships and other illegal activities, considerable ambiguity remains, for instance, when the JCG should decide to ask for JMSDF intervention, or what needs to be done when the JCG refuses to acknowledge that the situation is beyond its capacity to address.

As the institutions explore better inter-agency cooperation, the bias against the JSDF within Japanese society continues to present challenges. First and foremost, the extra-constitutional process with which the JSDF was created resulted in a lingering question on the JSDF's constitutional legitimacy. Worse yet, such a lingering question about its legitimacy, combined with the anti-military sentiment at the time of JSDF establishment, made the JSDF a near social-outcast for much of the first four decades of its history.

The Japanese government, having to justify the JSDF as a legitimate entity, created an extremely elaborate and meticulous legal argument on why the existence of the JSDF does not violate Article Nine of the Japanese constitution. The legal labyrinth created henceforth, together with JSDF's original nature as a constabulary force, has prevented the JSDF from gaining an identity as a professional military organization. The JSDF's non-military status has also been institutionalized in the Japanese legal framework. According to Japanese law, for instance, the legal status of its personnel, while being treated as military personnel abroad, is civil servant. This, which will be discussed in Chapter Five, subjects JSDF personnel to the same legal restrictions as police officers and JCG inspectors when they are mobilized for the operations other than defense of Japan. Many in the police organization still look at its role as "defending the people *from* the military (=JSDF)." [223] The Japanese government's response to JMSDF's accident with a fishing boat was illustrative of JSDF's awkward institutional status within Japan—it was the JCG, not JMSDF, which had the primary responsibility in investigating the JMSDF.

Japan's experience with a professional military organization before and during World War II makes it understandable that the JSDF was met with a great deal of skepticism in its early years. Given the important role that the JSDF has played since then not only in disaster relief within Japan but also in non-combat international activities, however, time is ripe for such a bias to change. Practically speaking as well, as the distinction between internal and external national security threats becomes less clear, the bias against the JSDF held among the law enforcement agencies must be set aside for effective operational cooperation. As long as such a mentality continues to exist among the uniformed institutions, it prohibits them from working together for a single goal—protecting Japan's national security interests.

-4-
INTELLIGENCE COMMUNITY

Intelligence is a critical component in a country's national security policy. Without good intelligence, a country's top leadership does not have the foundation to base policy addressing the security challenges of the country. And yet, the intelligence community is a component of a country's national security policy infrastructure that too often has its significance underestimated. Even in the United States, while calls for the need to reform the intelligence community began almost immediately after the Central Intelligence Agency was established by the 1949 National Security Act, it took the tragedy of the 9-11 terrorist attacks in 2001 to create any real momentum for intelligence reform. Although the intelligence reform was implemented with a great deal of support nationwide, a great deal of debate still remains over whether the 2004 intelligence reform indeed had the intended effects of reforming the US intelligence community.

In Japan's case, for most of its postwar history, the necessity of intelligence—let alone its importance—was hardly discussed. The reason can be found in Japan's wartime experience. In pre-1945 Japan, the country was put under the surveillance of Special Superior Police (*tokubetsu koto keisatsu*). Commonly known as *tokko,* the organization was part of the Interior Ministry (*naimusho*), the most powerful bureaucratic institution in pre-1945 Japan. The responsibility of *tokko* was, simply put, to take measures to ensure public order in Japan. During wartime, that meant to place the people under surveillance so that they would not hold anti-government ideas that lead to anti-government actions, and to arrest those who were suspected of taking in subversive ideas. Simply put, *tokko* in pre-1945 Japan is generally remembered as the "thought police" that suppressed the public. After Japan's surrender in 1945, *tokko* was dissolved along with the Interior Ministry, as well as the Imperial Army and Navy. To the General Headquarters (GHQ), which placed the highest priority to the democratization of Japanese society, *tokko* was one of the governmental institutions that symbolized undemocratic pre-1945 Japan.[224] Although the institution dissolved, the memory and image of *tokko*—a government institution that conducts secretive work to oppress the public's freedom of thoughts—stayed in Japanese society. It gave a negative image to any secretive activity by the government; thus, intelligence activities, secretive in their nature, have also been painted with a negative picture. It also has prohibited even the mere discussion of it. The very lack of a solidified translation of the term "intelligence" proves the scarcity of the discussion of this issue in Japan. Today, the term *joho* is most commonly used, but this often ends up confusing "information" and "intelligence."[225] Indeed, Japan is an unusual country that, despite its economic and (arguably) military power, does not have a government agency that is specialized in collecting, analyzing and distributing intelligence.[226]

Not having a discussion about intelligence does not mean Japan had no intelligence community, however. In fact, even during the Cold War, Japan's intelligence community was active. The intelligence organizations that handle public security within Japan—the Public Security Investigation Agency (PSIA) and National Police Agency (NPA)—remained vigilant in monitoring the activities of domestic political organizations that could potentially resort to violence to accomplish their goals, criminal organizations, and other organizations that could disturb public security.[227] As for foreign intelligence, then Japan Defense Agency (JDA) remained watchful of the movements by the former Soviet military in the Far East. The Ministry of Foreign Affairs (MOFA) collected intelligence worldwide through its diplomats dispatched to its embassies and consulates. However, Japan's intelligence community's activities during the Cold War seemed to have focused more on simply gaining a better understanding of domestic and international situations, rather than collecting and analyzing intelligence that could be used to address both short-term and long-term policy questions. Also, the intelligence community in Japan was stovepiped, with the agencies within the community barely engaging with each other. Furthermore, the community was decentralized, and it was not clear whether the prime minister could access all the intelligence he needed to make decisions in a timely manner.[xxxv] During the Cold War, when the distinction between the threats against internal security and those against external security was fairly clear, Tokyo at least could afford maintaining such a decentralized and stovepiped intelligence community.

The end of the Cold War, however, brought an end to such an era. When Japan suffered from a series of natural and manmade large-scale disasters during the 1990s, lack of the government's capability in collecting and analyzing relevant intelligence and communicating it to the top leadership in a timely manner came under severe criticism. When North Korea tested its ballistic missiles across Japan in 1998, the Japanese government's inability to detect the missile launch

---

[xxxv] Of course, Japan was not the only country whose intelligence community had very little intra-agency interaction and suffered from structural decentralization. In the United States, for instance, lack of communication and coordination between the Central Intelligence Agency (CIA), Department of Defense (DOD) and Federal Bureau of Investigation (FBI), as well as the lack of authority of the Director of Central Intelligence (DCI) have often been pointed out as the defect of the community and the proposed reform plans repeatedly attempted to rectify them.

and communicate it to top leadership in the Japanese government again came under criticism.[xxxvi] In context of the discussion on how to improve the Japanese government's crisis management system, the enhancement of the intelligence community began to be mentioned. The 9-11 terrorist attacks in 2001, as well as North Korea's missile and nuclear tests, renewed the call for the enhancement of the intelligence community in Japan.

Japan's intelligence community is still in the process of evolution. Following an overview of how Japan's intelligence community is structured today, this chapter first examines the government agencies that have formed the intelligence community in postwar Japan. Recent efforts on intelligence reform and the measures introduced will then be discussed. The chapter concludes by identifying the continuing challenges that the Japanese intelligence community faces.

INTELLIGENCE COMMUNITY IN JAPAN

In principle, Japan's intelligence community is decentralized. Rather than a centralized community that is managed by one agency/position which has the statutory mandate to manage the entire community, Japan's intelligence community resembles a loose coalition of the key government agencies.

Japan's intelligence community consists of five core government agencies that are attached to different government agencies as core members:[228]

- Cabinet Intelligence and Research Office (CIRO) (attached to the Cabinet Secretariat, and headed by the Director of Cabinet Intelligence (DCI));

- National Police Agency (NPA) (attached to the National Public Security Commission (NPSC));

- Defense Intelligence Headquarters (DIH)/Intelligence Division, Internal Bureau (attached to the Ministry of Defense (MOD);

- Intelligence and Analysis Service (attached to the Ministry of Foreign Affairs (MOFA); and

---

[xxxvi] Excellent narratives that describe the communication breakdown in these incidents during the 1990s can be found in Aso, Iku, *Joho Kantei ni Todokazu* (Information Did Not Reach Prime Minister) (Tokyo: Shincho-sha, 2001).

- Public Security Investigation Agency (PSIA) (attached to the Ministry of Justice (MOJ).

The activities of the intelligence community are coordinated at two levels—sub-cabinet and senior official. At the sub-cabinet level, the Cabinet Intelligence Council (*Naikaku Joho Kaigi*, CIC) meets twice a year. It is a vice-ministerial level meeting chaired by Chief Cabinet Secretary. In addition to the standing members of the Council, the representatives from other government agencies are invited to attend at the vice-ministerial level as necessary (Table 1-1).[229]

Table 1-1. Cabinet Intelligence Council

Chair: Chief Cabinet Secretary
Standing Members
Deputy Chief Cabinet Secretaries
Deputy Chief Cabinet Secretary for Crisis Management
Assistant Chief Cabinet Secretary in charge of National Security and Crisis Management
Director of Cabinet Intelligence (DCI)
Director-General, NPA
Vice Minister, MOD
Director-General, PSIA
Vice Minister, MOFA

The Joint Intelligence Council (*Godo Joho Kaigi,* JIC) is a senior official meeting that meets biweekly. Chaired by the Deputy Chief Cabinet Secretary for Administration, the JIC meetings are attended by the senior officials of the agencies that are standing members of the Cabinet Intelligence Council (Table 1-2).[230]

Table 1-2: Joint Intelligence Council

Chair: Deputy Chief Cabinet Secretary for Administration
Standing members
Deputy Chief Cabinet Secretary for Crisis Management
Assistant Chief Cabinet Secretary in charge of National Security and Crisis Management
DCI
Director-General, Security Bureau, NPA
Deputy Director, PSIA
Director-General, Intelligence and Analysis Service, MOFA
Director-General, Defense Policy Bureau, MOD

In addition, the Cabinet Satellite Intelligence Center (CSICE) and the Cabinet Information Collection Center support Japan's intelligence community.

The five core agencies in the Japanese intelligence community, while coordinating with one another, compete to have close relationships with the Japanese government's top leadership. They also approach their respective intelligence activities from different perspectives. For instance, the NPA and the PSIA approach is primarily law enforcement-oriented. This approach emphasizes intelligence activities that lead to the arrest and eventual prosecution of the perpetrator. On the other hand, the MOD (DIH in particular) looks at intelligence from national defense- and military-oriented perspectives. This puts a premium on the intelligence that leads to detection of the foreign military and other activities that can threaten the security of Japan and its people, so that it can take appropriate measures to eliminate such threats. Further yet, the foreign intelligence activities conducted by MOFA focus more on gaining a better understanding of the international environment so that Japanese policymakers can be better informed as they make foreign policy decisions.

Below, this section examines how each of the core organizations in Japan's intelligence community is organized. Where possible, it also discusses the challenges that each organization faces in strengthening its function.

Public Security Investigation Agency

The Public Security Investigation Agency, (*Koan Chosa Cho*, PSIA), an agency attached to the Ministry of Justice, is one of the law enforcement-oriented agencies in Japan's intelligence community. The PSIA was established in 1952 in order to ensure the enforcement of Prevention of Destructive Action Law (*Hakai Katsudo Boshi Ho*, better known for its shortened reference form *Habo-ho*).[231] Since the enactment of Law concerning the Restrictions against the Organizations that have engaged in Indiscriminate, Large-scale Murder (*Musabetsu Tairyo Satsujin Koui wo Okonatta Dantai no Kisei ni kansuru Houritsu*) in 1999, the PSIA also has a responsibility to ensure the enforcement of this law as well.

With these two laws providing the legal foundation for their mission, the PSIA today has two primary tasks. One is the enforcement of the above two laws. As the agency designated to enforce these laws, the PSIA not only regularly investigates the organizations in question and places them under surveillance, but also conducts on-site inspection of such organizations. For instance, Aum Shinrikyo (now renamed itself Alef) was put on probation in January 2000, the PSIA has conducted regular on-site inspection of the group's facilities. In 2007 alone, such on-site inspections took place at over forty facilities throughout Japan.[232]

The other aspect of PSIA tasks have to do with foreign intelligence. During the Cold War, the PSIA had collected and analyzed information on Japan's communist neighbors—North Korea, China and Soviet Union.[233] After the Cold War, in order to respond to the rising security concerns for terrorism (both homegrown and foreign-based), it has expanded the scope of investigation to include activities by terrorist groups.[234] The PSIA has made publically available part of its analyses on the challenges against Japan's public security, including the movements of terrorists, both in the annually-published *Naigai Jousei no Kaiko to Tenbo* (Situation in Public Security inside and outside Japan and their prospect) as well as regularly-published *Kokusai Terrorism Youran* (International Terrorism Report).[235]

The legal parameters within which the PSIA has to operate is carefully defined. For one, the PSIA can only function as the agency that collects intelligence. The two laws that authorize PSIA activities allow the PSIA to request the Public Security Examination Commission (*Koan Shinsa Iinkai*, PSEC)—a commission established as an affiliated agency of the Ministry of Justice that meets on *ad hoc* basis—that a restriction be placed against the organizations that are suspected of engaging in activities that can threaten public security.[236] However, it is the PSEC that has the authority to decide whether the organizations in question should have their activities restricted. The PSIA itself does not have the authority to make arrests, either. Further, PSIA cannot coerce cooperation from the witnesses and their information source: there must be voluntary cooperation.

Because of the inherent risk of abuse by the PSIA, both *Habo-ho* and the Law concerning the Restrictions against the Organizations that have engaged in Indiscriminate, Large-scale Murder aims have been controversial since their enactment respectively in 1952 and 1999.[237] Further, as mentioned earlier, the memory of *tokko* effectively playing the role of the Japanese government's thought police made any law that justified the government's restricting citizen's behavior a politically sensitive matter. Therefore, in order to alleviate concerns, both laws have clauses that explicitly prohibit any expansive interpretation of the law.[238] It also stripped the PSIA of authority to arrest and restricted PSIA's ability to coerce cooperation in its investigation.

This, as a result, has made the PSIA extremely cautious and hesitant in initiating the request to restrict the activities of questionable organizations to the Public Security Screening Committee. The Public Security Screening Committee was also very cautious in reviewing PSIA's request. In fact, the request for restriction was never made by the PSIA until it made its first request under *Habo-ho* in 1996 against Aum Shinrikyo. Despite the request being made one year after the sarin gas attack in the Japanese subway by the Aum Shinrikyo, the PSIA request was rejected.[239] The Law concerning the Restrictions against the Organizations that have engaged in Indiscriminate, Large-scale Murders Act had to be passed in 1999 before the Public Security Screening Committee finally decided to place the Aum Shinrikyo under the surveillance in January 2000.

The PSIA has three major institutional components: the internal bureau, facilities for training and research, and regional public security investigation bureaus (Chart 4-1-1).

Chart 4-1-1. Organizational Chart of the PSIA

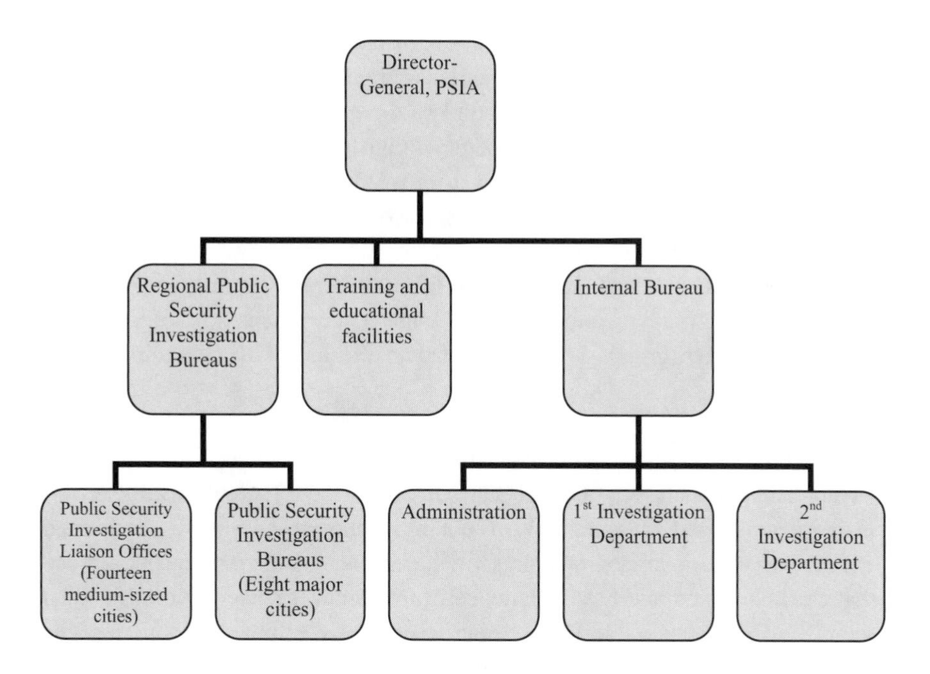

(Source: PSIA. http://www.moj.go.jp/KOUAN/shoukai2.html#02 (accessed 31 April 2008)).

Within the Internal Bureau of the PSIA, the First Investigation Department assumes the responsibility of collecting intelligence on developments within Japan. The targets of the investigation include labor unions, civic groups, left-wing and right-wing extremist groups and the Japan Communist Party. The Second Investigation Department is in charge of conducting investigations on developments outside Japan that could impact public security in Japan. Its surveillance targets include the Japan Red Army, a group that committed a hijacking, foreign workers in Japan, as well as the internal situation in the Korean Peninsula, China, Russia and other former communist countries. The Second Investigation Department also liaises with foreign intelligence communities.[240]

Since the 1990s, the PSIA began to explore ways to recast its role within Japan's intelligence community. Its effort was primarily driven by a survival instinct triggered by criticism the PSIA faced at the end of the Cold War. In particular, the PSIA's competence was brought under heavy criticism when, after the 1995 sarin gas attack by the Aum Shinrikyo, it was evident that the PSIA failed to monitor the Aum Shinrikyo as the organization accumulated the materials that were eventually used in the sarin gas attack.[241] Furthermore, the emergence of international terrorism as one of the biggest global security threats made the PSIA question whether the scope of its investigation and surveillance should be expanded beyond its conventional targets.[242] With growing pressure on Japanese political leaders to consolidate the government agencies that had been underutilized or ineffective through administrative reform, the PSIA spent much of the 1990s desperately trying to prove that it could re-invent itself to respond to the evolving post-Cold War security environment. The result of its effort culminated in a reorganization in May 1996 under which the focus of domestic surveillance was shifted away from the Japan Communist Party and other left-wing groups to other domestic subversive groups. Investigation of foreign subversive groups was also added to the list of PSIA's surveillance target.[243]

Today, PSIA's effort to reinvent itself continues. Particularly after the 9-11 terrorist attacks against the United States in 2001, the PSIA enhanced its effort in reorienting itself from an inward-looking agency that only was concerned with the activities—homegrown and foreign entities—to an intelligence agency that can collect and analyze intelligence from a broader perspective of national security. For instance, the PSIA began to explicitly emphasize its role as the agency that collects and analyzes intelligence in order to prevent terrorism incidents both home and abroad. Such references first appeared in PSIA's annual white paper *Naigai Josei no Kaiko to Tenbo* (*Review and Prospect of Internal and External Situations*) in 2005. Furthermore, "protection of Japan's free and democratic society and contribution to ensure peace and security of Japanese nation and its citizen" has been put forth as PSIA's mission since the *2006 Review and Prospect of Internal and External Situations*.[244] This suggests a conscious effort on the part of the PSIA to recast its institutional image as the agency that conducts comprehensive analyses on a broad range of security threats against Japan.

National Police Agency

The role of the National Policy Agency (NPA) as the agency that is primarily responsible for maintaining the public security in Japan was discussed in Chapter Two. What is often not known is that the NPA is also a significant player in Japan's intelligence community. In particular, the Security Bureau (*keibi-kyoku*) plays an important role.

Until its reorganization in 2006, intelligence-related matters were handled by several offices within the NPA. Domestic intelligence and counter-intelligence activities were handled by the Security Division in the Security Bureau (*keibi-kyoku*). Foreign intelligence-related activities (including counter-intelligence) were handled by the International Department (*kokusai bu*) in the Executive Secretariat and the Foreign Affairs Division (*gaiji ka*) within the Security Bureau. In 2006, the NPA realigned its organization with the major goals of (1) enhancing the capability to tackle organized crime, (2) streamlining and strengthening its counter-terrorism capacity, and (3) improving its capacity to respond to an increasing number of cyber crimes.[245] Under this reorganization initiative, all foreign intelligence-related activities were consolidated under the Foreign Affairs and Intelligence Department (*gaiji joho bu*) which was newly established within the Security Bureau (Chart 4-1-2).

Chart 4-1-2. Organization of the Security Bureau, NPA

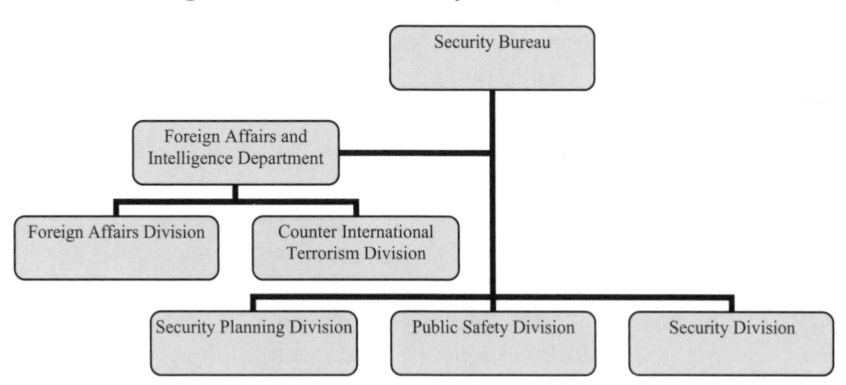

(Source: National Police Agency, http://www.npa.go.jp/english/kokusai/pdf/Poj2007-5.pdf (accessed 20 March 2008)).

Under the current structure, two divisions in the Security Bureau share the responsibility on domestic intelligence-related activities. The Security Planning Division has the responsibility in planning and research for the NPA's security operations. The Public Safety Division collects intelligence on the Japan Communist Party, right- and left-wing extremist organizations and other groups whose violent tendency provides a source of public security concern (such as the Aum Shinrikyo). Within the Foreign Affairs and Intelligence Department, the Counter International Terrorism Division collects the intelligence on the activities by the overseas-based terrorist groups. This division also has the authority to dispatch "International Terrorism Special Assault Team (*Kokusai Tero Tokubetsu Kinkyu Tenkai Butai*)". The Foreign Affairs Division has the responsibility for the NPA's counter-intelligence activities. Finally, the Security Division is responsible for operating Riot Police (*kido-tai*) which, if necessary based on the intelligence provided by the Public Safety Division, will mobilize to maintain public security.[246]

The NPA, the Security Bureau in particular, has been one of the key players in the Japanese intelligence community. To be sure, the NPA conducts its intelligence activities with a law enforcement mindset—the purpose of its activities is to prevent large-scale terrorist incidents in Japan from happening and, if prevention fails, to arrest the perpetrators. Still, the increasing difficulty of dividing domestic and international terrorism has driven NPA to expand the scope of its activities with larger presence in foreign intelligence-related activities. For instance, the NPA has been actively engaging in the discussion on transnational crimes (cyber crimes, money laundering, and counter-terrorism) in the framework of the G8 and other multinational frameworks.[247] It also has been seconding its officials to the Ministry of Foreign Affairs (MOFA) to serve as Police Attachés at Japanese embassies overseas. Also, unlike the United States that assigns the US military the responsibility to protect US embassies abroad, senior police officers (usually seconded from various prefectural polices) are often dispatched to Japanese embassies to take charge of the embassy security.[248]

With the divisions that engage in both domestic and foreign intelligence related activities under its jurisdiction, the Security Bureau will continue to play a central role in the NPA's intelligence related activities. In addition to its in-house capacity in intelligence activities, the Security Bureau's effort is supported by the activities of the Security Department (*keibi bu*) of prefectural polices throughout Japan. The direct command relationship established between the Security Bureau of the NPA and the Security Departments of prefectural police creates a nation-wide centralized intelligence network that helps the NPA's collection and analysis of the public security-related intelligence activities.[249] The cooperative relationship that the NPA established with foreign law enforcement and intelligence organizations through the cooperative investigative efforts helps NPA's capability in collection and analysis of foreign intelligence.

Defense Intelligence Headquarters, MOD

Defense Intelligence Headquarters (*Joho Honbu*, DIH) was established on 20 January 1997. Prior to the inauguration of the DIH, national defense-related intelligence activities (including counter-intelligence) were carried out by the intelligence units of three SDF services as well as the Joint Staff Council on the uniform side, and the Intelligence Division (*Chosa-Ka*) of the Internal Bureau of today's Ministry of Defense (MOD, then the Japan Defense Agency (JDA)) on the civilian side. JDA's signal intelligence (SIGINT) effort has been taken up by the Ground Self-Defense Force's Annex Chamber of the Second Section of the Intelligence Division (*Rikujo Jieitai Daini Chousa Besshitsu,* better known with its acronym *Cho-betsu*). The creation of the DIH consolidated all of these intelligence organizations within the MOD (Chart 4-1-3.)[250] Intelligence Division of the Internal Bureau of the MOD manages the DIH activities. It also develops internal guidelines on the issues such as intelligence classification and information security.

Having approximately 2,400 staff, the DIH today is the largest intelligence organization in the Japanese intelligence community.[251]

Chart 4-1-3. DIH Organization (simplified)

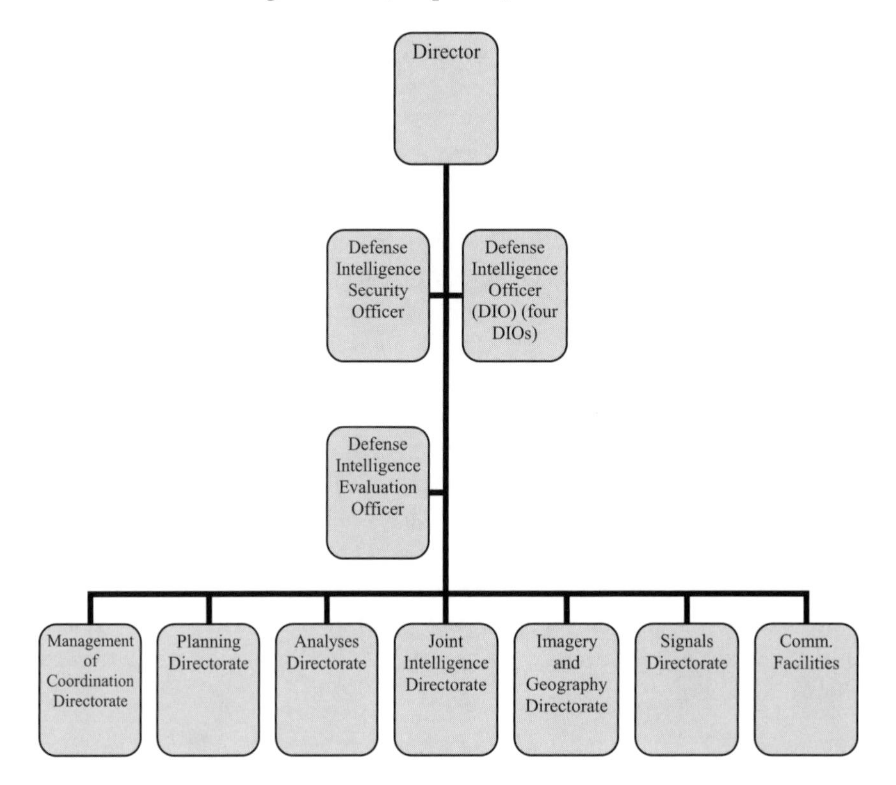

(Source: DIH. *Soshiki-zu* (Organizational Chart). http://www.mod.go.jp/dih/sosiki.files/slide0035.htm (accessed 9 April 2008)).

When first created, the DIH was an organization that supported the Chairman of the Joint Staff Council of the Self-Defense Forces (JSDF). However, as the JSDF's operational structure transitioned to a joint operational structure in March 2006, it became the organization that directly reports to the defense minister. When such a transition took place, in order to maintain the intelligence capacity to support the Chairman of the Joint Staff, the Joint Intelligence Department (J-6) was created within the Joint Staff Office.[252]

DIH is mandated to provide strategic intelligence necessary for MOD and JSDF operations. Retaining the organizational character from the era when it reported to the Chairman of the Joint Staff Council, the DIH is led by a uniformed officer (three-star). His/her deputy is a civilian MOD official. Supporting the DIH director and deputy director are four Defense Intelligence Officers (DIOs). Among the four, one is civilian and three are colonel/captain level JSDF officers. A civilian DIO handles country-specific information on defense policy, and JSDF officers are in charge of military intelligence.[253] The DIH liaises with the Intelligence Division of the MOD Internal Bureau to ensure that its activities are conducted in a manner that responds to MOD/JSDF's intelligence needs.

In addition to the Management and Coordination Directorate (*Somu-bu*) which handles human resources (including benefits of DIH staff), budget, acquisition, and the administrative procedures related to protection of classified information, five functional directorates support DIH's day-to-day operations.[254] The Planning Directorate (*Keikaku-bu*) forms DIH's intelligence collection and analyses plans. It also works as the point of contact when DIH needs to coordinate with other intelligence-related offices both within the MOD (e.g., the Intelligence Division of the Internal Bureau, the divisions that handle communication and information systems in each SDF service's staff office) and outside the MOD (e.g., US military intelligence organizations) as well as engages in information management.[255]

The Analyses Directorate (*Bunseki-bu*) collects all intelligence available to DIH (including the information in the public domain, imagery, signal intelligence, and intelligence that was obtained in the process of intelligence cooperation). Based on the information collected, the Analyses Directorate conducts all-source analyses in order to support MOD's policy decisions and SDF operations. When intelligence obtained is about the developments of foreign militaries and requires immediate processing and analyses to support the Joint Staff Office's decision-making on SDF operations, such intelligence is handled by the Joint Intelligence Directorate (*Togo Joho-bu*).[256] The Imagery and Geography Directorate (*Gazo Chiri-bu*) collects and analyzes satellite imagery. The imagery that is used for the analyses is most often purchased from the commercial earth-monitoring satellites. Based on its analyses, it crates digital maps, and also conducts analyses on topography.

The Signals Directorate (*Denpa-bu*) is Japan's only signal intelligence (SIGINT) organization. As such, it collects SIGINT from the communication facilities that are placed throughout Japan and conducts SIGINT analyses. The six communication facilities were used by the JGSDF's *Chobetsu* prior to the establishment of the DIH in 1997.[257] When the DIH was created and Signals Directorate absorbed *Chobetsu,* the six communication facilities were also transferred to support the Signals Directorate's operations. The Signals Directorate also conducts its own research and development of SIGINT technology and related equipments.[258] According to some accounts, approximately seventy percent of DIH staff belongs either to the Signals Directorate or one of the communication facilities in Japan.[259]

It has been a decade since the DIH was established. General Masahiro Kunimi, the first director of the DIH, expressed confidence that the establishment of the DIH would be able to (1) provide higher quality intelligence analyses and (2) develop the capability of intelligence analysts. He was also hopeful that the DIH, taking advantage of the fact that it could access foreign military intelligence through its exchanges with its counterparts in the United States and other countries, would be able to offer intelligence analyses with different perspectives to Japanese leadership.[260]

Despite General Kunimi's aspiration, however, it is questionable whether the DIH has lived up to its initial expectations. For one, insufficient communication and coordination between the DIH and the other intelligence-related offices within the MOD has been prevalent. Other intelligence-related offices in the MOD often are kept in the dark on DIH activities. Communication between MOD's intelligence-related offices including DIH and intelligence agencies of other countries is also not very well coordinated.[261] Further, the division of roles between the DIH and the other intelligence-related office within the MOD is often not clear. For instance, both DIH and the Intelligence Division of MOD's Internal Bureau communicate with US Defense Intelligence Agency. In such a case, it is often not clear which office has the lead in communicating with DIA on what issues.

Furthermore, the capacity of DIH analysts is still a work in progress, especially in the area of foreign intelligence. Two problems have often been identified for the slow development of the DIH's analytic capability. For one, the current criteria with which the DIH recruits its analysts may not be appropriate. This is particularly the case with foreign intelligence analysts who are often recruited based on their foreign language proficiency, not for their analytical capability or their expertise in the specific country or region. Therefore, the analytical product too often includes a mere translation of the information available in foreign languages into Japanese, without much insight or analyses attached to it.[262] Further, the career development of DIH analysts and technicians has much room for improvement. With the current system, while the DIH recruits its own staff, most of the senior positions within the DIH (section chief level and above) are held either by the MOD career bureaucrats and SDF senior officers who are not intelligence specialists, or by the detailee from the other government agency.[263] This makes it hard to incentivize the staff directly hired by the DIH.[264]

Intelligence and Analysis Service, MOFA

The Intelligence and Analysis Service (*Kokusai Johokan Soshiki*) is a foreign intelligence organization that resides in the Ministry of Foreign Affairs (MOFA). The organization was originally called the Information and Research Bureau (Joho Chosa Kyoku). The bureau was renamed to be the International Intelligence Bureau (*Kokusai Joho-kyoku*) at the time of reorganization in August 1993.[265] It was further renamed to have its current name—Intelligence and Analyses Services—at the time of MOFA reform that took effect in August 2004 (Chart 4-1-4).[266]

Chart 4-1-4. Organizational Chart of Intelligence and Analysis Service, MOFA

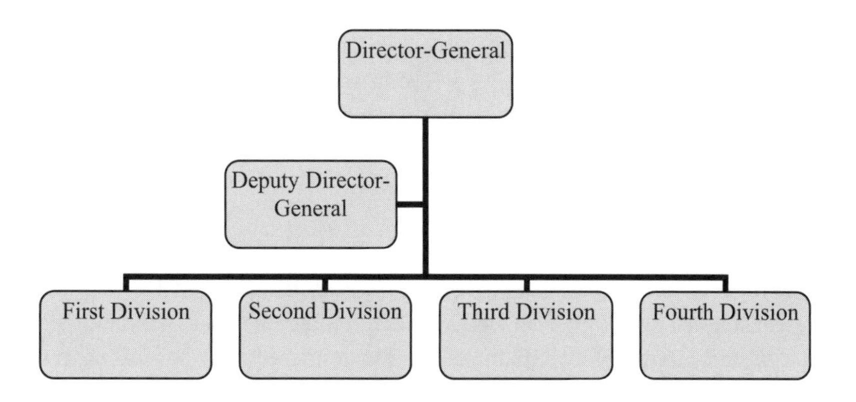

(Source: MOFA. *Saihen/Kyoka no Mokuteki* (The purpose of reorganization and enhancement (of Intelligence and Analysis Service). http://www.mofa.go.jp/mofaj/annai/honsho/kai_genjo/pdfs/koku_j.pdf (accessed 5 April 2008)).

The Intelligence and Analysis Service is led by the Director-General. The organization is divided into four divisions. The First Division plays a role of coordinator within the Intelligence and Analysis Service. It also gathers various types of information (e.g., publicly-available information, human intelligence, information obtained through the Japanese government's information-gathering satellites) and attempts to draw a comprehensive analysis out of them. The Second Division primarily handles information collection and analysis on functional issues. For instance, it covers terrorism, proliferation of weapons of mass destruction. The Third and Fourth Divisions primarily handle regional issues. The Third Division covers Asia and Oceania, and the Fourth Division looks at Europe, the Americas, the Middle East and Africa.[267] Each division is staffed with analysts that have expertise in one of the regional and/or functional issues.

The reorganization of MOFA's intelligence arm into the current structure under the Director-General of the Intelligence and Analysis Service was an attempt to respond to the anticipated growth of the need for intelligence analyses that effectively respond to the changing security environment. Therefore, the focus of the reorganization was placed on the four basic principles of (1) expertise, (2) agility, (3) efficiency, and (4) comprehensiveness. In this context, in order to allow agility within the organization, the aforementioned division of labor between the four divisions remains flexible. While each analyst has the issues that they are primarily responsible for, the Director-General, if necessary, can task them to support other analysts who are working on other issues so that they can conduct a more thorough and complete analyses. In case of North Korea's missile launch, for example, the director-general may guide the director of the Third Division to task imagery analysts (who are in the First Division), North Korean analysts (who are in the Third Division) and political-military analysts (who are in the Second Division) to work on the collection and analyses of the relevant information to assist MOFA senior officials to come up with a policy position.[268]

The purpose of reorganizing MOFA's intelligence arm seems to increase its in-house intelligence analyses capacity. However, it remains questionable whether the reorganization since 1993 indeed resulted in the increased capacity of MOFA's in-house intelligence organization. The primary reason for this is that the Intelligence and Analysis Service (as well as its predecessors) has never played a central role in collection and analysis of foreign intelligence within MOFA. Rather, such activities primarily take place in day-to-day work in other regional and functional bureaus that remain in close contact with overseas embassies and consulates. Beyond the analyses of technical data such as satellite imagery, other regional and functional bureaus within MOFA often have higher expertise, better information collection capacity, and are able to provide policy-relevant analyses in a timelier manner. Further, its small staff size—it is estimated by some that the Intelligence and Analysis Service has approximately 100 staff—limits what the organization can produce.[269] Despite the repeated reorganization, the Intelligence and Analysis Service in MOFA can be better described as a coordinator of intelligence analyses within MOFA rather than a major intelligence institution itself.[270]

Cabinet Research and Intelligence Office

The Cabinet Research and Intelligence Office (CIRO, *Naikaku Joho Chosa Shitsu*) is an intelligence organization of the Cabinet Secretariat. In the Japanese intelligence community, CIRO is probably the institution that has undergone the biggest changes in its function, personnel size, and capacity. The Research Office that was established in the secretariat of the Prime Minister's Office in 1952 was the origin of today's CIRO. With the reorganization of the Prime Minister's Office in 1957, the Research Office was transferred under the jurisdiction of the Cabinet Secretariat and was renamed to be the Cabinet Research Office. In 1986, the Cabinet Research Office was renamed as the Cabinet Intelligence Research Office.[271]

Today, CIRO has five departments and three centers (the Cabinet Information Coordination Center and Cabinet Satellite Information Center) within the organization (Chart 4-1-5).

Chart 4-1-5. CIRO Organizational Chart

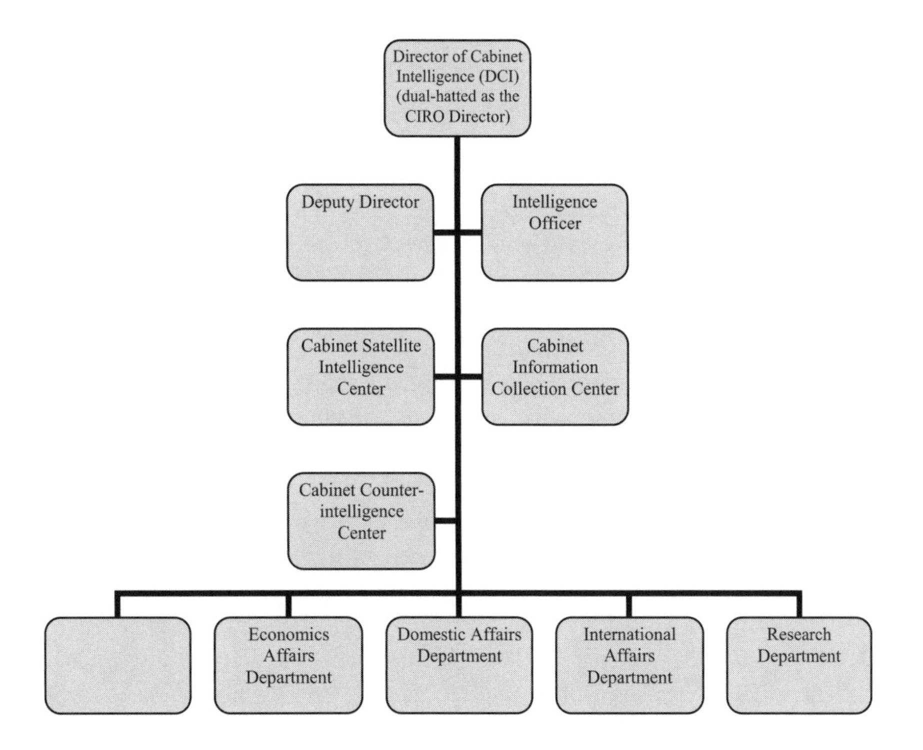

(Source: Cabinet Secretariat. *Naikaku Joho Chosa-shitsu* (Cabinet Intelligence and Research Office) http://www.cas.go.jp/jp/gaiyou/jimu/jyouhoutyousa.html (accessed 12 April 2008)).

Within CIRO, the Management and Coordination Department (*Soumu Bumon*) handles personnel, budget, and public relations. It also addresses the issues important to ensure that CIRO provides comprehensive intelligence analyses that integrate wide ranges of information. The Economic Affairs Department (*Keizai Bumon*) is in charge of collecting information on economic activities. The Domestic Affairs Department (*Kokunai Bumon*) collects information on domestic issues. The International Affairs Department (*Kokusai Bumon*) collects information on foreign affairs. The Research Department (*Kenkyu Bumon*) conducts in-depth analysis on foreign affairs.[272]

CIRO's effort to support the Cabinet Intelligence Officer is complemented by the two centers that are attached to CIRO: the Cabinet Satellite Intelligence Center (CSICE, *Naikaku Eisei Joho Center*) and the Cabinet Information Collection Center (*Naikaku Joho Shuyaku Center*).[273] The CSICE was established in 2001 after Japan formerly decided in 1998 to introduce a semi-indigenously developed information-gathering satellite (IGS). While it is called an "information-gathering (*joho shushu*)" satellite instead of "surveillance (*teisatsu*)" satellite and is described as a multipurpose satellite, it is mostly used for obtaining imagery for national security purposes.[274] The CSICS operates the IGS, obtains imagery from the IGS, analyzes them and shares its analyses with CIRO and the other Japanese government agencies that have interest in its analyses. The Cabinet Information Collection Center (*Naikaku Joho Shuyaku Center*) co-locates with the Cabinet Crisis Management Center in the Prime Minister's official residence. It has a twenty-four-hour operation system, and collects information on the incidents that could lead to national emergency. The information collected, analyzed and distributed by the Center is used by top Japanese leadership in order to prepare the government for potential national emergencies.[275]

As an intelligence organization attached to the Cabinet Secretariat, CIRO may look as though it is the most influential organization in the Japanese intelligence community. Indeed, the Director of Cabinet Intelligence (DCI) who is dual-hatted as CIRO regularly meets with the prime minister (the CIO briefs prime minister every week under normal circumstances, and more briefings are scheduled as necessary). The DCI is also one of the few officials that attend both the CIC and JIC.

Despite its position within the Cabinet Secretariat, however, the institutional strength of CIRO has constantly been in question. CIRO's biggest institutional weakness is the way that CIRO is staffed. As of April 2005, CIRO has approximately 170 staff. But approximately sixty percent of CIRO staff is on loan from other agencies within the Japanese government. According to

Shinichi Isajiki, who was serving as the CIRO Deputy Director in 2005, only seventy out of 170 CIRO staff were directly hired by the CIRO. Approximately forty staff were detailed from the NPA; approximately twenty from the PSIA, ten or so from the MOD, and several each from MOFA, Ministry of Internal Affairs and Communication, Japan Coast Guard, Ministry of Finance, and Ministry of Trade, Economy and Industry (METI).[276] In fact, until the creation of the position of the DCI, there was a bureaucratic custom that the senior NPA official who had had a long experience in public security, head CIRO, and a MOFA official who had had regional expertise, be appointed the deputy director of CIRO. Even following the creation of the DCI position in 2001, this tradition still continues.[xxxvii] Particularly, the perceived NPA dominance within the CIRO makes it very difficult for CIRO to play the role of "honest coordinator" of intelligence and exercise its influence as such in the Japanese intelligence community.[277]

Further, CIRO does not have its own information-collection apparatus. Unlike the DIH, NPA and MOFA, which all have information-collection capacity within their own organization—for instance, while the staff size of the Intelligence and Analysis Service of MOFA may be as small as 100, it still can collect information through the cable communication between MOFA headquarters and Japanese embassies and consulates abroad—CIRO does not have human resources that collect first-hand information. This means that, while the intelligence provided by the intelligence organizations of Japan's friends and allies under the government-to-government agreements is available, CIRO has to obtain most of its information from publicly-available sources, including domestic and foreign media reports and the information provided by the non-profit research organizations that are attached to CIRO that also suffer from a limited staff and resources.[278] This is why CIRO's "intelligence collection activities" sometimes faces the criticism that all they do is either clip newspapers or "cut and paste" the information that is provided by outside organizations. Setting such criticism aside, its limited staff size indeed constrains CIRO's capacity to develop its in-house information-collecting capacity.

INTELLIGENCE REFORM IN JAPAN

As examined in the previous section, the Japanese intelligence community remains decentralized, with each community member continuing to address the organizational challenges of its own. Naturally, many security experts in Japan

---

[xxxvii] The incumbent DCI Hideshi Mitani spent most of his career at the NPA as a public security official. He has also been detailed to the MOD (then still the Japan Defense Agency) Intelligence Division, and has served at the Japanese embassy in Washington, DC in the late 1980s.

argued for a long time that Japan needs to enhance its intelligence community's capability. In particular, many have argued for a more centralized intelligence community that better supports the prime minister's decision-making.

The concerns for Japan's lack of intelligence capability are not new. For example, the Liberal Democratic Party (LDP), the political party that dominated Japanese politics for most of Japan's post-World War II history, first studied the possibility of Japan acquiring its own surveillance satellite in 1982.[279] Intelligence activities by North Korean agents inside Japan were already stirring concerns among public security officials in Japan in the mid-1980s.[280] The adversarial impact of Japan's lack of intelligence capability on its foreign policy has repeatedly been pointed out. Even before the end of the Cold War, calls have been made for Japan to enhance its intelligence-gathering capability.[281]

Former Japanese ambassador to Thailand Hisahiko Okazaki was among the earlier advocates for the creation of an intelligence agency in Japan. Atsuyuki Sassa, former NPA official who also served as the director of the Cabinet Office of National Security Affairs (the predecessor of the Office of Deputy Chief Cabinet Secretary for Crisis Management) has also proposed that Japan should have its own intelligence agency.

It was not until a series of national emergencies hit Japan in the 1990s that the movement toward creating a stronger intelligence organization gained momentum. In particular, the Japanese government's inability to effectively respond to the 1995 Hanshin-Awaji earthquake was harshly criticized. Its inability to respond was largely attributed to its poor information-collection, analyses and reporting capability of the government. In order to address criticism, the government took several measures. The establishment of the Cabinet Information Collection Center in May 1996 is one of such measures taken by the government.[282] Also, the Cabinet Intelligence Committee (CIC) and the Joint Intelligence Committee (JIC) were created as venues to address intelligence-related issues. In short, during the 1990s, it was the demand for a more effective crisis management system that primarily drove the reform of intelligence community in Japan.

Since the 9-11 terrorist attacks in 2001, the Japanese government entered the second phase of reforming its intelligence community. In particular, when Shinzo Abe was elected to succeed Junichiro Koizumi as the prime minister in September 2006, the enhancement of the Cabinet's intelligence capability became one of the top policy priorities. In December 2006, Abe launched the Council on Enhancing Intelligence Function *(Joho Kino Kyoka Kento Kaigi)*. Along with the Council on Enhancing the Cabinet's Function in the Area of

National Security (*Kokka Anzen Hosho ni kansuru Kantei Kino Kyoka Kaigi*) and the Advisory Council on Rebuilding the Legal Foundation for Security (*Anzen Hosho no Houteki Kiban no Sai-kochiku ni kansuru Kondankai*) that explored the possibility of Japan exercising its right of collective self-defense, this council represented Abe's major policy initiatives in the area of national security.

When Abe stepped down from the premiership after serving barely for a year, many of Abe's initiatives on national security policies came to a halt. Interestingly enough, however, the effort to enhance the Cabinet's intelligence capability quietly continues today. After its establishment in December 2006, the Committee announced the basic conceptual framework within which it examines the means to enhance the Cabinet's intelligence capability on 28 February 2007. The report identified (1) a more clearly defined relationship between policy and intelligence, (2) strengthening of human intelligence (HUMINT) capacity, (3) improvement in collection, analyses and sharing of the information, and (4) establishment of necessary infrastructure that supports intelligence activities as the areas in which the Japanese government should put efforts in.[283] The report also identified the importance of information security, including the necessity to create government-wide criteria for classifying the information.[284] Further, in August 2007, the Council announced the basic principles for enhancing Japan's counter-intelligence capability.[285]

Building on the report, the Council issued another report on 14 February 2008. The report laid out the principles based on which the Japanese government should continue its effort in enhancing the Cabinet's intelligence capability. The principles proposed included:

- Reorganization of the Cabinet Intelligence Committee (CIC);

- Increased role of the Director of Cabinet Intelligence as the coordinator within the Japanese intelligence community on issues such as the prioritization and divisions of labor among the agencies within the intelligence community;

- Enhancement of HUMINT capacity;

- Enhancement of in-house information-collection capacity of the Cabinet; and

- Improvement of collection, analyses, and sharing of information through greater emphasis on all source analyses and facilitation of the engagement by the members of the "extended intelligence community (e.g., Japan Coast Guard, METI)."[286]

While the report of the previous year was issued while Abe was still in power, this report was released under Fukuda's watch. Further, some of the recommendations in the February 2008 report are already being implemented. For instance, the report called for the placement of several senior intelligence analysts with the title of Cabinet Intelligence Officer (*naikaku joho bunseki-kan*) in CIRO. Hired for his/her high level of expertise in one or more regional/functional areas with a long-term assignment that goes beyond three years, these senior intelligence analysts are expected to act as the primary drafter of intelligence estimates that will be eventually submitted to the CIC.[287] While not all the positions are filled yet, CIRO began the recruitment of the Cabinet Intelligence Officers in April 2008. Further, following up on the statement in the basic principles for counter-intelligence efforts announced in August 2007, the Counter-Intelligence Center was established within the CIRO in April 2008 as well. These all suggest that the intelligence reform remains the priority for the Japanese government today.

CHALLENGES

As mentioned above, Japan's effort to strengthen its intelligence community continues today. While progress has been made since the end of the Cold War, several challenges still need to be overcome for the Japanese intelligence community to be more effective and functional.

First and foremost, the perceived institutional characteristics of CIRO and that of the DCI need to be altered for CIRO to be truly functional as the coordinator within Japan's intelligence community. Yoshio Omori, former NPA official who served as CIRO Director before retiring from public service, offers an interesting observation in this regard. Being a strong proponent of Japan having a more centralized intelligence community, Omori, emphasizing the importance of information management, stressed the significance of unifying the Japanese intelligence community's point of contact with intelligence services of other countries in order to avoid the manipulation of the information. Further, despite himself being a former NPA senior official, he strongly insists that Japan's intelligence organization will become truly effective only when it achieves its independence from influence of the National Policy Agency. He also proposes that Japan needs to have an intelligence agency that specializes in foreign intelligence related activities.[288]

Secondly, Japan's intelligence community continues to face a human resource deficit. The source of the problem often originates in the hiring criteria during recruitment, and the professional development options for the analysts once hired. Often hired for their foreign language proficiency alone, the analysts are left untrained as intelligence analysts. None of the organizations in Japan's intelligence community offer an in-house system to train intelligence analysts. For instance, the DIH often relies on short-term training programs offered by US Defense Intelligence Agency and other intelligence services of the foreign country to train its analysts. CIRO recently began to send its analysts at policy research institutions overseas as a part of the training of its personnel, but it is too premature to assess its effect. Lack of sufficient incentives—in terms of the career path or otherwise—for intelligence analysts to improve their analytical skills has also resulted in low morale of the intelligence analysts.

Further, Japan still has a long way to go in its counter-intelligence capability. This is the issue that had been considered problematic since the 1980s but had not been seriously addressed.[289] The Counter-Intelligence Center within CIRO has only begun its operation in 2008, and it will take at least several more years for the Japanese government to be equipped with the system necessary for counter-intelligence (e.g., a government-wide security clearance system, identification of the accountability, introduction of the mandatory counter-intelligence training).

In addition, the Japanese government has to find a way to win back public confidence in its ability to spend intelligence activities-related resources appropriately without compromising the ongoing intelligence-related activities. In 2001, the government's resources for intelligence activities (commonly referred to as secret funds (*kimitsu-hi*)) came under sever criticism when it was revealed that MOFA officials spent these "secrets funds" inappropriately, authorizing Japanese embassies overseas to use such funds to entertain Japanese lawmakers or its own officials.[290] These secret funds came under even closer scrutiny when it was further revealed that a mid-level MOFA official used it for his private expenses.[291] Since then, the funds allocated for intelligence-related activities have been looked upon with suspicion. Of course, it is impossible to disclose the complete details of Japan's spending on intelligence-related activities; specifics on spending do not belong to a discussion in the public domain. Still, Japan's intelligence community needs to figure out the way in which it can satisfy public demand for transparency and accountability in government spending to some degree without giving out the details of the intelligence activities. Creating a system in which the government briefs to selected members of the Diet on the activities of the intelligence community (including its spending) in closed meetings, if a system that heavily penalizes the leaks from such discussion can be established, may be a possible solution.

Finally, enacting a law that codifies the protection of classified information is an urgent task. This clearly goes beyond the capacity of Japan's intelligence community, and must be tackled as a government-wide effort. While it is encouraging to see the initiatives launched by former Prime Minister Shinzo Abe in the area of intelligence reform continue, legislation to protect classified information shows no sign of being drafted, or introduced. The law to protect classified information is not only required for Japan to have a deeper intelligence cooperation with its friends and allies. It is also critical in order to maintain the accountability needed in a democracy without compromising the ongoing intelligence activities.[292]

-5-
LEGAL FRAMEWORK

Throughout most of its postwar history, Japan's national security policy lived in the gap between what its constitution allowed it to be and what it realistically had to be. This gap originates in Article Nine of the Japanese constitution, which reads as follows:

> *Aspiring sincerely to an international peace based on justice and order, the Japanese people forever renounce war as a sovereign right of the nation and the threat or use of force as means of settling international disputes. In order to accomplish the aim of the preceding paragraph, land, sea, and air forces, as well as other war potential, will never be maintained. The right of belligerency of the state will not be recognized.*[293]

When one literally interprets this article, Japan, under its constitution, is not allowed to have any military force. In reality, however, the Japan Self-Defense Forces (JSDF) has existed since 1954. Today, the JSDF has the fifth largest defense budget in the world, and is considered to be one of the most modernized militaries.[294] In order to justify the existence of the JSDF in light of the constitutional prohibition of possessing military force, however, the Japanese government has explained that the JSDF is not a military that possesses war potential. Rather, the Japanese government has argued that: (1) Article Nine of the constitution did not deny Japan its right of self-defense; (2) Japan, therefore, is allowed to possess the capability that is minimally necessary for self-defense; and (3) the JSDF is constitutional because it is not a military, but rather an organization that can use force to exercise Japan's right of self-defense.[295]

Such an ambiguous constitutional position has put the JSDF in a contradictory role because it is "treated as a military according to international law, but not so within Japan."[296] It has also forced the Japanese government—the Japan Defense Agency (JDA)/Ministry of Defense (MOD) and the Ministry of Foreign Affairs (MOFA) in particular—to struggle in order to justify all aspects related to the JSDF, ranging from its very existence to the capability it is allowed and the missions it is authorized to take up throughout most of its postwar history.

At an even more fundamental level, there has been a long-lasting question about the relationship between Article Nine of Japan's constitution and the existence of the JSDF. Throughout the post-World War II years, Article Nine of the constitution served as the most basic foundation on which Japan shaped its national security policy, symbolizing Japan's postwar determination that it would not enter into wars with other countries. If, then, Article Nine does not allow Japan to have a military force, what is the JSDF? As stated in the beginning, the Japanese government spent most of its postwar years trying to justify the existence of the JSDF. Tokyo's efforts in legitimatizing all aspects of the JSDF are based on the following logic:

- Japan, as a sovereign nation, has the right to self-defense as a measure of self preservation;

- Even Article Nine of its constitution does not deny Japan the right to possess the ability to defend its existence;

- Such an ability cannot necessarily be considered "war potential" (*senryoku*) because it is only used for self-defense;

- The JSDF is an organization for self-defense, not an organization to wage war against others;

- Therefore, possessing the JSDF does not contradict the spirit of Article Nine of the constitution;

- Since the JSDF is allowed to use force only for Japan's self-defense, the right of collective self-defense, while being acknowledged in the UN Charter, cannot be exercised by Japan; and

- The JSDF, as an enforcement organization for self-defense, cannot involve in actions that could be considered a use of force when abroad. Nor is it allowed to engage in activities that are an integral part of any use of force (*buryoku koushi tono ittaika*).[297]

Based on this logic, two fundamental operational principles for the JSDF were established. First, the JSDF, while being treated as a military force in the context of international law, is not "what is normally conceptualized as a military force."[298] Secondly, a JSDF operation must not involve use of force that is greater than minimally necessary. Finally, the JSDF personnel is allowed to use force only for individual self-defense. While the third principle was later slightly revised to enable JSDF personnel to use force not only to protect themselves, but also those that are subject to their protection, these two principles have set the parameters of the permissible JSDF operations at home and abroad since 1954.

These principles came under considerable challenge after the Cold War. In particular, Japan's self-imposed ban against exercising the right of collective self-defense and the prohibition against "integration with the use of force" posed a considerable problem as Japan struggled to identify ways to engage JSDF personnel in overseas operations. First, Japan's self-imposed ban on exercising the right of collective self-defense has proven to limit Japan's security cooperation abroad. For instance, Japan's inability to exercise the right of collective self-defense limited the types of missions that the JSDF could participate in overseas. It also created tension between Japan and the United States. The US-Japan alliance is reciprocal, yet fundamentally asymmetric: American soldiers are obligated to fight for Japan when JSDF soldiers are not. Japan's self-imposed ban on the right of collective self-defense left ambiguity in what the United States could expect from Japan when US forces engaged in conflict in East Asia. Although Tokyo and Washington attempted to diminish such an ambiguity when they revised the Guidelines for US-Japan Defense Cooperation in 1997, Japan's hesitance to engage with the United States on bilateral planning discussion for specific contingency scenarios (e.g., conflict on the Korean Peninsula, crisis across the Taiwan Strait) caused frustration in Washington.

The prohibition of the JSDF participating in activities that could be "integrated" with the use of force by other countries' military also places unrealistic limits on the scope of JSDF operations overseas. For instance, under the current premise, the JSDF engaging in rear-area support on a transport mission cannot transport soldiers, weapons, and/or ammunition, because it could be considered as "integrated with the use of force." But is it reasonable for the JSDF to be, simply put, "picky" about what it can and cannot transport? The principle against "integration with the use of force" is particularly aggravating because it includes use of force by the US military. For instance, when Japan detects that a ballistic missile is launched and heading toward the United States, the current Japanese interpretation of the constitution does not allow the JSDF to attempt to intercept the flying missile, because it will then be considered as Japan having exercised the right of collective self-defense. There was a serious debate in the Diet on whether sharing the information of missile launches with the United States could be interpreted as "integration with the use of force." It is not too difficult to envision the intense strain that prospects such as these put on the US-Japan alliance.

When pressure grew that Japan, along with other countries in the international community, send the JSDF personnel to take part in international efforts to maintain peace and security, the Japanese government struggled to find a legal explanation that justified JSDF operations overseas for UN-led peacekeeping operations without contradicting the past justification of the JSDF. Following the 9-11 terrorist attacks in 2001, Tokyo yet again scrambled to create a legal argument based on which the JSDF could participate in operations by coalition forces not organized as a UN force.

JSDF operations outside Japan are authorized based on the following premises at present:

- Its activities do not include use of force against foreign troops, or will not be integrated with any use of force by other countries;

- The area where it operates can be considered a "non-combat zone" (*hi sento chiiki*); and

- The purpose of a JSDF dispatch is not to support aggressive wars.

Unless the proposed operation is either in support of the mission that is granted an unambiguous mandate by the United Nations or is clearly considered to be international disaster relief activities, the Japanese government has to authorize each JSDF dispatch by enacting separate special measures law.

Further, with the exception of homeland defense, JSDF activities require legal justification through two types of laws—the law to authorize the particular operation, and the other to regulate what the JSDF is allowed to do during the proposed operation. This, needless to say, results in not only a complicated, but also a cumbersome legal framework that the JSDF must operate within. Nonetheless, examining the legal framework that dictates JSDF activities will provide us a useful window to view how Japan is enhancing (or not) its national security policy infrastructure in terms of its legal foundation.

This chapter therefore focuses on the legal framework with which Japan authorizes various JSDF operations. The chapter first provides an overview of the laws that authorize JSDF mobilization to demonstrate how strictly JSDF mobilization, even in Japan, has been regulated. The description of the laws that authorize JSDF overseas operation follows. After examining the laws that define what JSDF personnel are allowed to do while deployed, the chapter ends with a discussion of the prospect of future changes to the existing legal framework.

LEGAL FRAMEWORK FOR JSDF MOBILIZATION INSIDE JAPAN

The SDF Law is clear in acknowledging that defense of Japan is the primary (*shu taru*) mission for the JSDF.[299] The Self-Defense Forces Law (the SDF Law, *Jieitai-ho*) defines JSDF missions as follows:

> *The JSDF, in order to protect peace and independence of our country and preserve the security of the nation, shall have defense of our country against direct and indirect aggression and, when necessary, maintain public order.*[300]

In carrying out the homeland defense mission, the SDF Law authorizes JSDF mobilization inside Japan under the following circumstances—defense of Japan from (threats of) armed attacks, maintenance of public order, disaster relief and prevention/containment of disaster damage, and protection of critical facilities (including US military and diplomatic facilities) in Japan. Each SDF Law provision is often augmented by another law that dictates the process through which JSDF deployments are approved and ordered.

Defense of Japan from (threats of) armed attacks

When Japan is under an armed attack, or is facing an imminent danger of such a threat, the JSDF can be activated for "defense mobilization (*bouei shutudo*)." Defense mobilization can be ordered only by the prime minister when such a mobilization was considered necessary.[301] When the "defense mobilization" order is anticipated as imminent, the defense minister is also entitled to order the JSDF to stand-by for mobilization.[302]

Although the SDF authorizes JSDF "defense mobilization," it was not until June 2003 when the Japanese government enacted the Law on Ensuring the Nation's Peace and Independence, as well as the Security of the Nation and its People in case of Armed Attack, etc (*Buryoku Kougeki Jitai nado ni okeru Wagakuni no Heiwa to Dokuritsu narabini Kuni oyobi Kokumin no Anzen no Kakuho ni Kansuru Houritsu*, better known as the Armed Attack Response Law (*Buryoku Kougeki Jitai Taisho Ho*)) that the procedures for JSDF mobilization was established. These procedures include:

- Establishing the government's basic response principles (in which JSDF "defense mobilization" is included);

- Obtaining the consent of the cabinet to the plan; and

- Obtaining the Diet approval to the proposed basic response plan.[303]

Once mobilized, the JSDF is legally authorized to use weapons as necessary to defend Japan, as long as such weapons use does not go beyond what is considered reasonable and does not violate the generally accepted principles in international law and customs.[304] The JDSF is also authorized to command the Coast Guard in such cases as well.[305]

While conducting "defense mobilization," the JSDF can also take measures to protect the Japanese public. The Law Concerning the Measures to Protect the People in case of Armed Attack, etc. (*Buryoku Kougeki Jitai nado ni okeru Kokumin no Hogo no tameno Sochi ni kansuru houritsu*, better known as the Public Protection Law (*Kokumin Hogo Ho*)) authorizes such JSDF deployment at the request of the prefectural governors which must be made to the defense minister.[306] The defense minister, when the request is received and the prime minister approves the request, can then order the JSDF to deploy to support the prefectural governments.[307]

The provision for JSDF's "defense mobilization" has been written into the SDF Law since 1954. It is important to note, however, that the Japanese government did not have a statutory process through which JSDF "defense mobilization" could be ordered until it enacted the Armed Attack Response Law and the Public Protection Law respectively in 2003 and 2008. Even with the enactment of these laws, concerns remain that the Japanese government, the JSDF in particular, may lack a statutory authority in responding to a threatening situation. Among defense planners in Japan, there is a concern that the Japanese government may not be able to respond when Japan faces an imminent threat of attack, but it is uncertain whether "defense mobilization" should be ordered by the prime minister. For instance, in case of a suspected missile launch against Japan, the extremely short response time makes it questionable whether the Japanese government can (1) Confirm that a missile was indeed launched to attack Japan; (2) Draft the basic response principles and get the Cabinet to approve it; and (3) obtain Diet approval of the basic response principles. One can also envision other cases that do not reach the threshold for ordering "defense mobilization" (e.g., unintended accidental launch of ballistic missiles, falling meteors or debris from satellites and space stations) but do require action from the JSDF.

In order to alleviate the concerns that Japan may lack a legal framework to respond to such situations, the Japanese government revised the SDF Law in July 2005. The revised SDF Law now authorizes the defense minister, with the approval of the prime minister, to mobilize the JSDF to destroy objects that are entering Japanese territory. The prime minister must notify the Diet of the results of the defense minister's mobilization order as soon as the situation allows.[308] While this represents an important recognition that the existing legal framework for JSDF mobilization requires adjustment in order to better defend Japan from security threats, questions remain whether the current legal framework is designed on an inoperable concept, therefore inadequate for the Japanese government to appropriately order JSDF defense mobilization when necessary.

Maintenance of public security

Although the police organization is primarily responsible for protecting the people's lives and assets, as well as maintaining public order in Japan, the JSDF can be deployed to take part in activities that maintain public order and public security when Japan faces a national emergency which requires personnel beyond the regular police force.[309] This type of JSDF mobilization is referred to as "security mobilization" (*chian shutsudo*). It can be commenced either based on an order from the prime minister or requests by the prefectural governments.[310]

The SDF Law authorizes the prime minister to order JSDF's "security mobilization" when "it is considered that public security cannot be maintained by the ordinary police force in case of indirect attacks and other emergencies."[311] Unlike ordering "defense mobilization," prior approval of the Diet is not necessary for the prime minister to order for "security mobilization." However, the prime minister must begin the process of seeking the Diet approval within twenty days of issuing an order. Should the Diet disapprove of the prime minister's decision, the order must be retracted in a timely manner, and the JSDF must be withdrawn accordingly.[312] Prior to the prime minister's decision, the defense minister, in anticipation of his/her "security mobilization" order forthcoming, can direct the JSDF to go on stand-by. The defense minister can also order the JSDF to conduct intelligence-collection prior to the "security mobilization," and the JSDF personnel who engage in the activity are authorized to carry and use weapons for self-defense. The SDF Law obliges the defense minister to remain in close communication with the National Public Security Commission (NPSC), the highest-level decision-making organization on the issue of public security in Japan, under these circumstances.[313] Similar to the case of "defense mobilization," the defense minister can command the Coast Guard when JSDF "security mobilization" is ordered.[314]

In cases when the JSDF is activated for "security mobilization" due to the requests from prefectural governments, the actual JSDF dispatch still has to be ordered by the prime minister. The prime minister's initiates the order when the prefectural governments have a situation "that is grave and there is a critical need from the perspective of maintaining public security."[315] When there is no longer a need for JSDF dispatch, and when prefectural governments issue a request, the prime minister must order the withdrawal of the troops in a timely manner.[316]

In addition to "public security mobilization," there are two operations that can be ordered for the purpose of maintaining public security. One is maritime patrol operations (*kaijo keibi kodo*). Similar to the police force having the primary responsibility in maintaining public security and order inside Japan, the Japan Coast Guard (JCG) is primarily responsible for ensuring the security of Japan's territorial water.[317] However, when the JCG faces a situation that is beyond its capacity, the SDF Law authorizes the defense minister to, with an approval of the prime minister, order a JSDF dispatch to engage in maritime patrol operations.[318] Maritime patrol operations by the JSDF became well known to the Japanese public when, in 1999, Prime Minister Keizo Obuchi approved of then Defense Minister Hosei Norota to order this operation in response to activities by unidentified spy ships off Japanese shores. More recently, Prime Minister Junichiro Koizumi permitted then Defense Minister Shigeru Ishiba to order maritime patrol operations when Chinese submarines entered Japan's territorial water in 2004.[319]

The other is the counter-airspace incursion measures (*ryoku shinpan sochi*). Based on the SDF Law, the defense minister can order the JSDF (Air Self-Defense Force in this case) to intercept suspicious incoming aircraft that attempt to enter Japanese airspace in violation of international law and other aerospace regulations.[320] Although the maintenance of public security is primarily a responsibility of the police organization, counter-airspace incursion measures are taken exclusively by the JASDF, as the police force simply does not have such a capability. While the SDF Law allows the JASDF patrol aircraft to take "necessary measures" to conduct counter-air incursion operations, much ambiguity remains on what the appropriate rules of engagement should be, particularly as they relate to the criteria for weapon use.[321]

Disaster relief / Prevention or containment of disaster damage

Disaster relief is a mission that the JSDF has been engaged in throughout Japan since its establishment. In fact, it is the activity that the vast majority of the

Japanese public identifies the JSDF with.[xxxviii] It also is the activity that has contributed to promoting the positive image of the JSDF among the public. There are three types of JSDF mobilization under this category: disaster relief, containment of damage in the aftermath of earthquakes, and response to nuclear-related accidents.[322]

The SDF Law authorizes the JSDF to engage in disaster relief activities throughout Japan.[323] When the JSDF is dispatched to assist local governments with relief activities in the aftermath of natural or manmade large-scale disasters, there are two ways in which the JSDF can be mobilized—mobilization based on the requests from local government, and unilateral mobilization. When the governors of prefectural governments determine that a JSDF dispatch is necessary, they can request a JSDF dispatch to the defense minister or to the individual that the defense minster designates the recipient to be. When the heads of local communities (e.g., mayors) deem it necessary to have disaster relief assistance from the JSDF, they can request JSDF mobilization either to the governor, Commandant of the Japan Coast Guard, Director of the Coast Guard Office, or the director of the airport operation in their areas. The governors and others who received such requests, after determining that such requests are reasonable, will in turn make a request to the defense minister or a designated individual.[324]

Upon the requests from the governors, the defense minister, when he/she determines that a JSDF dispatch is absolutely necessary, can order JSDF mobilization for disaster relief. In making such a determination, three factors need to be considered:[325]

- Whether there is an urgent need;
- Whether there is no other appropriate option; and
- Whether a JSDF dispatch is appropriate from the perspective of maintaining public order.

Only when all of these conditions are met does the defense minister (or those who were designated) authorize JSDF mobilization.

[xxxviii] For instance, the 2006 opinion poll conducted by the Cabinet Affairs Office indicates that approximately 75 percent of the repondents identify the JSDF with disaster relief activities. See Cabinet Affairs Office "*Chosa Kekka no Gaiyo* (Executive Summary of the Poll Results)" *Jieitai Bouei Mondai ni Kansuru Yoron Chosa* (Pubic Opinion Poll regarding the JSDF and Defense Issues) February 2006, http://www8.cao.go.jp/survey/h17/h17-bouei/2-4.html (accessed 15 January 2008).

In principle, the MOD has to wait for the request from prefectural governors to be made in order to dispatch the JSDF for disaster relief. However, in exceptional cases in which damage from the disaster is so severe that it may cost lives to wait for the request to come in, the defense minister or his/her designee can order voluntary mobilization of the JSDF to the affected areas.[326] A voluntary JSDF dispatch may also happen when the areas that are in the vicinity of JSDF bases and other MOD facilities are affected by disasters, including fire.[327] When the relief activities by the JSDF is deemed no longer necessary, the JSDF will be withdrawn either at the request of prefectural governors or by the order of the commanding officer of the dispatched units.

The JSDF dispatch in response to large-scale earthquakes is dictated by the Special Measures Law in response to Large-scale Earthquakes (*Daikibo Jishin Tokubetsu Taisaku Sochi-ho*, commonly referred to as the Large-scale Earthquake Law (*Daishin-ho*)) which was enacted in 1978. When the Japan Meteorological Agency (JMA) issues a warning of an earthquake, the prime minister can issue a warning for earthquake damage with cabinet approval. When this warning is issued, the Earthquake Response Headquarters (*Jishin Taisaku Keikai Honbu*) is established, and the prime minister will serve as the chief of the headquarters.[328] The Large-scale Earthquake Law dictates that the chief of the Headquarters for the Response to Earthquakes (the prime minister, unless he/she is incapacitated) is authorized to request the JSDF dispatch for consequence management and execution of emergency relief on the ground.[329] While it takes the request of the prime minister to dispatch the JSDF, its withdrawal can be ordered by the defense minister.

The JSDF dispatch in response to nuclear power-related accidents is a category that was newly established following the accident at the nuclear fuel processing facility in Tokaimura in 1999. Being the first large-scale disaster caused by an accident at a nuclear power facility, there was heavy criticism against the government for not distributing information to the local residents, and not responding to the incident in a timely matter in the aftermath. In response to these criticisms and ensuring the more effective response by the Japanese government and other related parties, the government enacted the Special Measures Law regarding the Response to Nuclear Disaster (*Genshiryoku Saigai Taisaku Tokubetu Sochi-ho*, commonly known as the Nuclear Disaster Law (*Gen-sai Ho*)) in 1999.

The Nuclear Disaster Law dictates that, in the case of a nuclear power-related disaster, the prime minister should issue a "nuclear power emergency declaration," establish the Nuclear Power Disaster Response Headquarters (*Genshiryoku Saigai Taisaku Honbu*), and serve as the chief of the headquarters.

In his/her capacity as the chief of the Nuclear Power Disaster Response Headquarters, the prime minister can request the JSDF dispatch if he/she determines that it is necessary.[330] In addition, the Nuclear Disaster Law also entitles the heads of local communities to request the JSDF dispatch to their prefectural governors. Upon receiving such requests, the governors ask the prime minister to order the JSDF to dispatch to their local communities.[331]

Protection of military and other important facilities in Japan

Prior to the 9-11 terrorist attacks in 2001, the JSDF was not legally allowed to protect the security of its own forces and facilities, as well as US military facilities—unless the country were under attack; it was the police that were responsible for the security of those facilities. The only exception made to this practice was the protection of "weapons and other items" that included weapons, ammunition, gunpowder, ships, aircrafts, vehicles, radio communication equipment, and liquid fuel.[332]

The situation changed, however, after the 9-11 attacks in 2001. When the Japanese government enacted the Anti-Terrorism Special Measures Law (*Tero Taisaku Tokubetsu Sochi Ho*) in November 2001, the SDF Law was also revised to allow the prime minister to order JSDF mobilization to protect US military and SDF facilities, when the prime minister acknowledges that there is a sufficient threat of terrorism against these facilities.[333] However, being mindful of the law enforcement organization's primary responsibility to provide public security, the SDF Law also dictates that the prime minister, prior to ordering JSDF mobilization to protect JSDF and US military facilities, must consult with the prefectural governors that would receive the dispatched JSDF units. It also compels the prime minister to ensure that the defense minister and the chairman of the National Public Safety Commission discuss and agree on the facilities to be protected, and the time period of the JSDF dispatch. When the situation improves and the threat to those facilities no longer exists, the prime minister has to order the withdrawal of the JSDF immediately.[334]

The evolution of the legal framework for JSDF mobilization inside Japan is illustrative in demonstrating how Japan was legally ill-equipped for JSDF operations inside Japan. The SDF Law granted the statutory authority to JSDF mobilization for homeland defense and other domestic emergencies since 1954, but Japan lacked the legal foundation that was necessary for the prime minister to order JSDF mobilization which was not established until after the Cold War. Moreover, the existing legal framework for domestic JSDF mobilization suggests that JSDF operations in Japan are controlled very strictly. Not only does the proposed operation have to be authorized under the SDF Law, but an explicit statutory authority needs to be granted either to the defense minister or the prime minister to issue such orders under specific circumstances. While such tight legal control over JSDF mobilization is useful to prevent abuse, lack of flexibility can prevent the Japanese government from responding to the emergency in Japan in a timely fashion.

LAWS THAT AUTHORIZE JSDF OPERATIONS OUTSIDE JAPAN

When the JSDF was established in 1954, there was no political intention or plan to deploy it overseas. Such a sentiment is clearly reflected in the 1954 resolution passed by the House of Councillors (Upper House), which reads as follows:

> *At the establishment of the Self-Defense Forces, given the provisions in the Constitution and our people's strong love and support for peace, this House hereby reconfirms that the SDF will not engage in overseas activities.*[335]

As such, the overseas dispatch of the JSDF was simply out of the question for a long time. The only exceptions allowed were JSDF cooperation in the observation of Antarctica, and transportation of VIPs.[336] The SDF Law also authorizes the SDF to sweep mines at sea, but the Japanese government originally interpreted this provision as only authorizing the SDF to sweep mines in the vicinity of Japan.[337] Even when the International Disaster Relief Law was revised in 1987 to allow JSDF participation in international disaster/humanitarian relief operations (the SDF Law was also revised at the same time to reflect this revision), the norm that the JSDF cannot and should not operate outside Japanese territory remained.[338]

The Japanese government, prompted by the criticism from the international community for its unwillingness to commit its personnel to support the multinational forces after the 1990-91 Gulf War, began to revisit its position on a strict ban on JSDF's overseas activities. After successfully paving the way for, although in a limited manner, JSDF participation in peacekeeping operations led by the United Nations (UN) in 1992, Japan renewed its effort to push its legal framework to further broaden JSDF participation in multinational military operations abroad following the 9-11 attacks in 2001. New laws have been passed to authorize the SDF to engage in new types of activities abroad, and the SDF Law has also been revised in tandem to reflect such legislative developments.

At present, there are three basic categories of overseas operation that the JSDF has a statutory authority to participate in: UN-led peacekeeping operations, international disaster relief, and (although on case-by-case basis) multinational coalition forces operations that do not have explicit UN authorizations. In order to ensure that JSDF deployment to these missions remain consistent with the three principles for JSDF'S overseas dispatch—no use of force, activities in non-combat area, and no participation in invasion—the permissible scope of JSDF activities in these operations are carefully defined.

UN Peacekeeping Operations

In 1992, the Japanese government enacted the UN Peacekeeping Operations (PKO) Cooperation Law. Under this law, the SDF is authorized to undertake the following tasks:[339]

- Cease-fire monitoring and disarmament monitoring;
- Patrolling of buffer zones;
- Inspection of illegal weapon possession;
- Collection, storage or ridding of abandoned weapons;
- Assistance in defining a cease-fire line;
- Assistance in exchange of prisoners;
- Provision of medical services;
- Evacuation of victims of disasters and assistance of their return;
- Provision of sustenance (food, water, etc.) to disaster victims;
- Construction of the facilities for the evacuees;
- Reconstruction of damaged facilities and infrastructure;
- Decontamination of the environment in affected areas; and
- Provision of transportation as well as installation of storage, communication equipment, construction equipment and other machineries, as well as provide for their inspection and repair.

However, the so-called "PKO Five Principles"[340] that were attached to the passage and enactment of the original PKO Cooperation Law "froze" the SDF participation in what it described as the "PKO core mission" (*hontai gyomu*)—activities such as cease-fire monitoring, redeployment of the military, stationing and patrolling of a buffer zone, weapon inspections, collection of abandoned weapons, assistance in defining a cease-fire line, and assistance in prisoner exchanges. The "freeze" was initially put in place to alleviate the concerns in Japan at the time that JSDF participation in peacekeeping operations can open doors to JSDF military activities overseas.[341] By the time Japanese leaders debated over JSDF participation in UN peacekeeping missions in East Timor, however, the political environment had grown more permissible to lift this "freeze." JSDF's experience in participating in and successfully completing UN-led peacekeeping missions since its first deployment to UN peacekeeping operations in Cambodia in 1993, alleviated such initial concerns. Further, a growing number of opinion leaders and politicians in Japan began to push for lifting the "freeze" arguing it was unrealistic and presenting an obstacle for Japan to participate in international peace-building efforts in a meaningful manner.[342] These developments eventually led to eliminating the "freeze" on the SDF participation in PKO "core missions" when Japan revised the 1992 PKO Cooperation Law in 2001 in tandem with deciding to dispatch the JSDF to East Timor.[343] Still, considerable political sensitivity remains over the JSDF participation in "PKO core missions." In fact, while it has been seven years since the "freeze" was lifted, no JSDF troops have been dispatched to participate in PKO "core missions."

With the enactment of the UN PKO Cooperation Law, a new provision was added to the SDF Law to reflect the list of activities that the JSDF was now allowed to undertake. It also states that the JSDF may participate in "the activities that will benefit peace and security of international community, including our nation…in the way such a participation will not interfere with its primary mission (homeland defense) and will not lead to the intimidation by force or the use of force."[344]

Supporting US Military Operations in Case of Regional Contingencies

The Japan-US Joint Declaration on Security—Alliance for the 21st Century in April 1996, directed bilateral efforts to revise *the US-Japan Guidelines for Defense Cooperation* (referred to as the Guidelines hereafter), which was established originally in 1979.[345] Announced in 1997, the revised Guidelines clarified the role to be expected by the JSDF under three circumstances—peacetime, regional contingencies or "situation in the areas surrounding Japan (*shuhen jitai*)," and direct attacks against Japan. Among the three categories, what Japan should do in case of *shuhen jitai* was the most politically controversial, as it was not a clear case of armed attack against Japan, yet it called for Japanese assistance to US military action. The case of *shuhen jitai* was also written with the greatest ambiguity in the original 1979 Guidelines.

The actions that the Japanese government is allowed to take to support US military operations in case of situations in the areas surrounding Japan (*shuhen jitai*) were eventually codified as the Law to Ensure Japan's Peace and Security in the Situations in the Areas Surrounding Japan (so-called *Shuhen Jitai Ho*) in May 1999. In essence, the law authorizes the SDF to engage in the following activities at sea and in the airspace in the area surrounding Japanese territory:[346]

- Rear-area logistical support (replenishment, transport, repair and maintenance, medical services, communications, and administrative works at airports, seaports and bases);

- Rear-area search-and-rescue operations (replenishment, transport, repair and maintenance, medical services, communications, provision of accommodations and sanitation); and

- Ship inspections.

The law also clarifies the definition of the terms that describe specific actions to be taken by the SDF. It is in these charts that the Japanese government took pains to articulate that the JSDF will not provide ammunition and other weapons, and that the JSDF will not provide materials or services to US forces that are preparing to leave for combat missions. For instance, the term "medical" is defined as "the treatment of casualties, provision of sanitary instruments, as well as other related materials and services." Further, while the law authorizes the SDF to use force in order to protect their lives and possessions as well as those of their colleagues engaged in the same activities, the SDF is explicitly prohibited from taking measures that can appear to be construed as the use of force.[347]

Following the enactment of the *Shuhen Jitai Ho*, the revised Acquisition and Cross-Service Agreement (ACSA), signed between the United States and Japan in 1998, entered into effect in September 1999. This agreement also enabled the Self-Defense Forces to provide and receive goods and services from US forces in case of regional contingencies, in addition to when the SDF participates in joint training with US forces, UN peacekeeping operations, and international relief activities.[348]

Participation in Non UN-led Overseas Operations: Special Measures Laws

Since 2001, the Japanese government has chosen to enact special measures laws (*tokubetsu sochi ho*) to authorize the JSDF to participate in the operations that are not granted explicit authorization by the United Nations (e.g., in the form of Security Council resolution). This approach comes with one significant disadvantage: special measures law often has a time limit and thus has to be exposed to political discourse whenever its renewal needs to be debated. The disadvantage can work as an advantage at the same time, however. Because it has a time limit, it is easier for the Japanese government to get the Diet to agree on the bill, which accelerates the deliberative process. For instance, while it took only two months for the 2001 Anti-Terror Special Measures Law to be enacted, it took nearly two years for Japan to enact the Law regarding the Situations Surrounding Japan (*shuhen jitai ho*).

Since 2001, three special measures laws have been enacted to authorize the JSDF to participate in the multinational operations in Afghanistan and Iraq. In November 2001, the Japanese government enacted the Anti-Terror Special Measures Law so that the JSDF could engage in refueling operations in the Indian Ocean to support coalition operations in Afghanistan. With the initial time limit of two years (the time limit was extended to four years in a later revision in 2003), the law was renewed until it finally expired in November 2007. In order to resume the refueling mission in Afghanistan, Tokyo passed a new law, the Replenishment Support Special Measures Law, in January 2008 (which will expire in January 2009). Finally, the Iraq Reconstruction Assistance Special Measures Law was enacted in July 2003 with an initial time limit of six years.[349]

The Anti-Terrorism Special Measures Law

Enacted in November 2001, the Anti-Terrorism Special Measures Law authorized Japan to engage in (1) cooperative assistance, (2) search-and-rescue, (3) relief of the affected population, and other necessary activities in order to support US and other armed forces, and to respond to the request by international organizations.[350] The law justified Japan's engagement in these activities with the UN Security Council resolutions that denounced international terrorism, specifically UN Security Council Resolution 1368 that acknowledges the 9/11 terrorist attacks in 2001 to be a threat to peace and security.[351] The law also authorized SDF participation to provide material assistance and other support services to the multinational forces, and to engage in search-and-rescue activities.[352] Although the list of activities is quite extensive, several conditions are attached to them. First, the SDF was to operate only on the high seas and the airspace above it—it would not be able to operate on foreign soil without explicit consent from the host country.[353] Second, SDF activities could not include the use of force.[354] Finally, no combat should be ongoing in the areas in which the SDF is anticipated to operate.[355]

The Replenishment Support Special Measures Law

The Special Measures Law regarding the Replenishment Support Activities for Counter-Terrorism Maritime Intervention Activities (*Tero Taisaku Kaijo Soshi Katsudo ni taisuru Hokyu Shien Katsudo no Jisshi ni kansuru Tokubetu Sochi Ho*, more often referred to as the New Anti-Terrorism Special Measures Law (*Shin Tero Tokuso-ho*)) was introduced for deliberation by the Diet on 17 October 2007. It was submitted to replace the Anti-Terror Special Measures Law that expired on 1 November 2007. The Japanese government decided to submit this bill instead of pursuing further renewal of the Anti-Terror Special Measures Law when questions were raised regarding whether the refueling mission in fact supported not only the multination military operation in Afghanistan, but also operations in Iraq.[356] When the bill was approved by the House of Representatives on 14 November 2007, the bill was sent to the House of Councillors for consideration. Following the House of Councillors' rejection of the bill on 11 January 2008, the House of Representatives re-approved the bill with two-thirds majority that is required to overturn the decision of the House of Councillors. The bill was enacted into law on the same day.[357]

The law declares that the refueling mission is to take place either within Japanese territory or on the high sea and within the territorial waters of foreign countries where no combat is ongoing.[358] While the Anti-Terror Special Measures Law authorized the JSDF vessels to engage in refueling as well as search-and-rescue and relief activities, this new law only authorizes the JSDF to engage in refueling activities, defined as "provision of fuel and/or water."[359] Should combat begin (or be expected to begin) near the area where the JSDF operates, the operation must be suspended until the combat subsides.[360] The law imposes strict limits on the use of weapons by JSDF personnel engaging in the replenishment activities—they can use weapons only to protect themselves, those with them, and those who are under their protection when weapon use is absolutely necessary in order to protect their lives. Further, the extent of their weapon use is confined within what is considered as "self-defense" or "emergency evacuation" under the Japanese Criminal Code.[361]

The Iraqi Humanitarian and Reconstruction Assistance Special Measures Law

When the United States invaded Iraq in March 2003, Japan did not move as quickly as it did in the case of Operation Enduring Freedom. While some in the Japanese government first explored the possibility of deploying the SDF to provide rear-area support for the coalition forces, it decided against such an option for three reasons. First, such a dispatch would have necessitated the enactment of a new law: the deployment based on the PKO Cooperation Law would have been difficult given that the US decided to invade Iraq without an explicit authorization from the UN Security Council. Second, the Japanese government preferred to concentrate its legislative effort on enacting the Armed Attack Response Law at that time.[362] Finally, US invasion of Iraq was extremely unpopular among the Japanese public. For instance, the opinion poll conducted by *Kyodo News* indicated that nearly 80 percent of the respondents opposed the invasion of Iraq.[363] The same poll showed that over 90 percent of the respondents considered Prime Minister Koizumi's articulation of the reasons of his support for the US decision to invade Iraq insufficient. Therefore, the Japanese government determined that it would be politically impossible to send the JSDF to participate in a coalition operation in Iraq while the invasion continued. Still, Japan immediately expressed its support for US military action in Iraq. It also announced its intention to provide emergency humanitarian assistance to the affected areas, as well as other indirect measures, including enhancing the security of US military facilities in Japan.[364]

Once President Bush declared the end of the major combat mission on 1 May 2003, the possibility of deploying the SDF to take part in the reconstruction assistance efforts quickly emerged as a realistic possibility.[365] Unlike the overwhelming opposition to the invasion of Iraq, the poll results indicated that greater support existed for JSDF deployment to reconstruction and humanitarian assistance activities in postwar Iraq: even in the aforementioned *Kyodo News* poll, approximately 60 percent supported JSDF deployment to postwar Iraq.[366] The deliberation by the government accelerated after Prime Minister Koizumi, in his meeting with President Bush during his visit to the United States on 23 May 2003, indicated that Japan was ready to consider the deployment of the Air Self-Defense Force (ASDF)'s C-130 transport aircrafts to provide support in transport of goods in the region, and to examine what would be possible in order to make a "contribution that commiserates with Japanese national power."[367]

The Special Measures Law regarding Humanitarian Reconstruction Assistance Activities and the Activities to Support Ensuring Safety (usually shortened and referred as the Iraq Humanitarian Reconstruction Assistance Special Measures Law) was submitted to the Diet on 13 June 2003, and was enacted on 1 August

2003. The law authorized Japan to engage in activities of humanitarian reconstruction as well as in ensuring safety.[368] The scope of activities permissible under the law was also defined. According to the law, humanitarian reconstruction activities are defined as:

- Medical services;
- Assistance for the return of the affected people to their homes, provision of food, clothes, medicines and other daily sustenance, and establishment of boarding facilities for the affected people;
- Advice or guidance on administrative matters; and
- Other activities to save the victims, repair the damage, or support the reconstruction of Iraq, including transport, storage, construction, repair or maintenance, supply and sanitation.[369]

"The activities to assist ensuring safety" were defined as activities that assist the United States and other countries to restore safety and security in Iraq, including transport, storage, communication, construction, repair or maintenance, supply and sanitation.[370] It required the prime minister to obtain the cabinet's approval for the basic plan for any activity under this law, including when a SDF deployment is involved.[371] The law also required that the prime minister would have to notify the Diet of the basic plan for its approval, and terminate the activity in case the Diet rejects the plan.[372]

The law also imposed several restrictions on the operations the SDF would conduct. First, the law required that the SDF contingents would be sent to non-combatant areas: if fighting broke out near the area of the SDF operations, their activities would need to be suspended and the personnel be evacuated.[373] The SDF was also prohibited from transporting weapons (including munitions),[374] as well as providing fuel and maintenance to aircraft that are on stand-by prior to departing to engage in combat.[375] Furthermore, their use of weapons was authorized only when it was absolutely necessary in order to protect their lives or properties, their fellow SDF soldiers and other reconstruction assistance personnel and those who came under their protection.[376]

LEGAL FRAMEWORK FOR JSDF CONDUCTS WHILE IN OPERATIONS

As in all democracies, the JSDF deployment both at home and abroad requires statutory authorization. In addition to the law to justify its operations, the conduct by deployed JSDF personnel is also subject to another set of domestic laws. What is noticeable is that the provisions that define the police and other law enforcement organizations regulate most of JSDF operations—indeed, the only exception is when the JSDF uses force while being mobilized for homeland defense. Even then, use of force by the JSDF has to be restrained at the level "that is minimally necessary (to eliminate the threat)."[377] Specifically, the Law regarding the Execution of Policemen Duties (*Keisatsukan Shokumu Shikko-ho*) often provides the basic legal foundation based on which many aspects of the JSDF actions on the ground are regulated.

The regulation against the conduct of JSDF personnel is most strict in their use of weapons. The JSDF is not allowed to "use force" (*buryoku no koshi*) except when it is under defense mobilization based on Article Eighty-Eight of the JSDF Law.[378] In all other deployment, both at home and abroad, the JSDF personnel are subject to Article Seven of the Law regarding the Execution of Policemen Duties, which permits policemen to use weapons under the following circumstances:[379]

- In order to arrest the suspect, or to prevent the suspect from fleeing;
- To protect oneself or others; and
- To deter the resistance.

The provision also conditions the authorized weapon-use to "reasonable and necessary."[380] The same regulation applies to JSDF personnel when they use weapons in order to maintain order within the JSDF.[381]

Even when Article Seven of the Law regarding the Execution of Policemen Duties does not directly affect JSDF personnel, the core concept of Article Seven—one is only allowed to use weapons when doing so is considered reasonable and necessary, and is not allowed to harm others except for self-defense or for "emergency evacuation" (an action is taken because it is necessary to avert the dangers posed to the lives, bodies, liberty or properties of people[382])—is reflected in other applicable laws. For instance, the JMSDF personnel who engage in ship inspections are subject to Article Thirty-Seven of the Law Regarding the Control of Maritime Transport of Foreign Military and Other Items at the time of Armed Attack (*Buryoku Kougeki Jitai ni okeru Gaikoku Gunyou-hin nado no Kaijou Yusou no Kisei ni kansuru Houritsu*, more commonly referred to as the Maritime Transport Control Law (*Kaijo Yusou Kisei Ho*)). The article explicitly states that the JSDF personnel who engage in procedures specified in the Maritime Transport Control Law will have their weapon use subject to Article Seven of the Law regarding the Policemen Carrying Out Duties.[383] A similar restriction also applies when the JSDF personnel is dispatched to protect its weapons and/or facilities.[384]

When the JSDF engages in operations overseas (e.g., UN peacekeeping operations), its personnel are allowed to use weapons to protect themselves and those who come under their protection. Here, too, the condition under which the JSDF can use weapons is very similar to what is defined in Article Seven of the Law regarding the Execution of Policemen Duties:

- The degrees of weapon use must be restrained to what is considered "reasonable and necessary" in carrying out the mission; and

- No one must be injured or die as a result of the weapon use unless the weapon was used for the purpose of self-defense, or the requirements for the "emergency evacuation" was met.[385]

Further, the activities of the JSDF that are deployed for "security mobilization" operations are provided legal justification by the Law regarding the Execution of Policemen Duties. In addition to weapon use, the Law authorizes the deployed JSDF troops, while in "security mobilization," to:

- Questioning and collection of information necessary to execute the mission;

- Protection of those who need emergency care;

- Evacuation;

- Prevention and suppression of criminal activities;

- Aversion of risks, containment of the damage; and

- Entry into private land and facilities for rescue activities.[386]

The same regulations are applied to the JSDF troops mobilized for "protection mobilization."[387]

When the JMSDF engages in maritime security operation, it is subject to the regulations under the Japan Coast Guard Law (*Kaijo Hoan-cho Ho*). In addition to weapon use (Article 20-2);[xxxix] JMSDF engaging in maritime security operation is authorized to:

- Seek assistance from nearby ships;
- Order the captain of suspicious ships to submit appropriate documents;
- Conduct on-board ship inspection to confirm critical information about said ship, its load, and/or its navigation (e.g., final destination, discrepancy between the ship's load and its manifesto);
- Ask necessary questions to the crew and the passengers of said ship; and
- Take measures including the order not to continue the voyage, change the navigation route, impose restriction on the crew's off-boarding and unloading of its cargo to the port, or restrict communication with other ships or ground facilities.[388]

Also, in case of JSDF deployment for disaster relief in Japan, the articles of the Law regarding Execution of Policemen Duties, the Japan Coast Guard Law, and the Basic Law for Disaster Response (*Saigai Taisaku kihon Ho*) provide authorization for JSDF activities on the ground.[389] They include:

- Order evacuation;
- Entry into private land and properties;
- Request assistance from those who are nearby;
- Define Warning Area;
- Use of land and facilities that belong to individuals;
- Ridding of the objects that hinder execution of duties;

[xxxix] The article essentially seeks the legal justification of weapon use in Article Seven of the Law regarding the Policemen Carrying Out Duties, but has been enhanced so that use of weapon is allowed when the suspicious ship continues to flee and the on-board inspection is deemed critical in order to collect the information that can be useful to reduce the future risk. *Kaijo Hoan-cho Ho* (The Japan Coast Guard Law) Article 20-2. http://www.houko.com/00/01/S23/028.HTM (accessed 10 March 2008).

- Assign citizens for obligatory emergency relief work; and
- Tow abandoned vehicles.[390]

These various laws suggest that the JSDF operation is strictly controlled by the provisions for law enforcement organizations except for JSDF mobilization for national defense missions. What is extraordinary is that such restrictions apply even when the JSDF operates overseas (e.g., participation in UN PKOs). This has placed the JSDF under the extra restriction that no other foreign troops face when engaging in overseas missions. For instance, the existing restriction does not allow JSDF personnel to engage in overseas missions to use weapons except for self-defense (and protecting those who are under their direct care). This makes it impossible for the JSDF to assist foreign troops that operate next to it when they come under attack. If JSDF personnel facing such a situation feel compelled to assist such troops, they had to create a situation in which they could justify the use of their weapon for self-defense; that could mean he may literally have to throw himself at those who attack the troops. This is an example of how extending the restriction that envisions JSDF operations within Japan to JSDF overseas missions can create an unnecessary risk for the JSDF personnel deployed for overseas missions.

FUTURE PROSPECTS

In the last fifteen years, legal frameworks to authorize the JSDF to engage not only in homeland defense missions, but also in various other activities outside Japan have steadily evolved. In particular, there was no question that the 9/11 terrorist attacks against the United States was catalytic in triggering the legislative developments since 2001. Indeed, the 9-11 terrorist attacks presented Japan with a formidable challenge. At that time, neither Japan's legal system nor political atmosphere was permissive to sending the SDF to play an active combat role in the global war on terror. At the same time, however, it was clear that had Japan been unable to make a recognizable contribution to US-led multinational efforts, Japan would be exposed to even harsher criticism by the international community than it took after the 1990-91 Gulf War.

Prime Minister Junichiro Koizumi instinctively understood the potential impact on the US-Japan alliance in case of his government's inaction. Following the 9-11 attacks in 2001, he announced within ten days Japan's seven-point plan of assistance for the United States.[391] The plan included an SDF dispatch to support the military operations that would be led by the United States. Since there was no precedent for the SDF to participate in multinational military operation that had no explicit mandate by the United Nations, the Japanese government enacted the Anti-Terrorism Special Measures Law in November 2001.

The 2001 Anti-Terrorism Special Measures Law was a significant legislative development for Japan's national security policy. First and foremost, it established an important precedent for the legal approach to enable JSDF participation in non-UN-led multinational operations in the future. Without the Anti-Terror Special Measures Law, it is questionable whether Japan was able to enact the Iraq Reconstruction Special Measures Law, or the 2008 New Anti-Terrorism Special Measures Law. Furthermore, it demonstrated that enacting a special measures law can serve as a useful legislative compromise when the Japanese government urgently needs to make a certain national security policy decision on the issues that are politically too controversial to get consensus among legislators: with a time limit being attached to the law, it is easier to draw a compromise out of the opposition.

In addition to such legislative developments, a more fundamental change to the legal framework that JSDF deployments have been subject to seemed to be in the offing. The prospect of Japan lifting the ban on exercising the right of collective self-defense has been the subject of particular attention for the last few years.

Japan's self-imposed ban on exercising the right of collective self-defense and the challenges it posed against Japan playing a more visible and robust role both in the context of the US-Japan alliance and international security affairs have been discussed among defense policy experts for a long time. But when Junichiro Koizumi spoke about the necessity of constitutional revision soon after taking the office of the prime minister in April 2001, anticipation for an accelerated discussion about revising Article Nine of the Japanese constitution rose both inside and outside Japan.[392]

When Shinzo Abe became the prime minister in September 2006, he made the study of the Japanese government's current interpretation of Article Nine of the constitution one of the priorities for his cabinet.[393] In order to signal his determination, Abe established the Advisory Council on Re-establishing the Legal Foundation for National Security (*Anzen Hosho no Houteki Kiban no Sai-kouchiku ni kansuru Kondankai*), which he intended to chair himself, in April 2007 to deliberate on cases in which Japan should be allowed to exercise the right of collective self-defense.[394] Led by the former Japanese ambassador to the United States Shunji Yanai, this Advisory Council was to study four most likely scenarios that the Japanese government will face to explore whether the exercise of the collective self-defense would be required for Japan to adequately respond to the situation. In the event that any of the scenarios require Japan to exercise the right of collective self-defense, the Council was expected to recommend the re-interpretation of Article Nine.[395] Further, in order to pave the way for the eventual constitutional revision, his government enacted the Law regarding the Procedures for Revising the Constitution of Japan (*Nihonkoku Kenpou no Kaisei Tetsuduki ni kansuru Houritsu*, commonly referred to as the National Referendum Law (*Kokumin Touhyou Ho*)) in May 2007.[396] These developments between 2001-2007 heightened the expectation that Japan is at the cusp of allowing itself to exercise the right of collective self-defense.

As the Japanese government had to go under several rounds of enacting the special measures laws to authorize JSDF participation in the coalition operations in Afghanistan and Iraq, more people (mostly among officials at the Ministry of Defense and the Ministry of Foreign Affairs, as well as the politicians that have strong interests in national security and defense issues) began to argue for enacting a permanent law (generally referred to as general law (*ippan ho*) or permanent law (*kokyu ho*)). The purpose of the law would be to provide the basic criteria for JSDF overseas deployments regardless of UN authorization, and thereby establish a standard procedure with which the Japanese government can authorize JSDF dispatches overseas in a timely manner without relying on a case-specific special measures law. Political momentum appeared to develop behind enacting permanent legislation for JSDF's participation in international cooperation activities. In September 2005, the Liberal Democratic Party (LDP) incorporated the enactment of permanent legislation for JSDF's participation in international peace cooperation activities into the party's policy platform for the September election.[397] In August 2006, the LDP's Subcommittee on Defense Legislation under the Committee on National Defense released the proposed draft bill.

After several years of anticipation since 2001, however, not much tangible progress has been made either on the constitutional question or the permanent law. Particularly since the unexpected resignation of Prime Minister Shinzo Abe in September 2007, both of these developments have lost momentum. While the Advisory Council on Re-establishing the Legal Foundation for National Security was not disbanded with the resignation of Abe, it was clear that the Council had lost the political champion it once had under Prime Minister Abe. Following Abe's resignation, the Advisory Council did not convene until 11 April 2008—well more than six months since the previous Council meeting took place on 30 August 2007. When the Council issued its report and submitted it to Prime Minister Fukuda on 24 June 2008, it was clear that Fukuda was not at all interested in the content of the report: answering the question by the press on the same day, Fukuda disinterestedly replied he had not read the report yet, signaling that doing so was not his priority either. Although Prime Minister Taro Aso expressed his interest in tackling the issue soon after he became the prime minister, whether he can stay in power long enough to resurrect the issue remains highly uncertain.[398]

The political momentum behind the permanent law for JSDF overseas deployment also seemed to have lost steam. In the beginning, it enjoyed continued interest within the ruling coalition. In February 2008, the Liberal Democratic Party established a joint project team among its committees for national defense, foreign affairs and cabinet affairs. The joint project team aimed at submitting a bill to the Diet to begin debate before the conclusion of the 169th Ordinary Session of the Diet.[399] Built on the developments within the LDP, the LDP and the Komeito—the members of the current ruling parties—launched a project team to discuss the suggested content of the legislation in spring of 2008. However, as the approval rating for the Fukuda Cabinet plunges, the Komeito has turned lukewarm about submitting the bill to the Diet in the near future, having many supporters, particularly women, who are against JSDF's activity abroad, especially in the areas outside a "non-combat zone." While the ruling party's project team issued the interim report in late June, and the LDP still hopes to submit the bill to the Diet soon, the prospect of the bill is uncertain.[400] Given the low public approval rating of the current cabinet, as well as the primacy of domestic issues in the minds of Japanese legislatures these days, the outlook for the national security policy-related legislation getting the serious attention of Japanese leadership continues to be grim.

The legal framework for JSDF domestic and international operations have steadily evolved after the Cold War. Today, Japan is much better equipped legally to authorize JSDF operation; the concrete steps for the prime minister to make such decisions are also better established. Throughout this evolution, however, three fundamental principles for JSDF operation—JSDF is not considered a military force, its use of force must be restricted to what is minimally necessary to complete the missions, and the JSDF personnel is allowed to use force only for self-defense—remained unchanged. Over the years, these principles have been codified in the numerous existing laws to regulate JSDF—mostly focusing on preventing their abuse by JSDF rather than their practicality and applicability to the reality. In order for Japan to deploy the JSDF more effectively and responsively to the evolving security needs, the existing legal framework needs to be consolidated and simplified so that it is easy for Japanese decision-makers to understand and better articulate the rationale for their deployment decision to the public. Such a task cannot be completed, however, without revising the principles that helped to establish the current legal framework.

-6-
ASSESSMENT

Previous chapters have examined various aspects of Japan's national security policy infrastructure. How do they help Japan pursue its national security policy goals of: (1) defending Japan from security threats, and (2) participating in international efforts to create and maintain peace and stability? In this chapter, the key elements of Japan's national security policy infrastructure that were identified in Chapter One will be re-introduced. The institutions and frameworks examined in Chapters Two through Five will be assessed from the perspective of whether their current arrangements, as well as anticipated changes in the near future, help improve Japan's existing national security policy infrastructure in each of these key areas. Following this assessment, this chapter discusses the current political climate in Japan and evaluates the political winds surrounding the necessary changes for Japan to improve its national security policy infrastructure.

AN EVALUATION OF KEY ELEMENTS IN JAPAN'S NATIONAL SECURITY POLICY INFRASTRUCTURE

The goal of Japan's national security policy, as defined in the 2004 *National Defense Program Guideline*, is to defend Japan and to prevent threats in the international environment.[401] Further, the final report issued by the Council on Security and Defense Capabilities (the Araki Commission)—the document that Japanese government officials often refer to as a point of reference when discussing Japan's national security policy—suggests that Japan should develop an integrated approach to national security policy.[402] Chapter One identified four key elements that will be instrumental in facilitating Japan's quest to this end. They are: strong policy- and decision-making capability of the prime minister, the Cabinet's intelligence capability, better coordination among national security institutions in the Japanese government, and a legal framework.

ELEMENT ONE: CAPABILITY OF THE PRIME MINISTER

Examination of the civilian institutions in Chapter Two illustrated that the Japanese government, in essence, has a decentralized policy- and decision-making process. The prime minister is often the only actor in the process that can compel the bureaucracy to be more responsive and agile, forcing different agencies to work together when necessary. In times of crises, in particular, the prime minister needs to be able to make decisions based on the information and policy options that others present. In addition to his/her leadership quality, this requires a staff organization that supports the prime minister by (1) advising on policy issues, (2) presenting policy options, and (3) assisting the prime minister in supervising government agencies to oversee that the basic policy decided by the prime minister is maintained.

The prime minister, as the head of the Cabinet, is granted various rights by the Constitution, including:[403]

- Appointing and removing the members of the Cabinet (Ministers of States) as he/she chooses;
- Representing the Cabinet, submitting bills, reporting on general national affairs and foreign relations to the Diet, and exercising control and supervision over various administrative branches; and
- Countersigning all cabinet orders.

Based on the power vested in the prime minister by the Constitution, the Cabinet Law (*Naikaku Ho*) further specifies the authority of the prime minister to:[404]

- Convene and chair cabinet meetings either in response to the request from the Ministers of States or at his/her own initiative;
- Represent the Cabinet to the Diet, submit bills and budget proposals, and report on general national affairs and foreign relations to the Diet;
- Supervise and control the government agencies based on cabinet decisions;
- Referee the disagreements among the Ministers of States regarding the scope of their authorities and jurisdictions;
- Suspend the regulations and/orders issued by the government agencies; and
- Be dual-hatted as the Minister of State for the government agencies.

Looking at the legal authorities granted the prime minister, the prime minister appears to enjoy very strong authority. In reality, however, several institutional and political constraints have prevented past Japanese prime ministers from exercising strong leadership. First and foremost, the parliamentary cabinet system, unlike the presidential system, is designed to diffuse power among the members of the cabinet, limiting the prime minister's ability to lead.[405] While the prime minister represents the Cabinet to the Diet, the Cabinet Law vests the Cabinet as a collective entity with executive power.[406] The Cabinet can only make decisions with unanimous consent, which often delays the decision-making of the government.[407] Further, because of the prime minister's other role as the leader of the ruling political party under the current system, his/her effectiveness as a party leader, as well as the power base within the party, often have a direct impact on their performance as prime minister.[408] In short, it rarely has allowed the prime minister to fully utilize the authority attached to the position.[xl]

The efforts to enhance the support system for the prime minister, therefore, have a long history. As early as 1981, the report by Ad-hoc Research Committee on Public Administration (*Rinji Gyosei Chosa-kai*, often called *Dokou Rincho* (Dokou Ad-Hoc Committee)) proposed that the number of executive assistants for the Deputy Chief Cabinet Secretary and prime minister should be flexible, and that the prime minister should be allowed to appoint senior advisors at his/her discretion.[409] In the late 1980s, Prime Minister Yasuhiro Nakasone attempted to strengthen the capacity of the prime minister in policy-making by actively convening policy advisory councils (*shingikai*) that directly reported to the prime minister.[410]

The enhancement of the authority and function of the prime minister and expansion of the support staff for the prime minister were finally codified when the Hashimoto Cabinet enacted the Basic Law regarding the Reform of the Central Agencies and Other Organizations (*Chuo Sho-cho nado Kaikaku Kihonho*) in June 1999. The law defined the Cabinet Secretariat as the organization that should be managed by staff "directly appointed by the Prime Minister." It further included a provision that allowed flexibility in the number of advisors and executive assistants for the prime minister "in order to create the system that directly supports the Prime Minister."[411]

Almost ten years have passed since the enactment of the Basic Law. As Chapter Two examined, the Cabinet Secretariat has steadily developed as the institution that supports the Prime Minister. Under the provisions of the Cabinet Law, the Cabinet Secretariat has begun to emerge as the core player in Japan's national

---

[xl] In fact, in Japan's recent history, Yasuhiro Nakasone and Junichiro Koizumi were the only two that did so.

security policy, exemplified best by the central role it played in the process of dispatching the JSDF to the Indian Ocean and Iraq.[412] Further, when Japan revised its National Defense Program Guideline (NDPG) in 2004, the staff under the Assistant Chief Cabinet Secretary for National Security and Crisis Management played a far greater role in shaping the document compared to its first revision in 1995.[413] Thus, the Cabinet Secretariat has steadily evolved to support the prime minister in national security policymaking.

Still, the current arrangement prevents the prime minister from utilizing the Cabinet Secretariat truly as his/her policy planning support unit. The biggest reason is personnel—today, most of the staff in the Cabinet Secretariat is seconded from other agencies and given an assignment period that the human resources of their home agency decides. While the seconded staff in the Cabinet Secretariat may provide continuity and stability in the organization, they also limit the prime minister's ability to "think outside the box" and come up with new policy initiatives. Therefore, it is still desirable that the prime minister's personal staff can be brought into the Cabinet Secretariat, so that the organization does not stay complacent with the status quo.

In this context, the discussion toward establishing a Japanese National Security Council was the first serious attempt to institutionalize a system in which the policy staff personally chosen by the prime minister plays a major role in the Japanese government. To be sure, the proposed bill had many problems. For instance, the Council only included the Prime Minister, Chief Cabinet Secretary, Defense Minister and Foreign Minister as standing members. This invited criticism that the Council, if established, would merely serve as the body that manages the relationship between the MOD and MOFA. A question was also raised on the size of the envisioned Council. The proposed bill visualized that the Council would have a small number of staff (less than fifty people). Pointing out that the US National Security Council has over 130 staff, the critics argue that such a small number of staff in no way can engage in long-term policy planning for the prime minister while being involved in the day-to-day operation of the Cabinet, as well as coordination among the ministries.[414] Others question whether the envisioned NSC could identify and employ enough non-government experts to differentiate itself from the current staff in the office of Assistant Chief Cabinet Secretary for National Security and Crisis Management.[415] But the bill at least attempted to create a structure on which the prime minister could rely on for support in policy planning. After the Fukuda Cabinet decided not to continue the consideration of the law that would have served as the founding law for the revamped National Security Council of Japan, there is no sign that this law is going to be re-introduced to the Diet for deliberation. Thus, while the enhancement of the Cabinet Secretariat no doubt increased its relevance in the policy-making process in the Japanese government, the prime minister's ability to exercise leadership in policy- and decision-making through his/her own advisors will remain limited.

Element Two: Cabinet's intelligence capability

The prime minister requires intelligence and information in the decision-making process. This makes it critical that the capabilities to collect, analyze, and appropriately share and distribute salient information and intelligence reside in close proximity to the prime minister. As "domestic" and "international" security threats are becoming more difficult to distinguish, it is imperative that the intelligence community in Japan become as integrated as possible, with domestic intelligence organizations and foreign intelligence organizations cooperating with each other.

Calls for intelligence reform in Japan are not new. Overall, Japan's intelligence community is highly decentralized, with each member of the community maintaining its own intelligence assets, hiring and training its own analysts. These agency-attached assets, supposedly forming a "community," independently collect, analyze, assess, and distribute intelligence in reality. A community-wide common intelligence classification standard does not exist, and mutual trust among the intelligence organizations within the community is rare.

The enhancement of the Cabinet's intelligence capability has frequently appeared as a recommendation in the past reports released by advisory councils for the prime minister. For instance, the 1998 Final Report of the Administrative Reform Council, had already called for strengthening the Cabinet's intelligence capability. In particular, the report recommended:

- Establishing a section that supports the Cabinet in its intelligence capability within the Cabinet Secretariat. The section should be kept separate from the unit that manages strategic policy planning, as the independence of the intelligence must be maintained;

- Establishing the notion of "intelligence community" in order to facilitate mutual intelligence sharing among the relevant government agencies, as well as to promote the collection, analyses and assessment of the intelligence to the Cabinet;

- Making the Joint Intelligence Council into the formal organization of the Cabinet Secretariat and ensuring that it would work effectively; and

- Strengthening the Cabinet Intelligence and Research Office (CIRO) appropriately.[416]

When the Basic Law regarding the Reform of the Central Agencies and Other Organizations was enacted in June 1999, the Law gave the Cabinet Secretariat the mandate to, among other things, to collect and analyze intelligence, and authorized the Cabinet Secretariat to take appropriate measures to enhance this function.[417] The Cabinet Law gave the statutory foundation to the Director of Cabinet Intelligence, vesting him with the responsibility to manage the collection and analyses of the intelligence salient to important policy issues for the Cabinet.[418]

Since then, incremental efforts have been made to strengthen the Cabinet's intelligence capability. In particular, a number of crises drove efforts to reorganize and enhance the Cabinet's authority to collect intelligence analyses from Japan's intelligence community. For instance, the 1995 Hanshin-Awaji earthquake reminded Japanese political leaders of the importance of making all the information available to the prime minister and other top decisions makers in the Japanese government in case of national emergency. The experience led to the establishment of the Cabinet Intelligence Collection Center.[419] North Korea's Taepodong missile launch in 1998 exposed the Japanese government's dependency on the United States for national security intelligence. The revelation prompted Japan's decision to launch its own reconnaissance satellites and the decision to put the system in the hands of the Cabinet Satellite Information Center.

Most recently, under former Prime Minister Abe's auspices, the Japanese government explored ways to enhance the Cabinet's intelligence capability. Based on the recommendation by the Council, several new efforts have started. The reorganization of the Cabinet Intelligence and Research Office (CIRO) was central to this effort. With the reorganization, CIRO now has five senior intelligence officers supporting the Director of Cabinet Intelligence (DCI). The Counter-Intelligence Center was also newly established within CIRO. While the initiatives launched by the prime minister often are not inherited by the succeeding cabinet, the initiatives on strengthening the Cabinet's intelligence capability were a rare exception that had survived the political transition. For instance, when Prime Minister Abe resigned in September 2007, his effort in strengthening the Cabinet's resident intelligence capacity was succeeded by Yasuo Fukuda. When Prime Minister Taro Aso succeeded Fukuda in September 2008, his appointment of a former National Police Agency chief to the administrative Deputy Chief Cabinet Secretary signaled Aso's high interest in continuing this effort.

The efforts to enhance the Cabinet's intelligence capability still have left much to be desired, however. Ultimately, such efforts will remain cosmetic unless the status and authority of the DCI is considerably enhanced. The Cabinet Law currently does not provide the DCI authority to supervise other agencies in Japan's intelligence community.[420] This makes the DCI in today's Japanese intelligence community one of the peer principals of the community. For instance, the DCI briefs the prime minister twice a week; other organizations in Japan's intelligence community can and do enjoy more frequent and direct access to the prime minister than the DCI. The DCI does not represent the prime minister or the Cabinet at either the Cabinet Intelligence Council or the Joint Intelligence Council; either Chief Cabinet Secretary or the Deputy Chief Cabinet Secretary for administration represents the prime minister at these meetings. In short, the DCI is currently not in the position to serve the prime minister as his/her chief intelligence officer, providing integrated intelligence analyses to support his/her decision-making.[421]

Furthermore, as discussed in Chapter Four, the strengthening of CIRO as an intelligence organization is critical in improving CIRO's ability to support the DCI. In particular, the development of its in-house intelligence collection and analytical capability including an enhanced effort to recruit, train and retain capable analysts is urgently needed. The establishment of the basic protocol on intelligence classification and distribution which can be shared throughout Japan's intelligence community is just as important.

Element Three: Better coordination among the national security policy institutions

Today, the security threats that Japan needs to cope with have become transnational in nature, and amorphous in form. The activities that used to be law enforcement concerns (e.g., terrorism, smuggling) can easily turn into national security concerns. This makes it imperative that Japan's key national security policy institutions—the Ministry of Foreign Affairs, the Ministry of Defense, and the National Police Agency—have a close cooperative relationship in order to address security concerns.

This requires that MOFA and the NPA change the way they have looked at the MOD in the past: both agencies have to acknowledge that the MOD should not stay within the subordinate, and that it has to be regarded as a full partner in shaping and implementing national security policy in Japan. For instance, the NPA long identified one of the major roles of the police as defending the country *from* the Japan Self-Defense Forces. With Japan's new security challenges demanding that the domestic law enforcement and national defense organizations work together, the NPA must be more inclined to work *with* the MOD and the JSDF. For MOFA, it needs to acknowledge that, while the law grants the primary jurisdiction over national security policy to MOFA, it needs to work with the MOD as an equal partner in order for Japan's security policy to have any substance. The Cold War-era image of the MOD (then the JDA) as the inward-looking agency whose only mandate is to manage the JSDF and issues associated with US military in Japan needs to change.

At the same time, the MOD also has to prove that it has grown institutionally to have the capacity to play a major role in Japan's national security policy. Most importantly, it needs to improve its ability as the policymaking agency (*seisaku kancho*) and it can convince other agencies that it is no longer just a management agency (*kanri kancho*) for the JSDF. In other words, merely changing the name from the Japan Defense Agency (*Bouei Cho*) to the Ministry of Defense (*Bouei Sho*) is not enough.

This is all easier said than done. Old habits die hard. The NPA, while far more open to working closely with the MOD and JSDF to respond to emergencies, still strongly resists JSDF playing any role related to maintaining domestic security, particularly during peacetime. For instance, the NPA is said to be resentful that, with the revision of SDF Law after the 9-11 terrorist attack in 2001, the JSDF now is authorized to have its military police protect the facilities of US forces and its own even when Japan is not facing an armed attack. The NPA sees such a change as the MOD encroaching on the maintenance of domestic security, its primary area of responsibility.[422] In MOFA, as well, while there is a greater awareness that the MOD/JSDF has to be a major player in security policy for Japan to assert its presence in international security affairs, little willingness exists to acknowledge that reality. As one MOFA official describes it: "if you look at the growth in MOD capability from the Foreign Policy Bureau's perspective, for example, it is definitely a positive development… but if you are in the North American Bureau, you may actually miss the time when the MOD was still the JDA and much weaker. It is the matter of where in MOFA you are when you work with the MOD."[423] Meanwhile, the MOD has been plagued with one problem after another, raising questions of whether the MOD is institutionally capable of managing its organization, let alone playing a bigger role in Japan's national security policy.

Each ministry is currently engaged in its own efforts to streamline operations. However, few efforts have been made to improve the way in which national security policy institutions cooperate and coordinate among themselves. The attempt to enact the legislation to create a Japanese NSC, while criticized for only creating a mediation venue between the MOD and MOFA, at least attempted to institutionalize interagency coordination with some of the key players in Japan's national security policy. Now that effort has failed, with no sign of it being resurrected, leaving the Japanese government only with an informal regular discussion (either in person or via phone) between the Minister of Defense and Minister of Foreign Affairs. This is, however, an ad hoc arrangement, and can only function when the two ministers are on good terms—it can collapse any time because the discussion is not institutionalized. The NPA is not even involved in the discussion.[424] Aside from this arrangement, the modes of cooperation among the national security policy agencies have essentially not changed, which is hardly sufficient for Japan to meet its security policy goals in today's security environment.

Element Four: Adjustment of the legal framework

Japan, has to have all actions and authorities of its government supported by appropriate laws and regulations.[425] When the Japanese government needs to change its past practices, the appropriate laws and regulations need to be revised in order for such a change to be substantiated.

As discussed in Chapters Two thru Five, the legal framework for Japan's national security is exceedingly cumbersome, not allowing the Japanese government to be quick and decisive in its decisions. The current legal framework for JSDF overseas dispatch is a manifestation of the awkwardness of the existing system. Under the current system, if the proposed dispatch takes place outside the scope of the UN PKO Cooperation Law, International Disaster Relief Law, or the contingency legislation, each deployment-specific special measures law needs to be enacted. Once the deployment itself is authorized, the JSDF troops on the ground are placed under strict rules of engagement that more closely resemble police regulations rather than military regulations. Further, any institutional change intended for Japan's national security policy infrastructure requires that the related laws be changed accordingly. This often results in inflexibility—each time the institution tries to behave differently, or propose a policy initiative, the legal implications of the initiative must be discussed first. This tends to make the Japanese government passive, not able to present its policy option until the last minute.

To streamline the current legal framework, it is desirable for Japan to enact at least two laws. One is the basic law that defines how the Japanese government should organize itself to manage national security policy.[xli] The other is the law

---

[xli] The idea of enacting *Kokka Anzen Hosho Kihon Ho* (Basic Law regarding National Security) has been suggested in the past by the Diet members who are considered pro-strong defense and pro-US-Japan alliance. See, for example, Nagashima, Akihisa, *Nichibei Doumei no Atarasii Sekkei-zu:*

(the so-called General Law) that defines the conditions for the JSDF overseas dispatch, regardless of where the mandate comes from. While the cross-reference with the existing law (e.g., SDF Law) still needs to be in place, the general law will speed up the deliberation of the proposed overseas dispatch in the Diet, as the legislators can focus on whether the conditions for the overseas dispatch are met instead of first having to decide on which law the proposed dispatch will be based.

It should be reiterated, however, that the current complicated legal framework for Japan's national security policy stems from the fact that Japan has had to reconcile the gap between Article Nine of the Constitution and existing reality. Postwar Japan's national security policy revolved around arguing that the JSDF, while treated as the military abroad, was not considered a military in Japan. This, as a result, subjects the JSDF to the types of restrictions that militaries from other countries do not have. For instance, the JSDF is subject to the restrictions of law enforcement officers unless they engage in national defense operations. When opposition against the JSDF dispatches abroad is voiced, it is usually because the proposed operation may put the JSDF in a position where its personnel are compelled to use force while carrying out the mission. In other words, the JSDF, in the context of Japanese law, is a constabulary force that has a more powerful capability than the regular police force. Only a constitutional revision can bridge the current gap that exists between the Constitutional provisions and the reality in today's Japan.

The prospects for these necessary legal changes are not promising. At the most fundamental level, after Prime Minister Abe abruptly resigned and left the office in September 2007, the movement toward the constitutional revision was halted as Prime Minister Fukuda is clearly not interested in the recommendations submitted by the advisory council that examined the possible scenarios under which Japan should alter its current interpretation of not exercising the right of collective self-defense. While Prime Minister Aso indicates a strong interest in tackling this issue, the transition from Abe to Fukuda indicated that the support among Japanese political leaders on the constitutional revision is not widely shared.

While the Liberal Democratic Party (LDP) and Komeito (the current ruling parties) launched a joint task force to discuss the General Law with an eye on eventually drafting the bill and submitting it to the Diet, the political parties

---

Henbou suru Asia no Beigun wo Misuete (A New Blueprint for New US-Japan Alliance: Considering Evolving US Military Presence in Asia) (Tokyo: Nihon Hyoron-sha, 2002). The idea of the Basic Law regarding National Security was also proposed in the October 2005 proposal for a constitution revision by the Democratic Party of Japan.

cannot agree on the scope of the General Law. The original idea for the General Law was to include not only the provisions on the dispatch for UN PKOs and disaster relief, but also a provision authorizing the JSDF to participate in stabilization forces, provincial reconstruction teams (PRTs) and other multinational force operations that may lead to the JSDF operating outside the "non-combatant" area. However, recent political developments in Japan may significantly limit the scope of the proposed General Law, making it not much different than the UN PKO Cooperation Law. And the idea of the Basic Law for National Security has not been discussed outside a small community of security policy experts in Japan. With the exception of the legislative action to maintain status quo (e.g., continuation of the refueling mission in the Indian Ocean), a new legislative initiative to improve the legal foundation for Japan's national security policy is highly unlikely.

POLITICAL LEADERSHIP: POTENTIAL DRIVER FOR CHANGE

Progress in the four key elements of Japan's national security infrastructure so far has been limited. Even in the areas where some progress can be seen in recent years, these changes are not sufficient for Japan to act in a way that moves it closer to achieving its national security policy goals. Whether significant progress can be made in these elements depends on how the fifth element—political leadership in the area of national security policy—will evolve.

Much of the incremental progress toward the status quo in Japan's national security policy infrastructure has been established in the absence of interest and initiative by the political leaders. Changing the status quo ultimately is subject to the decisions of the political leadership in Japan. How much leadership authority should the prime minister be allowed? How should the prime minister be supported? How should the intelligence community be organized in Japan? How should the interagency coordination among the key national security agencies in Japan be institutionalized? How should the legal question in Japan's national security policy be addressed? These questions most likely cannot be fully addressed without changing the existing law (or the interpretation of the current law at minimum), which requires legislative action by the Diet. Many of the necessary changes are likely to be unpopular either in the bureaucracy or among the public, or both. Therefore, if Japan is to change the status quo in its national security policy infrastructure, a strong political will is imperative.

Since the end of the Cold War, the overall political attitude toward national security policy has been evolving. For instance, the Liberal Democratic Party

(LDP) and the Democratic Party of Japan (DPJ)—the larger of the ruling parties and the largest opposition party in today's Japan, respectively—agree that a more robust discussion must take place on constitutional revision. Both parties also agree that the current interpretation of Article Nine of the Constitution by the Japanese government is in effect hollowing out the Constitution, and that it should be revised.[426] This is a major shift from the Cold War era when the Social Democratic Party of Japan, as the biggest opposition party in Japan, stood proudly as the *goken seitou* (Constitution-protecting political party) and refused any discussion on constitutional revision. It is also important that Komeito, LDP's partner in the current ruling coalition, is also open to discussion on constitutional revision.[427]

The agreements among the LDP, DPJ, and LDP's coalition partner Komeito have led to important legislative achievements in Japan's national security policy since 2001. Such achievements include the enactment of the Anti-Terror Special Measures Law, Iraq Reconstruction Assistance Special Measures Law, the Armed Attack Response Law and the Public Protection Law. The upgrading of the Japan Defense Agency (JDA) to the Ministry of Defense (MOD) also could not have been achieved without legislative cooperation with the DPJ. Thus, one can argue that the political environment has become more favorable for the Japanese government to pursue additional measures to accelerate changes in Japan's national security policy infrastructure.

However, beyond the general agreement that Japan has to be more proactive to meet today's security challenges, there is surprisingly little consensus over the specific issues of Japan's national security policy. Take the issue of JSDF overseas deployment, for instance. In post-Cold War Japan, the debates over JSDF overseas dispatch have revolved around three main questions—whether the JSDF should be dispatched internationally, what the conditions for the JSDF's overseas deployment should be, and why Japan should deploy the JSDF.[428] From its first debate of this kind over the dispatch of the Japan Maritime Self-Defense Force (JMSDF) minesweepers to the Persian Gulf in 1990-91 to the most recent debate on the renewal of the JMSDF refueling mission in the Indian Ocean, little consensus emerged on the issue. In fact, more than fifteen years after Japan dispatched the JSDF for its first overseas mission, Japanese political leaders can barely agree on the desirability of SDF overseas deployment, its condition, and its reason. While they by and large agree that SDF deployment is a good, tangible way to demonstrate Japan's willingness to play a role in international activities, a great deal of differences remain on how much activity the SDF should be engaged in, and more importantly, why Japan should allow the SDF to participate in these activities to begin with.

Such a political environment ultimately is a reflection of the public mood in Japan. The Japanese government's past responses to the requests for JSDF overseas dispatch suggest that Japanese people are not sure whether they are willing to see the JSDF play a more robust role overseas in order to support Japan's national security policy goals. It is revealing that, in examining the past debates over the JSDF dispatch overseas, one issue always comes up as a potential show-stopper: the possibility of the dispatched JSDF personnel having to use weapons during the mission. The so-called "PKO Five Principles"—the five conditions that were attached when the Japanese government first enacted the PKO Cooperation Law in 1992—serve as a useful guide to gauge the level of JSDF overseas activities that the Japanese public is willing to see. The principles included the following:[429]

- Existence of a cease-fire agreement;
- Agreement of all the parties involved on Japan's participation in the PKO in question;
- Neutrality of the PKO forces in place;
- Japan's right to withdraw the SDF when these conditions are no longer met; and
- Minimum use of weapons.

In other words, the spirit of the Five Principles—the JSDF can be dispatched only to an area where it will not have to risk engaging in using weapons, reflected in the "minimum use of weapons" principle—may well represent the level of consensus over JSDF overseas deployment among the Japanese public today.

Junichiro Koizumi was the first Japanese prime minister who tried to push the public consensus beyond this point. When he came into the office, he discussed the need for Japan to recognize the JSDF as a military.[430] When defending his case for dispatching the JSDF to Iraq, he argued that the JSDF is "the only organization that can conduct effective reconstruction assistance activities in a sustainable manner."[431] Prime Minister Abe, following Koizumi's footsteps, also asserted his willingness to commit the JSDF to overseas mission when he spoke of Japan "no longer shying away from carrying out overseas activities involving the SDF, if it is for the sake of international peace and stability" at the North Atlantic Council in January 2007.[432]

The developments following Abe's resignation in September 2007 may suggest that the efforts by Koizumi and Abe may not be sustainable. Indeed, the two leaders may have been way ahead of the public on this issue. The 2006 public opinion poll by the Cabinet Affairs Office indicates that only less than 40 percent of the respondents think the JSDF should enhance its effort in international activities.[433] When asked whether the JSDF should increase, reduce or maintain the current level of international peace cooperation activities, over 50 percent responded that the JSDF should maintain the current level—those who supported the JSDF increasing the international peace cooperation activities only amounted to approximately 30 percent.[434] Complacency with the status quo among the Japanese public seems to result in the unwillingness to send the JSDF to missions whose scope is beyond the comfort zone of the public. This results in restricting the Japanese government's ability to be more responsive to international requests for JSDF dispatch.

For instance, when the Japanese government decided on dispatching the JSDF officers to the UN Mission in Sudan (UNMIS) in June 2007, Japan decided against sending JSDF engineering units due to concerns of the security situation on the ground, despite the strong request for them by both the Sudanese government and the United Nations.[435] Although the North Atlantic Treaty Organization (NATO) strongly requested Japan commit JSDF troops to provide rear-area support in transport and logistics either for the International Stabilization Force (ISAF) or the Provincial Reconstruction Team (PRT) in Afghanistan, Tokyo decided against pursuing the dispatch.[436] Both of these decisions were received with a great sense of disappointment. At minimum, this is hardly an appropriate decision for a government that has "improvement of the international security environment" as one of its national security policy goals.

Further, lack of consensus in the way of using the JSDF abroad continues to leave the Japanese government in the passive position whenever a need for multinational forces arises in the international arena. The initial comment made by then-Chief Cabinet Secretary Yasuo Fukuda on Japan's role in the war on terror in 2001 is quite telling of the mentality that is persistent among Japanese political leaders, and is also a telltale sign of Japan's inherently passive approach in determining whether it should dispatch the SDF overseas in any given situation: "(W)hat support we can give [to the US] will depend on what we are asked to do. We will consider Japan's actions after evaluating the responses of other nations."[437] In fact, examination of past debates over JSDF overseas dispatch among Japanese political leaders—from the PKO mission in Cambodia to East Timor to Iraq—illustrates that fear of international isolation, rather than a proactive will to shape the agenda has driven their decisions to dispatch the JSDF. It should be noted that even Koizumi, while trying to frame the debate in terms of Japan's national interests and Tokyo's responsibility as a major power in the international community in order to get the Diet to approve JSDF dispatch to Iraq, had to resort to the logic that was once tried by Prime Ministers Toshiki Kaifu when he first argued for the JSDF dispatch to support multinational forces during the 1990-91 Gulf War—if Japan does not do its share, it will face international isolation.[438]

No consensus exists on JSDF overseas dispatch beyond participation in international disaster relief operations. The political debate over the JSDF overseas dispatch has more or less stagnated, and has not progressed much since the debate first started immediately after the Cold War, despite the shock of the 9/11 terrorist attacks in 2001. Unless Japanese political leaders can make a convincing case to the public, the Japanese government will be forced to remain passive in deciding JSDF dispatch for overseas activities, continuing to take a minimalist approach in choosing the specifics of its actions.[439]

What is the prospect that political leaders in Tokyo will articulate the rationale for a more robust JSDF overseas deployment to the public? Unfortunately, the prospect does not look very encouraging. For the short-term, it appears that the Japanese political world is entering a period that looks similar to the early 1990s—a series of short-term governments led by politically weak prime ministers.[440] When the political landscape is uncertain, the governments, as well as political parties, tend to focus on the issues that bring them short-term gains—unless Japan faces another missile attack or an explicit attempt of armed invasion, national security is unlikely to become such an issue. Under such circumstances, there is a considerable risk that the issue is unnecessarily politicized in a way that may harm Japan's national interest. The success of the DPJ led by Ichiro Ozawa in suspending JMSDF refueling mission in the Indian Ocean by preventing the Replenishment Support Special Measures Law from being enacted prior to the expiration of the Anti-Terror Special Measures Law is a tantamount example of Japan's national interest being harmed for short-term political gain by a political party.

This puts the Japanese government in a difficult position. For one, it cannot pursue further changes to its institutional arrangement for national security policy without political support. Even if it can maneuver its way to achieve some of the changes by passing new laws and revising the existing ones, actual implementation of the new legal framework will be difficult in such a political environment. Citing the General Law as an example, several senior current and former MOD officials noted that the enactment of the General Law now will not allow Japan to dispatch the JSDF more actively to international operations as long as there is no new consensus on how Japan should utilize the JSDF abroad—rather, it may mean longer debate in the Diet on which provision should be applied to which proposed dispatch.[441] The fluidity in Tokyo's political environment will not likely foster the environment in which a serious national security policy debate can take place for some time to come.

DOES JAPAN HAVE THE CAPACITY TO EFFECTIVELY PURSUE ITS SECURITY POLICY GOALS?

Simply put, Japan's national security policy infrastructure today does not have the capacity to pursue its national security policy goals effectively. Its capacity in all of the five key elements is simply not enough for Japan to do so.

Japan's prime minister is institutionally inhibited from exercising strong leadership in setting policy agendas, providing strategic guidance and supervision of his/her government. The current arrangement compels the prime minister to rely too heavily on the expertise of a bureaucracy that is fundamentally risk-adverse, self-preserving and status quo-oriented. After the failure of the recent effort to establish a Japanese NSC in which the prime minister's personal policy staff can provide policy- and decision-making support, it is unlikely that similar efforts will get a second chance and succeed in the near term.

Similarly, Japan's intelligence community is too decentralized, with the Director of Cabinet Intelligence not having enough statutory authority to demand access to intelligence collected and analyzed by the intelligence organizations in other parts of the Japanese government. Further, because of the large percentage of staff at the Cabinet Intelligence Research Office being seconded from other government agencies (namely the NPA, MOD and MOFA) and occupying senior positions, the current arrangement prohibits CIRO's in-house capacity as an intelligence organization from further developing and maturing. This, again, forces the prime minister and his senior staff to rely heavily on agency-specific information, rather than integrated all-source analyses that ideally should be provided by the DCI. Further, absence of shared intelligence classification standards, including the clearance system of those who will be assigned to intelligence-related positions, creates confusion, and prevents the appropriate distribution of intelligence among the relevant parties.

Institutional relationships among MOFA, the MOD and NPA—the three key national security policy agencies in today's Japan—still leave a lot to be desired. While the improvements have been made on the ground on a case-by-case basis, little tangible efforts to learn from these positive experiences and institutionalize them at a higher level have been made. As a result, the relationship among these agencies still depends on person-to-person relations among the bureaucracy, which is fragile and unsustainable over the long-term. Ultimately, these three agencies are still too often preoccupied with how they can maintain (or, in case of the MOD, expand) their position as a major player in the national security policy community rather than work together toward a shared national security policy goal.

The legal foundation for Japan's national security policy is also problem-ridden. It is not only cumbersome, but it stands on legal assumptions that do not match the reality that Japan lives in today. The legal issue cannot be addressed without political leaders showing a strong commitment to do so. However, given today's political situation, the likelihood that Japanese political leaders turn their attention to the legal issues involving national security is very slim for some time to come.

Taken together, Japan's national security policy infrastructure is not in the shape to enable Japan to robustly pursue its national security policy goals. Recent developments in Japan discussed above—Tokyo's decision against pursing the dispatch of ground troops to Afghanistan and its decision against sending more substantial troops to the UN mission in Sudan—are signs that Japan has maximized its potential for its national security policy without considerably updating its security policy infrastructure. Given the political weakness of the current and likely near-term government, Japan may have to muddle through without being able to revamp its national security policy infrastructure for the foreseeable future.

-7-
EVOLVING US EXPECTATION OF JAPAN

"US-Japan relationship is the most important bilateral relationship in the world, bar none."

--Senator Mike Mansfield, US ambassador to Japan, 1977-1988[xlii]

"(O)ne of the most successful bilateral relationships in history..... Japan-US Security Relationship... remains the cornerstone for achieving common security objectives and for maintaining a stable and prosperous environment for the Asia-Pacific region"

--Japan-US Joint Declaration on Security: Alliance for the 21st Century[442]

"(T)he US-Japan partnership stands as one of the most accomplished bilateral relationships in history."

--The Japan-US Alliance for the New Century[443]

The leaders of two nations have repeatedly emphasized the significance of the bilateral relationship over the years. But will this premise hold even when Japan remains limited in the role it can and is willing to play as a US ally?

Previous chapters examined the key elements in Japan's national security policy structure in detail, with a conclusion that Japan's national security policy infrastructure is not yet strong enough to enable Tokyo to effectively pursue its national security policy goals, and engage more robustly in international efforts to maintain peace and security. It also appears that the current political climate in Tokyo will not facilitate its revitalization. Given such prospects, how should the United States approach the US-Japan alliance in the future? The answer depends on what the United States expects from Japan. Although difficult, this chapter attempts to trace the shift in US expectations of Japan through three phases—the Cold War era, post-Cold War period, and post-9/11, with particular focus on the post-9/11 period. The chapter ends with an assessment of whether current US expectations of Japan can be met, provided the evaluation in Chapter Six.

[xlii] Senator Mansfield recalled that he began to use this phrase in the early 1980s. See Mike Mansifled, *My Recollections* (Tokyo: Nihon Keizai Shimbun-sha, 1999).

EVOLUTION OF US EXPECTATIONS OF JAPAN: PRE-9/11

Cold War

The United States played an enormous role in shaping postwar Japan's identity. It was the US-led General Headquarters (GHQ), commanded by General Douglas MacArthur, that completely disarmed Japan after its unconditional surrender in 1945: Supreme Commander of the Allied Powers (SCAP) General MacArthur proposed the so-called "MacArthur notes" (*MacArthur San Gensoku*) to those in the GHQ who drafted the Japanese constitution. Hoping to make Japan into a "Switzerland of the Orient," MacArthur presented in "the MacArthur Notes" the following three principles based on which the Japanese constitution would be drafted:[444]

> *The Emperor: The Emperor is the head of the State. His succession is dynastic. His duties and powers will be exercised in accordance with the Constitution and the basic will of the people as provided therein;*
>
> *Renunciation of War: War as a sovereign right of the nation is to be abolished. Japan renounces it as an instrumentality for settling its disputes and even for its own security. It relies upon the higher ideals which are now stirring in the world for its defense and its protection. No Japanese army, navy or air force will ever be authorized and no rights of belligerency will ever be conferred upon by Japanese force;*
>
> *Elimination of the feudal system: The feudal system of Japan will cease. No rights or peerage except those of the Imperial Family will extend beyond the limits of those who now existent. No patent of nobility will from this time forth embody within itself any national of civic power of government. Pattern budget after British system.*

These principles were all reflected in the Constitution that Japan eventually adopted in November 1946. In particular, the second principle—renunciation of war—was incorporated into Article Nine of the Constitution and remains the core principle of Japan's national security policy today. As examined in Chapters Three and Five, it has prevented Japan from expanding its role in international security affairs.

However, it was the same MacArthur who pushed Japan to rearm once the Korean War broke out in July 1950. Wanting to relieve US forces in Japan from the duty of defense of Japan so that they could be deployed to the Korean Peninsula, MacArthur demanded that Japan build an armed force to complement US forces in Japan in maintaining public order, and issued the National Police

Reserve Ordinance on 10 August 1950. Based on the ordinance, the National Police Reserve (*Keisatsu Yobi Tai*) was inaugurated (the Coastal Safety Force (*Kaijo Keibi Tai*) was established in 1952). The National Police Reserve was re-organized into the Safety Force (*Hoantai*) in 1952 and merged with the Maritime Safety Force and eventually became the Self-Defense Force in 1954.[445]

When the United States and Japan signed the original *Security Treaty between Japan and the United States of America* in 1951, US government expected Japan to fulfill two roles. One was to allow forward-deployed US troops that could be used for military operations in East Asia to continue to station in Japan. The other was for Japan to develop its national defense capability. In fact, in the process leading up to the inauguration of the Japan Self-Defense Forces (JSDF), the United States had strongly pushed Japan to resume a full-scale re-armament, with over 400,000 troops, which the Japanese resisted.[446] The 1951 Security Treaty already included the provision that the United States, while willing to deploy its forces in Japan, requested that Japan gradually shoulder more responsibility in its own defense.[447] Following the conclusion of the Security Treaty in 1951, the United States readily provided the JSDF with armaments through the Military Assistance Program (MAP) so that Japan could quickly build up its national defense capability.[448] After Japan and the United States signed *the Mutual Cooperation and Security Treaty between Japan and the United States of America* in January 1960 to enter into a more reciprocal security arrangement, these elements continue to shape the core US expectation of Japan.[449]

It is worthwhile to note, however, that US motivation for entering into an alliance relationship with Japan was not driven only by military consideration from the beginning. In fact, the historical accounts of the bilateral negotiations for the 1951 as well as the 1960 Security Treaty reveals that US interest in the alliance with Japan was driven by the belief that a Japan that was economically strong and anchored in the community of Western democracies would be the strongest US ally in the Asia-Pacific region.[450] It is noteworthy that the strategic consideration for ensuring that Japan stands against the communist bloc by establishing the common sense of purpose and common objectives between the United States and Japan was a major factor in shaping US approach toward the revision of the US-Japan Security Treaty in 1960.[451]

During the Cold War period, the United States continued to urge Japan to develop its national defense capability. When the United States began to revise its global security strategy in the middle of the Vietnam War, US attempts to shift the primary self-defense responsibility on US allies became worldwide.

Such a US intention was announced as the "Nixon Doctrine" in 1969. In his speech on the "Vietnamization" of the Vietnam War in November 1969, President Richard Nixon reiterated the so-called "Nixon Doctrine," which was comprised of three principles:[452]

- The United States will keep all of its treaty commitments;
- The United States will defend its allies or the countries critical to US national interests if they face the threat of nuclear weapons; and,
- Other than nuclear threats, the United States, while keeping the treaty commitments, expects its allies to bear the primary responsibility in their own defense.

As part of bilateral efforts to confirm Tokyo's primary responsibility in defense of Japan, the two sides signed on to *the Guidelines for Japan-US Defense Cooperation* in 1978. This Guideline was established to outline the responsibilities to be shouldered respectively by US forces and the JSDF in defense of Japan.[453] The bilateral defense cooperation in case of regional contingencies in East Asia was left unaddressed in the 1978 Guidelines: both sides only agreed that bilateral defense cooperation under such circumstances needed to be jointly studied.[454] Further, as the Japanese economy grows, the expectation of Japan as a material supporter of US strategy in East Asia—an objective that was quietly pursued—began to be emphasized in a more visible manner in its demand for Japan's greater burden-sharing. Specifically, US presidents and senior officials began to talk more about Japan's host-nation support for US forces in Japan and Japan's procurement of US weapons—in fact the issue of host-nation support was among the first items mentioned in the May 1979 joint communiqué between US president Jimmy Carter and Japanese prime minister Masayoshi Ohira.[455]

By the 1970s, the foreign policy establishment within the US government also began to overtly encourage Japan to provide diplomatic support for US efforts worldwide. For instance, US Secretary of State Henry Kissinger discussed the shift in US foreign policy priority as building an international order that was based on balance, negotiation, and an inclination for global interdependence. He placed the US-Japan relationship as the core driver for promoting international peace and prosperity, and the foundation for US policy toward Asia.[456] Further, President Ford spoke to the importance of the partnership with Japan as a pillar of US strategy in Asia. In his speech in Hawaii, in which he laid out the principles of what later became known as a "new Pacific Doctrine," Ford emphasized his interest in seeing his government deepen non-military aspects of the US relationship with Japan, proclaiming that "(t)here is no relationship to which I have devoted more attention (then the US-Japan relationship)." He discussed the political partnership between Tokyo and Washington, and the prospect of working with Japan (along with other industrialized nations) on more global issues.[457] When Prime Minister Ohira visited the United States in 1979, President Carter and Prime Minister Ohira described the US-Japan relationship as a "productive" (*minori no aru*) partnership.[458]

In the 1980s the tension between the United States and Japan grew rapidly. The Japanese economy continued to grow, driven by its exports. The United States, the primary market of Japanese products, began to accumulate a trade deficit against Japan—by 1987, the US trade deficit against Japan rose to approximately 57 billion dollars.[459] The term "Japan bashing" began to be heard among those who blamed the US trade deficit with Japan on Japan's closed markets for foreign products.[xliii] As the trade conflict was growing into a serious bilateral issue, the US government attempted to call the attention to the security dimension of US-Japan relations, emphasizing that Japan is an important US ally in East Asia. For instance, President Ronald Reagan and Prime Minister Zenko Suzuki, during Suzuki's visit to Washington, DC in May 1981, referred to US-Japan relations for the first time as "alliance," reaffirming that the US-Japan Security Treaty was "the foundation of peace and stability in the Far East and the defense of Japan."[460] Prime Minister Yasuhiro Nakasone, in his first visit to the United States as the prime minister in January 1983, stressed that he deemed the US-Japan alliance critical not only for the security of Japan, but also for the Far East. When President Reagan visited Japan in November 1983, Nakasone reiterated his view that the US-Japan alliance is "the foundation of the peace and security of Japan and the Far East."[461] In response, Reagan referred to US forces in Japan, acknowledging that it was "essential not only to the defense of Japan, but also to contribute to peace and prosperity in the Far East."[462] In 1989, when the US and Japanese government reached an agreement over Japan's development of the FSX Support Fighter, President George Bush defended the administration's decision on US-Japan joint development of Japan's FS-X based on F-16 design because it would "contribute to the security of the United States and our major ally, Japan."[463]

Throughout the Cold War period, the US defense establishment remained primarily focused on encouraging Japan to build up greater national defense

[xliii] In the 1980s, a number of books were published on the US-Japan economic and trade friction. Clyde V. Prestowitz Jr., *Trading Places: How We Allowed Japan to Take the Lead* (New York: Basic Books, March 1988) is one such example.

capability.[xliv] The 1979 Carter-Ohira Joint Communiqué, while stressing the "productive partnership" between the two countries, continued to identify Japan's own effort to strengthen its defense capability as one of the examples of the elements that makes the US-Japan relationship "mutually beneficial."[464] In 1985, US Secretary of State George Shultz proposed that Japan should fill the gap between the publicly pronounced responsibility for its own defense and its actual capability.[465] Prime Minister Nakasone's unambiguous support for a successful conclusion of the Intermediate-range Nuclear Force (INF) Treaty and call for the Western bloc's solidarity at the 1983 Williamsburg G7 Summit was noted and highly appreciated by the United States.[466] Still, when Nakasone and Reagan met again in Tokyo in November 1983, Reagan noted that his government was "convinced that the most important contribution Japan can make toward the peace and security in Asia is for Japan to provide for its own defense and share more of the burden of our mutual defense effort."[467]

By the end of the Cold War, the United States has established three basic principles in its approaches to Japan—ask Japan to bear a greater responsibility in its own defense; to provide support (rhetorical and otherwise) for US diplomatic initiatives worldwide, and; to support US military operations in East Asia and beyond, primarily by continuing to support the presence of US forces in Japan.[468] While there certainly was an expectation that Japan would utilize its capability to support US military operations, Washington envisioned, with an exception of the request for the dispatch of minesweepers to the Middle East in the 1980s, that such support would be provided within the Asia-Pacific region.

Post-Cold War

When the Cold War ended, the United States had barely begun to recover from its recession. As US preoccupation with its domestic economic situation deepened, Washington began to look to its allies to shoulder more responsibility, not only in their own national defense, but also toward regional and global security. The US government's expectations of Japan also began to shift: it began to expect Japan to shoulder a greater burden not only in Asia but also other parts of the world in more tangible terms. From the alliance manager's perspectives, Japan building up its own defense capability and providing host nation support for US forces in Japan were no longer sufficient. The US government, particularly its defense establishment, began to urge Japan

---

[xliv] Hidetoshi Sotooka, Masaru Honda, and Toshiaki Miura, eds. *Nichi-Bei Doumei Han-Seiki: Anpo to Mitsuyaku (Half Century of the US-Japan Alliance: Security and Secrete Agreements)* (Asahi Shimbun-sha, 2001) provides a very detailed account of the bilateral negotiation over the terms of US-Japan Security Treaty and the evolution of US policy toward Japan during the Cold war, based on declassified documents of US Department of State.

to support US (and US-led multinational) military operations by committing the JSDF. Japan's failure to respond to such requests caused the first "drift" in the US-Japan alliance.

At the time of the 1990-91 Gulf War, the United States asked Japan to participate in the efforts of the international community to restore the independence of Kuwait by providing transport support.[469] However, Japan was unable to allow JSDF troops to participate in the multinational force operations during combat operations. While it tried to provide logistical support by enacting the International Peace Cooperation Law, the bill was not approved by the Diet. In the end, Japan contributed approximately thirteen billion dollars for the war chest, which largely went unnoticed; rather, the dispatch of the minesweepers after the war attracted much greater attention. Japan, already relying on the Middle East for seventy-five percent of its oil, was heavily criticized for "buying safety."[470]

Japan also failed to respond to US calls for cooperation in the first North Korean nuclear crisis. The first North Korean nuclear crisis began with North Korea's declaration that it intended to withdraw from the Nuclear Nonproliferation Treaty (NPT) in March 1993. Following the declaration, the North Korean government, despite the decision to suspend its withdrawal decision, continued to violate the security provisions set by the International Atomic Energy Agency (IAEA) and began to extract nuclear fuel rods from its reactors at Yongbyong. When the IAEA Board of Directors ruled to suspend all assistance to North Korea (except for medical assistance) in May 1994, North Korea immediately announced its intention to withdraw from the IAEA. The crisis was averted in the eleventh hour when former president Jimmy Carter travelled to Pyongyang and reached an agreement with Kim Il-song in October 1994.[471]

During this crisis, the United States came extremely close to taking military action on the Korean Peninsula. William J. Perry, who served as the Secretary of Defense at that time, later recalled that the United States was "within hours" from launching a strike against North Korea.[472] As the United States prepared for war, US and Japanese defense officials discussed what Japan could do in support of US military operations should a military conflict break out on the Korean Peninsula. Through this bilateral discussion, it became clear that there was little Japan was able—and frankly, willing—to do to support such a US operation. Although the two countries had already embarked on the basic technological study on the feasibility of bilateral cooperation in a theater missile defense (TMD) system by launching the TMD Working Group (TMD-WG) in December 1993,[473] the inability of the US-Japan alliance—or rather, the prospect of Japan's inability to support the United States even in a military contingency in East Asia—greatly disappointed US defense planners.[474]

While the sense of uncertainty about the validity of the US-Japan alliance began to mount among US defense planners, the Department of Defense was also concerned that the ongoing economic and trade friction with between the United States and Japan might aggravate the political relationship between the two countries which, in turn, could undermine the alliance. In 1995, the Department of Defense issued *the United States Strategy for East Asia-Pacific Region* (EASR). Led by Joseph S. Nye Jr., then serving as Assistant Secretary of Defense for International Security Affairs, the report aimed at reassuring US allies in the Asia-Pacific region that the US military will continue to maintain a sizable presence in the region despite the end of the Cold War. In regards to US security relations with Japan, the report referred to the US-Japan alliance as having served as a "linchpin" of US security strategy in Asia.[475]

The two incidents—particularly the 1994 North Korean nuclear crisis—only added to the urgency of strengthening the US-Japan alliance by redefining its meaning and modernizing the alliance cooperation mechanism. The US government's effort in this endeavor was led by the Department of Defense, but with a close consultation with the Department of State. In *the Japan-US Joint Declaration on Security* in April 1996, the United States and Japan reaffirmed that the US-Japan alliance provides the cornerstone of peace and stability in the Asia-Pacific region.[476] Following the 1996 joint declaration, the two governments accomplished one of the most important tasks of the alliance redefinition in 1997—the revision of the 1978 Guidelines for Japan-US Defense Cooperation. Recognizing that the 1978 Guidelines lacked the clarity in defining the role of Japan and the United States under various scenarios, the revised Guidelines (more commonly referred to as the new Guidelines), adopted in September 1997, outlined the respective responsibilities of Japan and the United States under three circumstances—peacetime, wartime, and "situations in the areas surrounding Japan" (*shuhen jitai*).[477]

While the redefinition of the Guidelines was certainly a positive step forward for the US-Japan alliance, US defense planners were still left with a dose of frustration. For instance, when discussing the geographic scope of the situation in the areas surrounding Japan, Japanese defense planners were highly reluctant to explicitly define geographic scope of the term. Concerned that the redefinition of the alliance would upset China, they preferred to maintain the position that the "situation in the areas surrounding Japan" represented a functional concept and referred to a situation in which the incidents that occur nearby Japan have the potential to gravely impact Japan's security. Similarly, due to the prohibition of exercising the right of collective self-defense, US defense planners found it extremely difficult to engage their Japanese counterparts in the discussion of potential scenarios on regional contingencies.

Practically speaking, too, US alliance managers were frustrated that Japan's inability to exercise the right of collective self-defense and the constraint emanating from it continued to limit the types of support Japan could offer the United States in its military operations in the situations in the areas surrounding Japan. For instance, under the new Guidelines, Japan could provide logistical support for US military operations, but only the kind of support that the Japanese public and Diet would not consider as integrated with the use of force. This meant that the logistical support that the JSDF can provide is limited: for instance, the JSDF could not transport ammunition to the US troops engaging in combat on the frontline.

The ban on the right of collective self-defense also complicated bilateral discussions on defense cooperation in other areas, such as missile defense. In the beginning, Japan was only willing to engage in joint "technical study (*gijutsu kenkyu*)" of missile defense with the United States. When asked about the development or the introduction of the system, its leaders evaded the question by insisting that the development and introduction of the missile defense system will be decided independent of the decision to enter joint study with the United States.[478] Those who belong to the Social Democratic Party of Japan also criticized Japan's participation in joint technological study with the United States as violating the 1969 Diet resolution on peaceful use of space.[479]

In October 2000, the Institute of National Strategic Studies (INSS) issued a Special Report "The United States and Japan: Advancing Toward a Mature Partnership" (known as the Armitage-Nye Report), which was intended as a blueprint for the next administration's policy toward Japan. The report reflected expectations of US policymakers for Japan. Citing the US-UK alliance as the future vision for the US-Japan alliance, the report argued that a "real" US-Japan defense partnership would lower the risk of instability in the Asia-Pacific region. The report praised the 1997 *Guidelines for US-Japan Defense Cooperation* as the basis for bilateral defense planning, but also argued that the document should be regarded as the starting point from which Japan would expand its role in the US-Japan alliance. The authors of the report pronounced expectations for Japan in several specific areas to:[480]

- Enact crisis management legislation;
- Fully participate in UN PKO activities, with Japan lifting its self-imposed restriction; and,

- Broaden the scope of the cooperation with the United States on missile defense.

Most importantly, the report addressed the issue of Japan's inability to exercise the right of collective self-defense, bluntly arguing that it is "a constraint on alliance cooperation."[481] Although suggesting that Japan decide how it should address the issue, the report, by unambiguously referring to the issue, alerted that the decision-makers in Japan should be aware of the constraining effect that the ban on the right of collective self-defense poses on the alliance cooperation with the United States. It was also clear from this report that US senior policymakers focus on the US-Japan alliance strongly hoped that the United States would be able to have a more robust defense cooperation with Japan.

In the first decade after the end of the Cold War, US alliance managers' expectations of Japan went beyond those held in the Cold War-era. Japan was not only expected to continue to build up its own capability and provide host nation support for US forces in Japan, but was also expected to participate in the military operations outside Japan. When US defense planners looked to Japan for the support for US military operations, however, it found Japan reluctant and, constrained by the ban on the right of collective self-defense and other postwar national security policy principles, unable to engage much. Although some positive steps were taken on overall modernization of the mechanism of the US-Japan alliance (e.g., redefinition of the alliance under the *US-Japan Alliance:* revision of the Guidelines for Japan-US Defense Cooperation), US alliance managers were left with the sense that the most critical part of its expectations of Tokyo—an alliance partner with less self-imposed restriction on its actions—was not quite realized.

POST-9/11: HEIGHTENING EXPECTATIONS OF JAPAN

Under Prime Minister Junichiro Koizumi, Japan took a number of national security policy decisions which raised the US government's, particularly alliance managers, expectations to an all-time high.

The US government's first surprise came in the aftermath of the 9-11 terrorist attacks in 2001. Koizumi responded extremely quickly after learning about the attacks. Having issued a statement strongly condemning the terrorists' action on 12 September,[482] he quickly convened the Security Council (*Anpo Kaigi*)—the cabinet-level meeting to make decisions on important national security issues—on the same day and issued six principles of the Japanese government's response, including cooperation with the United States and other countries while enhancing the patrolling and security of US facilities in Japan.[483] Most surprising was his next move. Within one week, Koizumi convened a press conference where he announced the six-point plan to support the United States in its fight against terrorism. The plan included:[484]

- Taking necessary measures to enable JSDF dispatch for the purpose of supporting US and other countries' armed forces in the areas of medical services, transport, and other rear-area support;

- Taking steps to strengthen the security of US military and other facilities in Japan;

- Dispatching JMSDF vessels for intelligence-gathering;

- Strengthening the information exchange to strengthen border controls;

- Providing emergency aid to Pakistan and India, and other countries that may be affected by this incident; and,

- Exploring JSDF dispatch for humanitarian assistance including assistance for refugees.

US government officials, particularly those who were involved in US policy toward Japan, were pleasantly surprised with Koizumi's response. First, the timing of his proposal was very swift. Furthermore, the plan included the dispatch of the JSDF, which was completely unprecedented. Also to the surprise of the United States, the Koizumi cabinet succeeded in getting the Anti-Terrorism Special Measures Law passed by the end of October 2001, ordering the first group of JMSDF vessels to the Indian Ocean in early November.

When the United States, in the face of a great deal of reluctance by the international community, decided to wage war against Iraq, Koizumi's reaction was promptly noted among senior US government officials. Within a few hours of being informed of the beginning of the combat operation in Iraq, Koizumi convened a press conference in which he pronounced unambiguous support for the United States.[485] By December 2003, he had enacted the Iraq Reconstruction Assistance Special Measures Law to authorize JSDF dispatch to Iraq to engage in reconstruction activities in Iraq.[486] In the end of December 2003, the JSDF advance team received a deployment order and departed for the Middle East.

For those in the US government who were in charge of US-Japan security relations, these decisions by Koizumi were unprecedented both for their swiftness (relatively speaking) and their scope. It was only a little over ten years before that Japan under Prime Minister Toshiki Kaifu, after several months of confusion without no clear indication of what type of support Japan might be willing to provide, failed to enact a law that would have authorized JSDF dispatch to engage in a rear-area transport mission in support of Operation Dessert Storm. Koizumi not only developed with the support package that included JSDF dispatch from the start, but also delivered on his commitment by enacting the authorizing legislation in short order. The United States also noted that the argument Koizumi made to defend his decision in front of the Diet and to the press appeared different than his predecessors. He frequently used the terms such as "proactive" (*shutaiteki/ sekkyokuteki*), "Japan's national interest" (*nihon no kokueki)*, and "responsible member of the international community" (*kokusai shakai no sekinin aru ichiin*), rather than "international contribution" (*kokusai kouken*), the term his predecessors preferred when discussing Japan's expanded role in international security affairs. To US policymakers who remember Japan's "too little, too late" response at the time of the 1990-91 Gulf War, Koizumi's achievements suggested that Japan might finally be more willing to expand its role in the global security arena.

In addition to Japan's activities in the Middle East, three additional developments came about inside Japan that boosted the optimism of US policymakers with regard to Japan becoming an alliance partner more willing to expand its role both within the alliance and in the world. In December 2003, just as Koizumi announced the dispatch of JSDF to Iraq, the Japanese government also announced that it would introduce a ballistic missile defense (BMD) system and would begin JSDF reorganization to facilitate its introduction.[487] Even having engaged in joint technological study through the TMD-WG from the early 1990s, Japan had long hesitated to decide on the introduction of the system. Even though the system is considered "defensive" (*bougyo-teki*) and thus its introduction would not violate Article Nine of the Constitution, the potential integration of Japanese and US systems had been controversial as it raised the questions of Japan exercising the right of collective self-defense. Therefore, the decision to introduce the BMD was seen as a sign that Japan might be willing to revise its standing interpretation of the right of collective self-defense.

Further, in October 2004, the Council on Security and Defense Capability—the prime minister's advisory council—issued its report. More commonly known as the Araki Report, the Council called Japan to search for an integrative security strategy that would flexibly use three approaches (Japan's own efforts, cooperation with allies and friends, and engagement in international efforts to maintain global peace and security) to pursue Japan's national security interests.

The report also pronounced that Japan would need a multi-functional and flexible defense capability to support such a security policy approach. Citing the qualitative changes in global security threats, the report further recommended that Japan revisit some of the self-imposed constraints on the conduct of its national security policy, including the three principles of arms exports. It further proposed that, while conducted cautiously, the discussion of the constitutional question—the issue of the right of collective self-defense, in particular—must begin.[488] It was the first time that an advisory council appointed by the prime minister discussed openly the need to address the constitutional issues, which had long been untouchable in Japan.

Finally, in December 2004, the Japanese government approved the revised National Defense Program Guideline (NDPG) and the related Mid-Term Defense Program (MTDP). Incorporating many of the elements in the aforementioned report by the Council on Security and Defense Capabilities, the 2004 NDPG essentially pronounced a departure from the Basic Defense Capability Concept (*Kiban-teki Bouei-ryoku Kousou*) as the organizing concept for the build-up of its defense capabilities. Rather, under the concept of multi-functional and flexible defense capability, the NDPG stressed the importance of technology and qualitative enhancements, including integration of the three JSDF services and enhancement of its intelligence capability. Further, for the first time, the NPDG framed JSDF's international activities as its core mission (*hontai gyomu*).[489]

Parallel to the internal developments in Japan were the bilateral efforts to update the US-Japan alliance to reflect the reality of the post-9/11 global security environment. As part of the Global Posture Review (GPR), the United States embarked on the Defense Policy Review Initiative (DPRI) in December 2002. Through the DPRI, Washington hoped to have a comprehensive discussion about how the two countries could develop a deeper defense cooperative relationship that extended beyond the Asia-Pacific region. Washington hoped to discuss issues including US and Japanese security strategies, how US military transformation would impact US military presence in the region including Japan, and how the US and Japan should coordinate their respective force transformation efforts. Eventually, the DPRI produced a set of three documents by the time it concluded in May 2006.

In *Joint Statement: US-Japan Security Consultative Committee*, released on 19 February 2005, the two countries reconfirmed common strategic objectives for the US-Japan alliance that included a wide range of regional (e.g., peaceful resolution of North Korea's nuclear problem, stability of the Taiwan Strait, cooperative relationship with China), as well as functional (proliferation of weapons of mass destruction, terrorism, energy, UN Security Council reform) issues.[490] In October 2005, the two sides issued the Security Consultative Committee (SCC) document *US-Japan Alliance: Transformation and Realignment for the Future*, outlining the basic principles for US force realignment in Japan as well as identifying the activity areas in which US forces and the JSDF should intensify cooperation.[491] Finally, in May 2006, the two sides released the third SCC document *United States-Japan Roadmap for Realignment Implementation*, detailing how the US forces in Japan will be realigned over the next eight years and defining the cost-sharing arrangement for the realignment.[492]

By 2005, there was a general recognition that the US-Japan alliance was at its apogee. General consensus existed that a personal relationship contributed a great deal to it. Almost all US policymakers referred to a close personal relationship forged between President Bush and Prime Minister Koizumi—as one former US government official noted on many occasions, when Bush considered foreign policy options, he almost always asked his staff, "what does Koizumi think?"[493] US Ambassador to Japan Howard Baker also stated: "Many say that the rapport they have established equals or exceeds that of the famed affection and goodwill that existed between former Prime Minister Nakasone and President Ronald Reagan. President Bush and everyone in this administration involved with Japan respect your Prime Minister's energy, decisiveness, and imagination. His rise and the leadership he has shown have brought Japan heightened respect and admiration from the world community."[494] Such a positive assessment of the US-Japan alliance and Japan's development as an important ally of the United States did not stop at senior Asia policy experts in the United States. For example, Lincoln P. Bloomfield, Jr, former Assistant Secretary of State for Political-Military Affairs, recognized Japan's decisions under Koizumi in a speech, saying: "the U.S. cannot help but recognize and acknowledge with appreciation that Japan has adapted its own role in the international arena to carry a larger share of the burden in bending international trends toward a stable and prosperous environment conducive to democracy and economic freedom.... Japan's leaders have grasped the new strategic reality that the path to its own economic security goes through political and security channels as well."[495]

Aside from the close personal relationship between the two leaders, many Asia policy experts in Washington also began to openly ponder whether a major transformation in Japan's national security was in the offing. In particular, the expectation that Japan might revisit the issue of the right of collective self-defense heightened. For instance, while cautioning against a revolutionary change, former Principal Deputy Secretary of State for East Asia and Pacific

Affairs Rust M. Deming thought that "Japan is turning a historic corner toward amending Article IX of the Constitution."[496] While standing by the judgment in the 2000 Armitage-Nye Report that Japan's inability to exercise the right of collective self-defense served to constrain the US-Japan alliance, James Przystup, one of the contributing members of the 2000 Armitage-Nye Report, still noted, "Issues related to constitutional reform is now front page news. Politically… Japan appears to be restructuring… with security issues becoming the matters of substantive debate rather than dogmatic polemics."[497] While many recognized the difficulty that Japanese leaders were likely to face in dealing with constitutional revision, there was a certain degree of optimism that Japan was moving to revise Article Nine—it was just a matter of time. The February 2007 CSIS Report *US-Japan Alliance: Getting Asia Right* (more commonly known as the second Armitage-Nye Report) was illustrative of the optimism prevailing in Washington. Noting the developments between 2001-2007, the report discussed the maturity of the US-Japan alliance and described the debate on the Constitution, as well as the discussion on the General Law, as "encouraging."[498]

The proponents of a stronger US-Japan alliance, particularly those who support Japan playing a greater role within it, heightened their expectation of Japan when Shinzo Abe succeeded Prime Minister Koizumi in September 2006. Abe, known for his conservative views that resembled those of his grandfather, former Prime Minister Nobusuke Kishi, had openly talked about the need for Japan to revise its constitution before he assumed the position of prime minister. In his first press conference, Abe spoke about the necessity for Japan to study whether there may be cases in which Japan should be able to exercise the right of collective self-defense.[499] In December 2006, he talked about his strong desire to accomplish constitutional revision "while I am in the office."[500] In May 2007, the Diet passed so-called National Referendum Law laying the groundwork for putting the constitutional revision to the vote. Abe also convened a study group to examine the cases in which Japan could be allowed to exercise the right of collective self-defense. His strong interest in the study group's deliberation was manifested in the fact that, although the group met frequently (they met five times in the three and a half months before Abe resigned), Abe always attended the session. For the first time in its postwar history, Japan had a prime minister who seemed willing to invest his political capital in constitutional revision. It was only natural that the optimism toward constitutional revision prevailed in Washington.

Anticipating that Japan would address the constitutional restraint sooner rather than later, senior US experts on the US-Japan alliance, many of whom left the government by 2007, envisioned an ambitious agenda for Japan, encouraging it to:

- Adopt stronger national security institutions that would allow Japan to make decisions with speed, agility and flexibility while protecting appropriate information;

- Address the issue of the right of collective self-defense and other legal obstacles in a way to enable Japan to become an alliance partner with greater flexibility in its actions; and

- Alleviate the fiscal constraints on the defense budget.

As the Second Armitage-Nye Report put it: "(T)he cooperative efforts that marked Japan's support for the United States in Afghanistan, its contribution to postwar reconstruction in Iraq, and its early participation in the Proliferation Security Initiative have set a firm foundation for closer future cooperation... to those to whom much has been given, much will be expected."[501]

US EXPECTATION OF JAPAN: IS THERE A GAP?

During the Cold War, US policymakers have held three core expectations for Japan. They were:

- Japan develops the military capability enough to defend itself from external threat;

- Japan remains a strong political and economic partner of the United States; and

- Japan hosts the forward-deployed US forces that can be deployed not only to support the defense of Japan but also to support US military operations in the Asia-Pacific region.

The end of the Cold War brought an expansion to US expectation of Japan. No longer was it sufficient for Japan to focus on its own defense capability, provide host-nation support to maintain US forces in Japan, and support US foreign policy to meet US policymakers' expectations of Japan. In the post-Cold War era, the United States increasingly focused on how much Japan can support US military operations not only in East Asia, but also in other areas. While aware of constitutional constraints that the Japanese government had to be mindful when it makes decisions to deploy the JSDF abroad, US government officials, particularly those in the Department of Defense, strongly encouraged their Japanese counterparts to invest efforts in expanding the scope of permissible JSDF operations abroad. US alliance managers also strongly hoped that Japanese leadership self-initiates efforts to take steps (political and legal) to relax the existing constraints.

It was in the area of relaxing the existing constraints on the JSDF that the US policymakers raised their expectation after the 9/11. With all the developments that occurred since 2001 first under Koizumi and then Abe, it seemed as though the United States might finally see Japan meeting its expectation to evolve into a full alliance partner. They were particularly hopeful that the debate over the right of collective self-defense would encourage Japan—political leaders, media, government officials, and the public—to engage in a more extensive discussion on what the Japanese national security policy goal in the post-9/11 world should be, how the US-Japan alliance will help Japan in achieving such goals、 and how Japan should respond to the post-9/11 security environment.[502]

However, Abe unexpectedly resigned in September 2007 following the Liberal Democratic Party (LDP)'s historic defeat in the July 2007 election for the House of Councillors, and the optimism rapidly began to fade. Yasuo Fukuda, who succeeded Abe, struggled to pass his legislative agenda through the Diet: the Democratic Party of Japan (DPJ), together with other opposition parties, now has a majority in the House of Councillors and stands ready to vote down any government bill. Ichiro Ozawa, the DPJ leader, seeing an opportunity to bring down the LDP-led coalition government, is determined to politicize any issue to the benefit of his party in the next election for the House of Representatives. National security is no exception. In fact, failing to renew the Anti-Terror Special Measures Law before its expiration to sustain Japan's participation in OEF were early legislative victories in Ozawa's book.

Further, Fukuda, either because of his preoccupation with domestic issues or because of his disagreement with Koizumi and Abe on some of the fundamental issues in Japan's national security policy, did not follow-up on most of the national security policy-related initiatives launched by Abe. He was quick to abandon the bill that would have established a Japanese-style National Security Council.[503] And he was not at all interested in the study group on the right of collective defense that Abe had convened to explore scenarios in which Japan may be allowed to exercise the right of collective self-defense. Although Fukuda managed to enact the Replenishment Support Special Measures Law in January 2008, which authorized the resumption of the JSDF refueling mission in the Indian Ocean, his government decided to withdraw the Japan Air Self-Defense operation in Kuwait in support of the coalition operation in Iraq at the end of 2008.[504] While the Ministry of Defense had examined the possibility of dispatching an additional JSDF contingent to support the coalition operation in Afghanistan, Prime Minister Fukuda decided against pursuing it after all.[505]

In the prevailing political environment, critical changes in Japan's national security infrastructure that are necessary for the Japanese government to enhance its national security policymaking capacity are likely to remain unaddressed. One exception will be the reform efforts at the Ministry of Defense. As Chapter Two briefly mentioned, *Boueisho Kaikaku Kaigi* (the MOD Reform Council) was convened by the Chief Cabinet Secretary in December 2007 following a series of scandals, topped with the procurement scandal that involved former vice minister Takemasa Moriya. After meeting roughly once a month, the MOD Reform Council submitted the final report to Prime Minister Fukuda on 16 July 2008. The report proposed a considerable reorganization of the MOD and the JSDF, essentially streamlining the line of communication to improve transparency and increase accountability.[506] Numerous scandals and incidents—from intelligence leaks and acquisition scandal to maritime accidents—that involved the MOD personnel raised many questions about the MOD's ability to function responsibly as the institution primarily responsible for national defense.[507] A great deal of political and public pressure that continues to exist will continue to drive MOD reform.[xlv]

The report by the MOD Reform Council also includes a series of recommendations of reform and reorganization outside the MOD, particularly in the Cabinet Secretariat. For instance, it strongly argues that the enhancement of the policy support system for the prime minister is an essential factor in revitalizing the civilian control of the JSDF.[508] Specific recommendations for enhancing Japanese government's strategy-planning capability included:

- Enhance the existing Security Council (*Anpo Kaigi*) to serve as an organization where national security strategy is developed;
- Utilize the existing Security Council to integrate development of national security strategy and defense planning;
- Utilize the existing informal policy coordination framework among the chief cabinet secretary, foreign minister and defense minister in support of the deliberation at the Security Council; and

[xlv] Most recently, the MOD and the JSDF have become the subject of renewed intense criticism after it was revealed that a JMSDF sailor who was undergoing the training for JMSDF's special security forces died during the training under questionable circumstances.

- Institutionalize a support for the prime minister in policymaking by appointing a group of security policy experts as advisors that directly report to the prime minister.[509]

However, given the reluctance to tackle reform of national security institutions among Japanese political leaders, it is unlikely that these recommendations will be fully implemented in the near future.

Japan's intelligence community will remain decentralized. The Director of Cabinet Intelligence has no statutory authority to manage the community and therefore remains one among many peers. Few efforts have been made in standardizing administrative procedures, such as the classification of information, clearance of new employees, and their training. Although the strengthening of intelligence capability was one of few policy initiatives that Fukuda chose to inherit from Abe, his decision of doing so was primarily driven by the concerns for information safety emanating from the intelligence leak incidents in the MOD, not by his interest in strengthening analytical capability of Japan's intelligence community.

The uniform institutions face a different set of problems. Similar to their civilian counterparts, they have challenges with coordination and cooperation among themselves. Rivalries and a strong sense of jurisdiction often prevent efficient cooperation among these agencies. In addition, the uniformed institutions also face the challenge of building up the physical capabilities that can support the national security policy goals set by the civilian leaders. So far, the JSDF, Japan Coast Guard, and the police force all face the task of transforming their organization and equipment to meet the new security challenges of the post Cold War world. But in many cases (this is particularly so in case of the JSDF), the uniform institutions have to make their acquisition and posturing decisions based on the speculation of what their civilian leaders may decide. This often results in conservative assessments, inhibiting decisive steps toward much needed transformation, constraining their ability to pursue more dynamic operational cooperation with their US counterparts.

Legal challenges are equally formidable. Particularly in an environment in which Japan's political leadership will remain unstable for some time to come, decisive action on issues that require legislative action for their resolution are not to be addressed. Simply put, now that Abe disappeared from the front stage of Japanese politics for a while, Tokyo will not see a political leader that is popular or politically strong enough while also being committed to investing his/her political capital in helping Japan overcome the existing constitutional and other legal obstacles. If neither Koizumi nor Abe—both of which had public popularity behind them to overcome the political opposition and push their agenda—could deliver on constitutional revision, the prospect for an alternative political leader emerging that can deliver is not very good. Whether Taro Aso can follow the footsteps of Koizumi and Abe remains highly uncertain. Without Japan resolving the existing legal challenges, there is very little room for progress that the United States and Japan can make in the area of security cooperation.

It is clear that Japan's national security policy infrastructure does not have the capacity to fulfill US alliance manager's expectations for a more robust JSDF engagement overseas. Japan's national security institutions, while on the path of gradual centralization, remain decentralized with insufficient staff support for the prime minister. Lacking a support system for the prime minister independent of the bureaucracy, the prime minister's ability to exercise leadership in policy- and decision-making will continue to depend on his/her personal management style, popularity and/or the political base in his/her political party. While interagency relations among the civilian institutions are improving, there are still no procedures to enforce the coordination. Each institution continues to compete for greater influence in Japan's national security policymaking, and for its own institutional access to the prime minister and other senior political leaders. Japanese intelligence community remains decentralized, inhibiting the Japanese government from quickly developing policy responses to security challenges that will be necessary for Japan to proactively engage in dialogues with the United States and other countries. Finally, there is little prospect that Japanese leaders will begin tackling the legal challenges that has fundamentally constrained the scope of Japan's national security policy to present. Under such circumstances, Japan will not be able respond to US calls for a more robust engagement in international security affairs, particularly by committing the JSDF to wider types of missions overseas.

—CONCLUSION—

The outlook for Japan's national security policy in the near-term is not encouraging. Internally, the debate toward constitutional revision completely stopped with Abe's departure. It is also unlikely that the bill for the General Law, which would provide an overarching legal framework for all types of JSDF overseas deployment, will be introduced to the Diet in the near future. Finally, the bill to establish the National Security Council as the staff support system for the prime minister is unlikely to be reintroduced to the Diet at least until after Japanese politics overcomes the current period of volatility and uncertainty.

Externally, Japan's profile in international security has steadily declined. Instead of continuing on the path of playing a greater security role, Japan has been retracting. With the withdrawal of the Air Self-Defense Force (JASDF) from the Middle East looking certain by January 2009, the refueling mission in the Indian Ocean will be the only support Japan is providing to the coalition operations in the Middle East, either for Afghanistan or Iraq. Recent press accounts suggest that the Japanese government considered several options for dispatching additional JSDF contingents to engage in rear-area support and/or surveillance in support of NATO force's operation in Afghanistan but ultimately abandoned the idea. The Japanese government's decisions not to send the JSDF to Afghanistan due to concerns about the security situation on the ground hints at the possibility that Japan may reverse its attitude toward JSDF's international operation and go back to the risk-averse posture of the 1990s. The recent decision by the Japanese government to dispatch several JSDF officers to support the UN peacekeeping operation mission in Sudan at the headquarters instead of deploying JSDF troops on the ground also suggest that Japan is not willing to send JSDF personnel to the international mission which may present a higher risk of casualties.

Even the future of the refueling mission in the Indian Ocean looks unclear—with the special measures law that authorizes the operation due to expire in January 2009, the Japanese government yet again faced an uphill battle in getting the Diet's approval for renewal. It looks almost certain that the renewal proposal will be rejected by the House of Councillors, where the opposition party now has a majority. Similar to January 2008 when the Diet first approved the Replenishment Support Special Measures Law, the current Japanese government resorted to "super majority rule"—the House of Representatives can override the disapproval of the House of Councillors if it can re-approve the bill with two-thirds majority—to renew the special measures law. Still, it remains unclear whether the refueling operation can be extended again beyond 2010.

The prospects for the US-Japan alliance are not promising, either. The implementation of the Defense Policy Review Initiative (DPRI) has been slow. The discussion on the roles, missions and capabilities between the two militaries has not progressed significantly. The most disappointing development (although not surprising) has been the delay yet again to implement the plan to relocate the Marines in Okinawa to Guam. In particular, Japan's domestic process to build the Futenma Relocation Facility (FRF) has been delayed by familiar factors—the resistance from Okinawa prefecture and the delay in the work plan established by the Japanese government. In the absence of high-level attention from Japanese leadership, DPRI implementation has been left with MOD bureaucrats, currently distracted by the upcoming substantial reorganization. Having lost the momentum to achieve transformation and realignment goals, the US-Japan alliance appears to have lost focus, entering into the second period of "drift."

Why is this happening? Simply put, Japanese leaders are now paying the price for not investing efforts in building a national consensus that Japan needs to be more actively engaged internationally, and the JSDF should be utilized more robustly to that end. As popular as Koizumi and Abe were, both leaders did not spend enough time in articulating why they thought it was important for them to expand the scope of JSDF activities abroad. And yet, they had clearly taken Japan too far into the direction of robust overseas engagement beyond the comfort level of the Japanese public. It is no accident that the latest public opinion poll on constitutional revision taken by *the Yomiuri Shimbun* in March 2008 indicated that the Japanese public is still very divided on whether or not to change the Constitution: in the poll, 42.5 percent of the respondents supported constitution revision while 43.1 percent opposed it.[510] The same *Yomiuri* poll indicates that the public is even more divided over what to do with Article Nine of the Constitution: thirty-six percent of the respondents supported continuing the current practice of interpreting the Article on a case-by-case basis, with thirty-one percent advocating the revision and twenty-seven percent supporting a strict application of the letters of Article Nine.[511]

How long will the current situation in Japan continue? Will Japan come back to focus on its national security policy issues? With the LDP's historic defeat in the House of Councillors election in July 2007, as long as the LDP-led government stays in power, the "twisted Diet *(nejire kokkai*)" will continue at least for the next three years. This will force the Japanese government and the ruling LDP-Komeito coalition to focus on policy issues that have direct appeal to the voters in the short-term. Unless Japan falls victim of a large-scale attack (through either conventional or non-conventional means), national security issues do not help gain votes. Further, as discussed in Chapter Seven, the leadership style of Junichiro Koizumi is an anomaly in the Japanese political culture. Shinzo Abe, although very popular, tried to follow Koizumi's leadership style and ultimately failed. Looking at the political landscape in Japan, it is very unlikely that Japan will see another dynamic leader like Koizumi soon. Therefore, it is very probable that Japan, at least for the next few years, remains complacent in the status quo, shrinking its commitments in the area of international security.

Why did the United States not anticipate these developments in Japan? In hindsight, the United States misread the developments in Japan after 2001 by overly focusing on Koizumi, regarding his actions and decisions as representative of the consensus in Japan. As discussed in Chapter Six, Koizumi so far has proven to be an anomalous political figure in recent political history in Japan. Several domestic political factors—demise of the factional politics in the ruling Liberal Democratic Party, the failure of the Democratic Party of Japan (DPJ) in capturing voter's imagination and confidence, Koizumi's unusual skills in translating his views on policy into phrases that resonated with ordinary voters—allowed him to become one of the longest-serving Japanese prime ministers in Japan's postwar history, but his views on foreign policies are not among the major reasons. In other words, the Japanese people did not support him because of his advocacy for a more proactive Japan in the international security affairs. Although the prime minister has more support for his decision making residing in the Cabinet Secretariat compared to a decade ago, the Japanese decision-making system by and large still works in a bottom-up, consensus-based manner. Overcoming this system requires an unusual political figure, which Koizumi was. In the absence of such a personality, the system will go back to its default.

Further, the US government (particularly the alliance managers) may have misread Koizumi's decision to dispatch the JSDF to the Indian Ocean and Iraq as Japan being on its way to reach a consensus on expanding the scope of JSDF's overseas engagements. It is true that the JSDF has been more active in international operations. However, it is noteworthy that their activism has been demonstrated in humanitarian and disaster relief, the area that Japan had always felt comfortable seeing the JSDF engaged in. Outside that, Japan has remained as reluctant to commit the JSDF as they were in the 1990s. In 2006, a MOD official who served as a civilian advisor to the commander of the JSDF operating in Iraq, describing the attitude of Japanese people, said "Japanese people do not want to see the JSDF pointing guns at the people of other countries in foreign lands. The Japanese public supported JSDF activities in Iraq because they were essentially in Iraq to repair roads, hospitals and schools."[512] His statement is supported by the poll results as well. In the February 2006 public opinion poll on the JSDF and defense issues conducted by the Cabinet Affairs Office of the Japanese government, over seventy-five percent of the respondents identified the JSDF with disaster and humanitarian relief activities. When asked what kind of activities the JSDF should put greater efforts in, only approximately thirty-six percent identified international peace-keeping activities. Further, the poll results showed that approximately fifty percent thought the JSDF's engagement in international activities should be sustained at the current level.[513] These results portray an image of Japan that it is willing to see the JSDF engaged in international activities primarily in the context of humanitarian and disaster relief missions, and not much else. This is hardly a path that Washington hoped Japan was heading down.

Finally, the United States might have underestimated the impact of questions over US security policy decisions to the attitude among the Japanese public toward the United States. Iraq and North Korea loom large as the reasons behind declining confidence in the United States among Japanese public. The US decision to invade Iraq without seeking an explicit UN authorization was met with strong disapproval among the Japanese public. The public opinion poll conducted by *Nihon Hoso Kyokai* (NHK, Japan Broadcasting Corporation) in the eve of the US military attack against Iraq in March 2003 indicates that 80 percent of the respondents disapproved of US military action in absence of a clear UN mandate.[514] Even the NHK opinion poll conducted after the collapse of the Saddam Hussein regime suggest that the Japanese public remains unsure whether or not to support US military action in Iraq: A May 2003 poll indicates that 54 percent of the respondents still do not approve of US military action against Iraq.[515] Further, divergence of policy toward North Korea between Tokyo and Washington contributed to the worsening image of the United States among Japanese. When US State Department first decided to de-list North Korea from the list of state sponsor of terrorism in the summer of 2008, a *Yomiuri Shimbun* poll revealed that approximately 80 percent of the respondents were not convinced by the US decision.[516] The recent US final decision to de-list North Korea from the list of state sponsors of terrorism is already met by skepticism about its effect on the Six Party talks, raising questions about US commitment to the resolution of the abduction issues.[517]

Combined, these factors have contributed to the declining confidence in the United States among the Japanese. The public opinion polls jointly conducted by *Yomiuri Shimbun* and Gallup indicates that the number of Japanese who positively evaluate the US-Japan relations have been steadily declining since 2000.[518] What is noticeable is the increasing number of Japanese who think the United States "untrustworthy:" the November 2007 poll indicates that the majority of the respondents (54 percent) consider that the United States is not to be trusted—the trend which has continued since 2002.[519] Under such circumstances, DPJ leader Ichiro Ozawa's proposition that Japan should base its policy decisions on global security issues on the authorization granted by the United Nations and other international institutions, for instance, resonates among the Japanese public.[520]

What does it mean for the US government, particularly those who have invested in developing the US alliance with Japan? First and foremost, adjustment of expectations is called for. In a sense, the United States became too accustomed with a Japan being led by Koizumi. US policymakers should recognize that the Koizumi era has so far proven to be an anomaly, not the norm. They will then need to maintain a pragmatic attitude in dealing with Japan, assuming that Japan will re-enter a period of short-term governments. Washington should expect the Japanese political situation to resemble the early 1990s, when the LDP fell from power and was replaced by a series of weak coalition governments, only to come back into power with the very unlikely bedfellow—the Social Democrats.

Secondly, US policymakers should focus more on "multinationalizing" its bilateral alliances and security partnerships in Asia. In a sense, Washington had already begun this effort in its focus on "mini-laterals" that includes both the United States and Japan. The expansion of US-Japan-Australia and US-Japan-India trilateral dialogues appear promising in this regard. These arrangements have helped encourage Japan to consider the potentials for security cooperation with other US allies, exemplified by Tokyo's deepening security relationship with these two countries in the last several years.[521] In the future, they will also likely prove to be a useful venue in which Japan, in an amicable atmosphere, can still be reminded that it is not *the* only ally for the United States in the Asia-Pacific region, and that it cannot expect the US national security establishment to invest its time in its relationship with Tokyo if Tokyo has nothing to offer. The mini-laterals are also useful in reiterating US interest and commitment to the region.

Finally, US policymakers should consider beginning the discussion of policy options in regards to its alliance with Japan, based on alternative visions for Japan's future. For instance, those who develop US Asia strategy need to discuss how the United States should approach the US-Japan alliance if Japan is not able to overcome the institutional, legal and political challenges that need to be overcome to engage more actively with the United States and the rest of the world in security affairs for the foreseeable future. Currently, most US policymakers who are involved in the alliance management continue to operate on the assumption that Japan will eventually overcome these hurdles and will be able to engage more robustly in military activities both in the context of the US-Japan alliance and beyond. If Japan continues to contract in international engagement, it requires US policymakers to consider alternative approach toward security cooperation with Japan.

Among the three options, the last—consideration of the alternative policy options—may be the most daunting for US alliance managers, because a strong US-Japan alliance has been one of the pillars for US security policy in Asia for the last six decades. In the last several years, in particular, US alliance managers have shaped its approach to Asia with the assumption that Japan would be a strong US ally willing to more robustly engage the JSDF in overseas missions in support of military operations around the world. That this premise may be untenable require a considerably different thinking in developing US policy toward Asia. Clearly, that is not a good option for the United States. However, US policymakers should at least consider the possibility that the current stagnation in Japan on security policy may continue for some time, with little prospect of its national security policy infrastructure being further strengthened. At some point, US alliance managers may have to determine whether Japan after all is an ally that is neither capable nor willing to share risk in military operations outside Japan.

The combination of adjusting the expectation and developing policy alternatives may be the most pragmatic course for the United States. Adjusting US expectation of Japan's willingness to use the JSDF deployment to overseas missions as its primary way of engaging in international security affairs will help ease the tension between Tokyo and Washington, particularly when Japan cannot respond to the US call to consider JSDF deployment to international missions positively. Developing alternative policies that do not focus so much on the activities that do not bring up the question of the right of collective self-defense will also help in maintaining the positive tone of the overall bilateral relationship. For instance, encouraging Japan to take a leadership role in orchestrating international efforts to develop capacity for humanitarian and disaster relief will likely be more successful because there is a strong domestic (public and political) support for JSDF to engage in such activities abroad. Identifying non-traditional security challenges (e.g., energy security, food security, global climate change) as the high-priority areas of cooperation between Japan and the United States will also be helpful in maintaining a forward-looking agenda between the two allies. While these approaches do not solve the existing challenges in the alliance (e.g. US base realignment), it nonetheless enables US alliance managers to articulate to their leadership why the US-Japan alliance continues to matter.

This volume attempts to capture the institutional dynamics within Japan's national security policy infrastructure and the political atmosphere that surrounds it. It is my hope that this will provide a window through which US policymakers understand the internal workings of Japan's national policy security infrastructure, which they then can utilize the understanding they gain in developing their policy toward Japan. I hope that this volume provides US policymakers a tool to do so.

ABOUT THE AUTHOR

Yuki Tatsumi was appointed Senior Associate of the East Asia Program at the Henry L. Stimson Center in September 2008. Prior to her appointment to be Senior Associate, she served as Stimson's Research Fellow, the position she took in July 2004.

Tatsumi's research career in Northeast Asian security began in 2000 when she joined the Stimson Center as a research associate. In August 2001, she joined the International Security Program of the Center for Strategic and International Studies (CSIS) where she focused on Northeast Asian security issues as a research associate. Since her departure from CSIS, she continues to serves as CSIS's Adjunct Fellow. Tatsumi also served at the Embassy of Japan in Washington, D.C., from 1996 to 1999 as special assistant for political affairs. During her assignment, she monitored key developments in US policy toward Asia.

Her analyses on Japanese security policy, Japanese defense policy, US-Japan alliance and Japanese domestic politics frequently appear in PacNet Newsletter, CSIS Japan Watch, Japan Digest, Japan Times, and the International Herald Tribune. She has also contributed articles to Japanese journals, including Ronza and Sekai Shuho. She also appears frequently in CNN International, Voice of America, BBC International, and CNBC-Asia. In addition, she has participated in the discussions on the US-Japan alliance, Japanese security policy and Northeast Asian security issues as a panelist, as well as given a lectures at various institutions including the Center for Strategic and International Studies, Foreign Service Institute, Japan Society, National War College, and the Paul H. Nitze School of Advanced International Studies. She has also testified before the House Committee on International Relations of US Congress in September 2006.

Tatsumi holds a B.A. in liberal arts from the International Christian University in Tokyo, Japan, and an M.A. in international economics and Asian Studies from the Paul H. Nitze School of Advanced International Studies (SAIS) at Johns Hopkins University in Washington, D.C

ENDNOTES

[1] *Koizumi Naikaku Souri Daijin Kisha Kaiken* (Press Conference by Prime Minister Koizumi) 27 April, 2001, http://www.kantei.go.jp/jp/koizumispeech/2001/0427kisyakaiken.html (accessed 13 February 2008).

[2] Security Consultative Committee, *Joint Statement* 19 February 2005. http://www.mofa.go.jp/region/n-america/us/security/scc/joint0502.html (accessed 15 February 2008).

[3] Tatsumi, Yuki, "U.S.–Japan Security Consultative Committee: an assessment." *PacNet Newsletter* No.10. 10 March 2005.

[4] The White House, "The Joint Statement: The Japan–US Alliance of the New Century," 29 June 2006 http://www.whitehouse.gov/news/releases/2006/06/20060629-2.html (accessed 14 January 2008).

[5] Speech by Prime Minister Shinzo Abe at the North Atlantic Council, "Japan and NATO: Toward Further Collaboration" 12 January 2007, http://www.mofa.go.jp/region/europe/pmv0701/nato.html (accessed 15 February 2008).

[6] Sunohara, Tsuyoshi, *Doumei Henbou: Nichi-bei Ittai-ka no Hikari to Kage (Alliance Transformed: Light and Shadow of US–Japan Integration)* (Nihon Keizai Shimbun-sha, 2007).

[7] Interview with a senior MOFA official, Tokyo, Japan: 13 December 2006.

[8] Interview with a Cabinet Secretarial official, Tokyo, Japan: 15 December 2005.

[9] Mochizuki, Mike M. and Yuki Tatsumi. "Conclusion" in Tatsumi, Yuki and Andrew L. Oros, eds. *Japan's New Defense Establishment: Institutions, Capabilities and Implications.* (Washington: The Henry L. Stimson Center, 2007). 119.

[10] *Ibid.,* 122-123.

[11] Tanaka, Akihiko, *Anzen Hosho* (Security) (Tokyo: Yomiuri Shimbun-sha, 1997): 122–25, 138.

[12] *Heisei 17-nendo ikou ni kakawaru bouei keikaku no taikou* (National Defense Program Outline FY 2005), http://www.mod.go.jp/j/defense/policy/17taikou/taikou.htm (accessed 10 December 2007).

[13] Ministry of Defense Japan, *Heisei 19 nendo Bouei Hakusho* (Defense of Japan 2007) (Ministry of Defense 2007) 439.

[14] Merriam-Webster Online http://www.m-w.com/dictionary/infrastructure (accessed 3 February 2008).

---

[15] Kubo, Fumiaki, "*America no Seijika ha dou Sodaterare te iruka* (How American Politicians are being nurtured.)" *Asuteion* vol. 66 (2007) 25–44. For general overview of the evolution of the political processes theory, see, for instance, Andrew S. McFarland *Neopluralism: The Evolution of Political Process Theory* (University Press of Kansas, 2004).

[16] Samuels, Richard J., "New Fighting Power!" *International Security.* Vol. 32, No. 3 (Winter 2007/2008) 84–112.

[17] An interview with a MOD official, Tokyo Japan: 8 May 2008.

[18] Hughes, Christopher W., *Japan's New Security Agenda: Military Economic & Environmental Dimensions* (Boulder: Lynne Rienner Publishers, 2004): 17–22.

[19] Tanaka, *Anzen Hosho,* 1–6.

[20] The White House, "Joint Statement: The Japan–US Alliance of the New Century," 29 June 2006, http://www.whitehouse.gov/news/releases/2006/06/20060629-2.html (accessed 14 January 2008).

[21] The White House, "President Bush and Prime Minister Abe of Japan Participate in a Joint Press Availability," 27 April 2007, http://www.whitehouse.gov/news/releases/2007/04/20070427-6.html (accessed 14 January 2008)

[22]Sakamoto, Kazuya *Nichi-bei Doumei no Kizuna (The Connection of the US–Japan Alliance)* (Tokyo: Yuhikaku, 2005) provides an excellent analyses of the dynamics during the revision of the US-Japan Security Treaty.

[23] *Nihon-koku to America Gasshu-koku no Aida no Anzen Hosho Jouyaku* (The Security Treaty Between Japan and the United States of America.), signed 8 September 1951, http://www.ioc.u-tokyo.ac.jp/~worldjpn/documents/texts/docs/19510908.T2J.html (accessed 1 March 2007)

[24] *Nihon-koku to America Gasshu-koku tono aida no Sougo Kyoryoku oyobi Anzen Hosho ni kansuru Jouyaku* (The Treaty of Mutual Cooperation and Security Between Japan and the United States of America), signed 19 January 1960, http://www.mofa.go.jp/mofaj/area/usa/hosho/jyoyaku.html (accessed 1 March 2007).

[25] Giarra, Paul S. and Akihisa Nagashima, "Managing the New US–Japan Security Alliance: Enhancing Structures and Mechanisms to Address Post-Cold War Requirements" in Michael J. Green and Patrick M. Cronin ed. *The US–Japan Alliance: Past, Present and Future* (New York: Council on Foreign Relations, 1999): 94-113.

[26] Eto, Shinkichi and Yoshinobu Yamamoto, *Sogo Anpo to Mirai no Sentaku* (Comprehensive Security and the Choices for the Future) (Tokyo: Kodan-sha 1991): 67.

[27] The Study Group on Comprehensive Security, *Sogo Anzen Hosho Kenkyu Group Houkoku-sho* (Report by the Study Group on Comprehensive Security, 2 July, 1980, http://www.ioc.u-tokyo.ac.jp/~worldjpn/documents/texts/JPSC/19800702.O1J.html (accessed 18 January 2008).

[28] *Ibid.*

[29] *Ibid.*

[30] *Ibid.*

[31] *Kokubo no Kihon Houshin* (Basic Principles of National Defense), 20 May 1957, from *Bouei Handbook 2007* (Handbook for Defense 2007) (Tokyo: Asabumo Shinbum-sha 2007):17.

[32] The Constitution of Japan, Article 9, http://homepage1.nifty.com/gyouseinet/kenpou/eiyaku.htm (accessed 3 February 2008).

[33] Tanaka, Akihiko, *Anzen Hosho* (Security) (Tokyo: Yomiuri Shimbun-sha, 1997): 177–185.

[34] *The Treaty of Mutual Cooperation and Security between Japan and the United States of America,* http://www.ioc.u-tokyo.ac.jp/~worldjpn/documents/texts/docs/19600119.T1J.html (accessed 12 January 2008).

[35] Tanaka, *Ibid.*

[36] Pyle, Kenneth, *Japan Rising: The Resurgence of Japanese Power and Purpose* (New York: Public Affairs, 2007): 256–257.

[37] Pyle, *Ibid.,*, 257-259; Ministry of Foreign Affairs of Japan, *Gaiko Seisho: Waga Gaikou no Kinkyou 1990-nen ban (Dai 34 Go)* (Diplomatic Bluebook: Recent Developments in Japan's Diplomacy 1990 edition (vol. 34) Chart 7, 1990, http://www.mofa.go.jp/mofaj/gaiko/bluebook/1990/h02-fufyou.htm#a3 (accessed 15 June 2008).

[38] *Buki Yushutu San Gensoku* (Three Principles on Arms Exports), 1967, in *Bouei Handbook 2007* (Defense Handbook 2007) (Tokyo: Asagumo Shimbun-sha 2007): 796.

[39] *Buki Yushutu ni Kansuru Seifu Touitsu Kenkai* (Government's Unified View on Arms Exports) 27 February 1967, in *Ibid..,* 796.

[40] Oros, Andrew L., *Normalizing Japan* (Palo Alto: Stanford University Press, 2008): 90–92.

[41] House of Representatives of Japan, *Wagakuni ni Okeru Uchu no Kaihatsu oyobi Riyou no Kihon ni Kansuru Ketsugi* (Resolution on Japan's space development and its utilization), 9 May 1969, http://kokkai.ndl.go.jp/SENTAKU/syugiin/061/0001/06105090001035c.html (accessed 23 January, 2008).

[42] *Uchuu Kaihatsu Jigyodan Ho* (NASDA Law) Article 1, enacted 23 June 1969, http://law.e-gov.go.jp/haishi/S44HO050.html (accessed 2 September 2008).

[43] Beckner, Christian, *US–Japan Space Policy: a framework for 21st century cooperation* (Washington: Center for Strategic and International Studies, July 2003): 7–8, 21–22.

---

[44] *Uchu Kihon Ho* (Basic Law for Space), Article 3, enacted 27 August 2008, http://law.e-gov.go.jp/announce/H20HO043.html (accessed 15 September 2008).

[45] Prime Minister Nobusuke Kishi's statement at the Cabinet Affairs Committee, the House of Councillors. 18 April 1958; Statement by Kaneshichi Masuda, JDA Director-General, at the Budget Committee, the House of Councillors, 4 April 1968.

[46] *Genshi-ryoku Kihon-ho* (Nuclear Power Basic Law) Article 2, enacted 19 December 1955, http://law.e-gov.go.jp/htmldata/S30/S30HO186.html (accessed 3 February 2008).

[47] Declared by then Prime Minister Eisaku Sato in response to the question at the Budget Committee of the House of Representatives, Tokyo: 11 December 1967. In Maeda, Tetsuo and Shigeaki Iijima, ed. *Kokkai Shingi kara Bouei-ron wo Yomitoku* (Understanding National Defense Debate through Diet Deliberations) (Tokyo: Sansei-do, 2003): 73.

[48] Sato, Eisaku, *Dai-58-kai Kokkai niokeru Shisei Hoshin Enzetsu* (Policy Speech to the 58th Ordinary Session of the Diet) 30 January 1968, in Maeda and Iijima, *Ibid.,* 73.

[49] Eto, Shinkichi and Yamamoto Yoshinobu. *Sougou Anpo to Mirai no Sentaku* (Comprehensive Security and the Choice of the Future) (Tokyo: Kodan-sha 1991): 159–160.

[50] *Ibid,* 249–252.

[51] Akiyama, Masahiro, *Nichibei no Senryaku Taiwa ga Hajimatta* (US–Japan Strategic Dialogue Begins) (Tokyo: Aki Shobo, 2002): 95–97.

[52] National Defense Program Outline, October 29, 1976.

[53] Statement by the Chief Cabinet Secretary, October 29, 1976.

[54] National Defense Program Outline, October 29, 1976.

[55] National Defense Program Outline, October 29, 1976.

[56] Tatsumi, Yuki, "Self-Defense Forces Today—Beyond an Exclusively Defense-Oriented Posture?" in Tatsumi and Oros eds. *Japan's New Defense Establishment: Institutions, Capabilities, and Implications* (Washington: The Henry L. Stimson Center): 23–24.

[57] Hughes, Christopher W., *Japan's Security Agenda*, (Boulder: Lynne Reinner Publishers, 2004), 160.

[58] Masahiro, Akiyama, *Nichi-bei no Senryaku Taiwa ga Hajimatta (Japan-US Strategic Dialogue Betgins)* (Tokyo: Aki Shobo 2002) 234–243.

[59] *Ibid.,* 310-315.

[60] The Advisory Council on Defense Issues, *Modality of the Security and Defense Capability of Japan: The Outlook for the 21st Century,* (1994) 5–7.

---

[61] *Ibid.,* 7.

[62] *Ibid.,* 7.

[63] *National Defense Program Outline,* November 28, 1995.

[64] *US–Japan Security Declaration: The Alliance for the 21st Century*, April 17, 1996. http//www.mofa.go.jp/region/namerica/us/security/security.html (accessed 15 February 2008)

[65] Murayama, Tomiichi. *Nento shokan: Souzou to Yasashisa no Kunidukuri no Vision* (New Year's Message: A Vision for Creative and Compassionate Nation-Building) Prime Minister's Office, 1 January 1995, http://www.kantei.go.jp/jp/murayamasouri/speech/greeting.html (accessed 25 January, 2008); Murayama, *Dai Hyaku Sanju Kai Kokkai ni okeru Shoshin Hyomei Enzetsu* (Policy Speech to the 130th Diet Session) 18 July, 1994, http://www.kantei.go.jp/jp/murayamasouri/speech/murayama.html#Heiwa (accessed 25 January, 2008); or Murayama, *Dai Hyaku Sanju-yon Kai Kokkai ni okeru Shoshin Hyomei Enzetsu* (Policy Speech to the 134th Diet Session) 29 September 1995, http://www.kantei.go.jp/jp/murayamasouri/speech/kokkai-134.html (accessed 25 January, 2008).

[66] Hashimoto, Ryutaro, *Dai Hyaku Yonju-ni Kai Kokkai ni okeru Shisei Hoshin Enzetsu* (Policy Speech to the 142nd Diet Session) 16 February, 1997, http://www.kantei.go.jp/jp/hasimotosouri/speech/1998/0216sisei.html (accessed 25 January 2008).

[67] Obuchi, Keizo, *Dai Hyaku Yonju-go Kai Kokkai ni okeru Shisei Hoshin Enzetsu* (Policy Speech to the 145th Diet Session) 19 January, 2000, http://www.kantei.go.jp/jp/obutisouri/speech/1999/0119sisei.html (accessed 25 January, 2008).

[68] Ministry of Foreign Affairs of Japan, *Ningen no Anzen Hosho Kikin* (Human Security Fund), 2007, http://www.mofa.go.jp/mofaj/press/pr/pub/pamph/pdfs/t_fund21.pdf (accessed 25 January, 2008).

[69] Tanaka, *Anzen Hosho* (Tokyo: Yomiuri Shimubn-sha, 1997): 319.

[70] Statement by Shuzo Hayashi (Director, Cabinet Legislative Bureau) in response to the question by Honorable Kokichi Yagi at the Budget Committee, House of Representatives, the 31st Session, 19 March 1959. In Maeda and Iijima eds. *Kokkai Shingi kara Bouei-ron wo Yomitoku:* 189–190.

[71] Seisuke Ohmori (Director, Cabinet Legislative Bureau) in response to the question by Honorable Kazuo Shii at the Special Committee on the US-Japan Guidelines for Defense Cooperation, House of Representatives, the 145th Session. 26 March 1999. In Maeda and Iijima. *Ibid.* 203-204.

[72] Statement by Masahiko Koumura (Minister of Foreign Affairs) in response to Honorable Hideyo Fudesaka at the Special Committee on the US-Japan Guidelines for

Defense Cooperation, House of Councillors, 145th Session, 10 may 1999 in Maeda and Iijima, *Ibid.* 199-200

[73] Council on Security and Defense Capabilities, Japan's *Vision for Future Security and Defense Capability,* October 2004, 1.4–11

[74] *Ibid.*

[75] *National Defense Program Guideline for FY 2005 and After,* 10 December 2004, *http://www.mod.go.jp/e/policy/f_work/taikou05/fy20050101.pdf*

[76] *Ibid.*

[77] *Ibid.*

[78] For the discussion of the national security policy infrastructure, see, for example, Joseph S. Nye, Jr and Anne-Marie Slaughter, "Report of the Working Group on Foreign Policy Infrastructure and Global Institutions," The Princeton Project on National Security (Fall 2006), http://www.princeton.edu/~ppns/conferences/reports/fall/FPIGI.pdf (accessed 15 January 2008).

[79] Shinoda, Tomohito, "Japan's Top-Down Policy Process to Dispatch the SDF to Iraq." *Japanese Journal of Political Science* Vol. 7 No. 1 (2006): 71-91.

[80] Pyle, Kenneth, *Japan Rising: The Resurgence of Japanese Power and Purpose* (New York: Public Affairs 2007): 225-229.

[81] The Ministry of Foreign Affairs Establishment Law (*Gaimu-sho Secchi ho).*Article 3, http://www.kantei.go.jp/jp/cyuo-syocho/990427honbu/gaimu-h.html (accessed 14 April, 2008).

[82] *Ibid,* Article 4 –I, (accessed 14 April 2008).

[83] The Ministry of Foreign Affairs, *Heisei 19-nendo ban Gaiko Seisho* (Diplomatic Bluebook 2007) http://www.mofa.go.jp/mofaj/gaiko/bluebook/2007/html/framefiles/honbun.html (accessed 14 April 2008).

[84] Ministry of Foreign Affairs of Japan, *1992-nen-ban Gaiko Seisho* (1992 Diplomatic Bluebook), http://www.mofa.go.jp/mofaj/gaiko/bluebook/1992/h04-4-1.htm#m1 (accessed 15 April 2008).

[85] *Gaimusho Kinou Kaikaku Kaigi* (MOFA Functional Reform Council), *Teigen* (Recommendations), 24 April 2001, http://www.mofa.go.jp/mofaj/annai/honsho/kaikaku/teigen_2.html#teigen (accessed 15 April, 2008).

[86] The Ministry of Foreign Affairs of Japan, *Gaimusho Kaikaku "Kodo Keikaku"* (MOFA Reform "Action Plan"), 21 August, 2002, http://www.mofa.go.jp/mofaj/annai/honsho/kai_genjo/actpln/kodo.html#12 (accessed 16 April, 2008).

[87] The Ministry of Foreign Affairs of Japan, *Korekaka no Gaimusho: Wagakuni no Anzen to Hanei no Tameni* (MOFA for the Future: Toward Japan's Security and Prosperity), 23 July, 2004. 2, http://www.mofa.go.jp/mofaj/annai/honsho/kai_genjo/pdfs/korekara.pdf (accessed 1 March 2008).

[88] *Ibid.,* 19; The Ministry of Foreign Affairs of Japan, *Sougou Gaikou Seisaku Kyoku no Kinou Kkyoka* (The Enhancement of the Foreign Policy Bureau), http://www.mofa.go.jp/mofaj/annai/honsho/kai_genjo/pdfs/sogo.pdf (accessed 1 March 2008). Also, on MOFA's Japanese language website, it is clear that the National Security Policy Division is designated as having the primary jurisdiction on Japan's national security policy. See http://www.mofa.go.jp/mofaj/annai/honsho/sosiki/sogo.html (accessed on 2 March 2008).

[89] Sunohara, Tsuyoshi, *Doumei Henbo: Nichi-bei Ittai-ka no Hikari to Kage* (Alliance Transformed: Light and Shadow of the Integration of the United States and Japan) (Tokyo: Nihon keizai Shinbun Shuppan-sha 2007): 62-63.

[90] The Police Law *(Keisatsu-ho),* Article 5.2–5.17, http://www.npa.go.jp/syokanhourei/soumu1/20070326-1.pdf (accessed 2 March 2008).

[91] *Ibid.,* Article 71, http://www.npa.go.jp/syokanhourei/soumu1/20070326-1.pdf (accessed 2 March 2008).

[92] *Ibid.,* Article 72, http://www.npa.go.jp/syokanhourei/soumu1/20070326-1.pdf (accessed 2 March 2008).

[93] *Ibid.,* Article 1, http://www.npa.go.jp/syokanhourei/soumu1/20070326-1.pdf (accessed 2 March 2008).

[94] *Ibid., Article* 5.6-b, http://www.npa.go.jp/syokanhourei/soumu1/20070326-1.pdf (accessed 2 March 2008).

[95] *Ibid., Article* 5.10, http://www.npa.go.jp/syokanhourei/soumu1/20070326-1.pdf (accessed 2 March 2008).

[96] *Ibid.,* Article 5.4-c, http://www.npa.go.jp/syokanhourei/soumu1/20070326-1.pdf (accessed 2 March 2008).

[97] *Ibid.,* Article 21-1, http://www.npa.go.jp/syokanhourei/soumu1/20070326-1.pdf (accessed 2 March 2008); NPA Organizational Chart http://www.npa.go.jp/english/kokusai/pdf/Poj2007-5.pdf (accessed 3 March 2008).

[98] *Ibid.,* Article 21-4, 21-20, http://www.npa.go.jp/syokanhourei/soumu1/20070326-1.pdf (accessed 2 March 2008).

[99] *Ibid.,* Article 23, 23-2-1, 23-2-2, http://www.npa.go.jp/syokanhourei/soumu1/20070326-1.pdf (accessed 2 March 2008).

[100] *Ibid.,* Article 24, http://www.npa.go.jp/syokanhourei/soumu1/20070326-1.pdf (accessed 2 March 2008).

[101] Ministry of Defense of Japan, http://www.mod.go.jp/j/defense/mod-sdf/index.html (accessed 25 February 2008).

[102] The MOD Law, Article 3, 8-1, 8-2, and 8-3, http://law.e-gov.go.jp/htmldata/S29/S29HO164.html (accessed 15 January 2008).

[103] *Ibid.,* Article 8-4, http://law.e-gov.go.jp/htmldata/S29/S29HO164.html (accessed 15 January 2008).

[104] Ministry of Defense of Japan, *Defense of Japan 2007* 196, http://www.mod.go.jp/e/publ/w_paper/pdf/2007/30Part2_Chap3_Sec3.pdf (accessed 25 January 2008).

[105] Ministry of Defense of Japan, http://www.mod.go.jp/j/defense/mod-sdf/sosikizu/inner/index.html (accessed 10 February 2008).

[106] Ministry of Defense, *Defense of Japan 2007* 196, http://www.mod.go.jp/e/publ/w_paper/pdf/2007/30Part2_Chap3_Sec3.pdf (accessed 25 January 2008).

[107] *Ibid.*

[108] Tatsumi, Yuki and Ken Jimbo. "From the JDA to the MOD- a step forward, but challenges remain." *PacNet Newsletter* No. 3A (2 January 2007), http://www.csis.org/media/csis/pubs/pac0703a.pdf (accessed 23 January 2008).

[109] *Ibid.*

[110] Author's private conversation with a MOD official, 1 March 2008.

[111] "*Bouei-sho Saihen Honkaku Chakushu he-'Seifuku' 'Sebiro' Tougou ga Shoten* (The MOD Reorganization began to move—Integration of Civilian and Uniform as a Focus)" *Yomiuri Shimbun,* 4 March 2008, http://www.yomiuri.co.jp/feature/20080219-1263180/news/20080303-OYT1T00794.htm (accessed 8 March 2008).

[112] Author's interviews with the members of the Advisory Council on the MOD Reform, Tokyo, Japan: 12–15 May 2008.

[113] Cabinet Secretariat, *Naikaku Kanbo no Gaiyo* (Overview of the Cabinet Secretariat), http://www.cas.go.jp/jp/gaiyou/index.html (accessed 2 March 2008); Cabinet Law (*Naikaku-ho*) Article 12, Enacted 16 January 1947, most recently updated 16 July 1999. http://www.cas.go.jp/jp/hourei/houritu/naikaku_h.html (accessed 2 March 2008).

[114] *Naikaku-ho* (Cabinet Law), Article 19, http://www.cas.go.jp/jp/hourei/houritu/naikaku_h.html (accessed 2 March 2008).

[115] Cabinet Law, Article 13, http://law.e-gov.go.jp/htmldata/S22/S22HO005.html (accessed 1 March 2008).

[116] Customarily, Chief Cabinet Secretary holds a press conference once a day; *Naikaku Kanbo Chokan* (Chief Cabinet Secretary); Wikipedia http://ja.wikipedia.org/wiki (accessed 28 February, 2008).

---

[117] Aso, Iku. *Joho Kantei ni Tassezu* (Information did not reach the Prime Minister) (Tokyo: Shincho-sha, 2001), for instance, provides a good narratives of how the Japanese government responded through various national crises in the 1990s.

[118] Cabinet Law, Article 15, http://law.e-gov.go.jp/htmldata/S22/S22HO005.html (accessed 1 March 2008).

[119] "*Naikaku Kiki Kanri-kan* (Deputy Chief Cabinet Secretary for Crisis Management) *Wikipedia* http://ja.wikipedia.org/wiki (accessed 1 March 2008)

[120] Author's interview with MOD official, 13 May 2008.

[121] Cabinet Law, Article 18, http://law.e-gov.go.jp/htmldata/S22/S22HO005.html (accessed 2 March 2008).

[122] Aso, Iku, *Joho Kantei ni Todokazu* (Information Not Reaching to the Prime Minsiter) (Tokyo: Shincho-sha, 2001).

[123] *Naikaku Angen Hosho-shitsu* (Cabinet Office of National Security) *Wikipedia* http://ja.wikipedia.org/wiki (accessed 1 March 2008).

[124] Schoff, James L. ed. *Crisis Management in Japan and the United States* (McLean: The Institute for Foreign Policy Analyses, Inc/Brassey's, Inc., 2004): 83-84.

[125] Tatsumi, Yuki and Andrew L. Oros, "Japan's Evolving Defense Establishment" in Tatsumi, Yuki and Andrew L. Oros eds. *Japan's New Defense Establishment: Institutions, Capabilities, and Implications* (Washington: The Henry L. Stimson Center, 2007): 17.

[126] *Ibid.*, 18–20.

[127] Author's interview with a Cabinet Secretariat official, Tokyo, Japan: 13 May 2008.

[128] Author's interview with a retired senior Japanese government official, Tokyo, Japan: 13 May 2008.

[129] Author's interview with a former MOD official, Tokyo, Japan: 8 May 2008; author's interview with a MOD official. Tokyo, Japan: 8 May 2008; author's interview with METI officials, Tokyo, Japan: 15 May 2008.

[130] Author's interview with a MOD official, Tokyo, Japan: 8 May 2008.

[131] Unclassified fact sheet on the Cabinet Satellite Information Center provided to the author by the former Cabinet Secretariat official, Tokyo, Japan: 8 May 2008.

[132] Author's interview with a MOD official, Tokyo, Japan: 8 May 2008; author's interview with a senior MOD official, Tokyo, Japan: 15 May 2008; author's interview with a MOFA official, Tokyo, Japan: 13 May 2008.

[133] *Ibid.*

---

[134] Author's interview with Cabinet Secretariat officials, Tokyo Japan: 13 and 15 May 2008; author's interview with a retired senior Japanese government official, Tokyo, Japan 13 May 2008.

[135] Author's interview with a Japanese government official, Tokyo, Japan: 13 May 2008.

[136] Author's interview with a Cabinet Secretariat official, Tokyo, Japan: 13 May 2008.

[137] Author's interview with MOFA officials, Tokyo, Japan: 12 May 2008; author's interview with a former senior Cabinet Secretariat official. Tokyo, Japan: 15 May 2008.

[138] Japan Defense Agency Establishment Law (*Bouei-Cho Secchi Ho*), adopted 9 June 1954, http://law.e-gov.go.jp/htmldata/S29/S29HO164.html (accessed 23 April 2007)

[139] Self-Defense Forces (SDF) Law (*Jieitai Ho*), adopted 9 June 1954, most recently revised 2 May 2008, http://law.e-gov.go.jp/htmldata/S29/S29HO165.html (accessed 1 March 2008).

[140] *Ibid.,* Article 3. http://law.e-gov.go.jp/htmldata/S29/S29HO165.html (accessed 1 March 2008).

[141] Constitution of Japan, Adopted on 3 November 1946, http://www.ndl.go.jp/constitution/e/etc/c01.html#s2 (accessed 2 March 2008).

[142] Whitestone, Yuko, "*PKO Sanka to Jiei-kan no Shokugyo-teki Identity no Henka* (Participation in Peacekeeping Operations and Changes in Professional Identities among the SDF Personnel)*" Kokusai Anzen Hosho* (The Journal of International Security) Vol. 35, No. 3 (December 2007) 28.

[143] Samuels, Richard J, "New Fighting Power!: Japan's Growing Maritime Capabilities and East Asian Security." *International Security* Vol. 32, No. 3 (Winter 2007/08): 86.

[144] Ministry of Defense, *Wagakuni no Bouei to Yosan: Heisei 20-nendo Yosan no Gaiyo* (Japan's Defense and Budget: Overview of Japan's Defense Budget for FY 2008-09), 23, http://www.mod.go.jp/j/library/archives/yosan/2008/yosan_gaiyou.pdf (accessed 3 March 2008).

[145] Institute of International Strategic Studies (IISS), *Military Balance 2008* (New York: Routeledge 2008): 384.

[146] The SDF Law, Article 9, http://law.e-gov.go.jp/htmldata/S29/S29HO165.html (accessed 2 March 2008).

[147] *Ibid.,* Article 7, http://law.e-gov.go.jp/htmldata/S29/S29HO165.html (accessed 2 March 2008).

[148] Ministry of Defense. *Ibid.,* 19, http://www.mod.go.jp/j/library/archives/yosan/2008/yosan_gaiyou.pdf (accessed 3 March 2008).

---

[149] Japan Air Self-Defense Force (JASDF), *Koku Jieitai no Yakuwari* (Role of the Air Self-Defense Force), http://www.mod.go.jp/asdf/english/mission/index.html (accessed 5 March 2008); JASDF *Koku Jieitai no Yakuwari: Sora karano Bouei* (The Role of the JASDF: Defense from Air), http://www.mod.go.jp/asdf/mission/mission01.html (accessed 6 March 2008).

[150] JASDF. *Koku Jieitai no Yakuwari: Daikibo Saigai-nado he no Taiou* (The Role of the JASDF: Responses to Large-Scale Disasters and Other Situations), http://www.mod.go.jp/asdf/mission/mission04.html (accessed 5 March 2008).

[151] *Ibid.*

[152] JASDF. *Koku Jieitai no Yakuwari: Kokusai Koken Katsudo no Jisseki* (The Role of the JASDF: Past Accomplishments in International Contribution), http://www.mod.go.jp/asdf/mission/mission09.html (accessed 5 March 2008).

[153] JASDF, *Koku Jieitai no Soshiki* (JASDF Organization), http://www.mod.go.jp/asdf/english/formation/index.html (accessed 5 March 2008).

[154] Security Consultative Committee (SCC), *US–Japan Alliance: Transformation and Realignment for the Future.* 29 October 2005, http://www.mofa.go.jp/region/n-america/us/security/scc/doc0510.html (accessed 3 March 2008).

[155] International Institute of Strategic Studies (IISS), *The Military Balance 2008* (IISS 2008): 386.

[156] Lind, Jennifer, "Pacifism or Passing the Buck?" *International Security* Vol. 29, No. 1 (Summer 2004), 97–98.

[157] *Ibid.*

[158] US Department of Defense, "Military Capability of the People's Republic of China," 3 March 2008; 5, http://www.defenselink.mil/pubs/pdfs/China_Military_Report_08.pdf (accessed 5 March 2008).

[159] Defense Department Appropriations Act, FY 1998, Public Law 105-56 enacted 8 October 1997, http://frwebgate.access.gpo.gov/cgi-bin/getdoc.cgi?dbname=105_cong_public_laws&docid=f:publ56.105.pdf> (accessed 3 March 2008).

[160] An interview with a JASDF officer, Tokyo, Japan: 12 May 2008.

[161] Ministry of Defense, *Wagakuni no Bouei to Yosan: Heisei 20-nendo Yosan no Gaiyo* (Japan's Defense and Budget: Overview of Japan's Defense Budget for FY 2008-09) 23, http://www.mod.go.jp/j/library/archives/yosan/2008/yosan_gaiyou.pdf (accessed 4 March 2008).

[162] *Ibid.*

[163] Japan Ground Self-Defense Force, "*Yakuwari* (Our Role)" http://www.mod.go.jp/gsdf/about/yakuwari.html (accessed 6 March 2008).

[164] Wikipedia, "*Unzen Dake* (Mount. Unzen)," http://ja.wikipedia.org/wiki (accessed 6 March 2008).

[165] Wikipedia, "*Chikatetsu Sarini Jiken* (Subway Sarin Incident)," http://ja.wikipedia.org/wiki (accessed 7 March 2008).

[166] Ministry of Defense, "*Heisei 20-nen Iwate Miyagi-nairiku Jishin no Taiou ni Tsuite* (Response to the 2008 Iwate-Miyagi Earthquake)" 19 June 2008. http://www.mod.go.jp/j/news/2008/06/19b.html (accessed 20 June 2008).

[167] Ministry of Defense, "*Heisei 19-nen ban Nihon no Bouei* (Defense of Japan 2007)" 131, July 2007.

[168] Ministry of Defense, *Heisei 19-nen ban Nihon no Bouei* (Defense of Japan 2007) 107, July 2007; Japan Ground Self-Defense Force Central Readiness Force (JGSDF CRF), http://www.mod.go.jp/gsdf/crf/pa/ (accessed 6 March 2008).

[169] JGSDF CRF, "*Chuo Sokuo Shudan no Hensei* (Organization of the Central Readiness Force)," http://www.mod.go.jp/gsdf/crf/pa/ (accessed 6 March 2008).

[170] Ground Research and Development Command, http://www.cpi-media.co.jp/shiokawa/message/kenkyu-honbu.html (accessed 8 March 2008); JGSDF, "*Rikujo Jieitai no Soshiki to Haichi* (Organization and Distribution of the JGSDF) http://www.mod.go.jp/gsdf/about/chutonchi/index.html (accessed 6 March 2008).

[171] Ministry of Defense of Japan, *Heisei 19-nen ban Bouei Hakusho* (2007 Defense White Paper) 108.

[172] Ministry of Defense of Japan, *Ibid.*, 107.

[173] *Ibid.*

[174] Ministry of Defense, *op. cit.*. 108

[175] Ebata, Kensuke, *Nihon no Bouei no Arikata* (The Modality of Defense of Japan) (Tokyo: KK Bestsellers, 2004): 245–257.

[176] For a detailed explanation of JGSDF's definition of logistics, see, for example, Azuma, Shun, "*Jieitai no Kouhou to ha Nani ka* (What is JSDF's logistics)." *Securitarian* (September 2002): 16–19.

[177] Ministry of Defense, *Wagakuni no Bouei to Yosan: Heisei 20-nendo Yosan no Gaiyo* (Japan's Defense and Budget: Overview of Japan's Defense Budget for FY 2008-09), 19, http://www.mod.go.jp/j/library/archives/yosan/2008/yosan_gaiyou.pdf (accessed 15 April 2008).

[178] Japan Maritime Self-Defense Force (JMSDF), "*Kaijo Jieitai no Bouei-ryoku* (Defensive Capabilities of the JMSDF)," http://www.mod.go.jp/msdf/formal/about/bouei/index.html (accessed 10 April 2008).

[179] Auer, James. E., "*Aitsugu Bouei-sho Fushoji: Seiji to Kokumi no Sekinin ni Me wo Mukeyo* (Ministry of Defense Scandals Continues: Responsibility of Political Leaders and

Public Must be Questioned).” *Wedge* (July 2008): 88-90; Agawa, Naoyuki, “*Umi no Yujo: Beikoku Kaigun to Kaijou Jieitai* (Friendship of the Sea: US Navy and the Maritime Self-Defense Force)” (Tokyo: Chuo Koron Shinsha, 2001).

[180] JMSDF, “*Keikai Kanshi* (Surveillance and Reconnaissance),” http://www.mod.go.jp/msdf/formal/about/keikai/index.html (accessed 5 April 2008).

[181] JMSDF, “*Kokusai Koken* (International Contribution),” http://www.mod.go.jp/msdf/formal/about/kouken/index.html (accessed 3 April 2008).

[182] JMSDF, “*Saigai he no Taiou* (Response to Disasters),” http://www.mod.go.jp/msdf/formal/about/saigai/index.html (accessed 2 April 2008).

[183] “*Aegis-kan Mamoru Shinei-kan 19DD wo Chotatsu* (Acquisition of 19DD, a new destroyer that will protect Aegis ships),” *Asagumo News*, 14 December 2006, http://www.asagumo-news.com/news/200612/061214/06121411.html (accessed 1 May 2008).

[184] MSDF Ohminato Regional District Force, “*Ohminato Chiho Sokan Takeda Yoshikazu* (Ohminato Regional District Commander ADM Yoshikazu Takeda),” http://www.mod.go.jp/msdf/oominato/soukan/soukan.htm (accessed 1 May 2008); MSDF Maizuru District Force, “*Maizuru Chiho Sokan karano Goaisatsu* (Greeting from the Commander of Maizuru District Force),” http://www.mod.go.jp/msdf/maizuru/ (accessed 1 May 2008).

[185] Ebata, Kensuke. *Nihon no Bouei no Arikata.* 27–28.

[186] Discussion on the JMSDF contribution to US naval deterrent strategy during the Cold War can be found in Auer, James E., “*Aitsugu Bouei Fushouji: Seiji to Kokumin no Sekinin ni Me wo Mukeyo* (Continuous scandals by the Ministry of Defense: Responsibility of Politicians and the Public needs to be Examined).” *Wedge* (July 2008): 88-90. A more comprehensive discussion can be found in Agawa, Naoyuki, “*Umi no Yuujo* (Friendship at Sea)” (Tokyo: Chuo Koron Shin-sha, 2001).

[187] Ministry of Defense, “*Heisei 17-nendo ikou ni Kakawaru Bouei Keikaku no Taiko ni Tsuite* (National Defense Program Guideline in and after the Japanese FY 2005),” 10 December 2004, in *Defense of Japan 2007*, 462–469, http://www.mod.go.jp/e/publ/w_paper/pdf/2007/44Reference_1_63.pdf (accessed 30 March 2008).

[188] “16DDH ‘13,500 ton’ Class,” *Globalsecurity.org,* http://www.globalsecurity.org/military/world/japan/ddh-x.htm (accessed 6 May 2008).

[189] The Joint Staff Office, http://www.mod.go.jp/jso/english/e-responsibility.htm (accessed 5 March 2008).

[190] Joint Staff Office, “*Togo Bakuryo Kanbu no Shosho Jimu* (The responsibility of the Joint Staff Office),” http://www.mod.go.jp/jso/folder/jurisdiction.htm (accessed 5 March 2008).

[191] Interview with the JSDF officers at the JMSDF Sasebo Regional District, Nagasaki, Japan: 30 January, 2007; Interview with the JGSDF officers at the Western Regional Army Headquarters, Kumamoto, Japan: 31 January 2007.

[192] Tatsumi, Yuki, "Self-Defense Forces Today—Beyond Exclusively Defense-Oriented Posture?" in Tatsumi and Oros eds., *Japan's New Defense Establishment: Institutions, Capabilities and Implications* (Washington: The Henry L. Stimson Center, 2005) 41–43.

[193] Armitage, Richard L. and Joseph S. Nye, Jr., *The US-Japan Alliance: Getting Asia Right Through 2020* (Washington: Center for Strategic and International Studies, 2007): 22.

[194] Japan Coast Guard (JCG) Law (*Kaijo Hoan-cho Ho*), Article One, adopted 27 April 1948, most recently revised 2 May 2008, http://law.e-gov.go.jp/htmldata/S23/S23HO028.html (accessed 10 May 2008).

[195] *Ibid.,* Article 2, http://law.e-gov.go.jp/htmldata/S23/S23HO028.html (accessed 10 May 2008).

[196] *Ibid.,* Article 5-12, 5-13, 5-14, 5-15, 5-16, 5-17, http://law.e-gov.go.jp/htmldata/S23/S23HO028.html (accessed 10 May 2008).

[197] *Ibid,.* Article 28-2, http://law.e-gov.go.jp/htmldata/S23/S23HO028.html (accessed 10 May 2008).

[198] The Japan Coast Guard, "*Kaijo Hoan Report 2007 nen-ban* (Maritime Security Report 2007),"
http://www.kaiho.mlit.go.jp/info/books/report2007/kakudai/p039_kakudai01.html (accessed 1 March 2008).

[199] *Ibid.*

[200] The Maritime Safety Agency (MSA), *Annual Report on Maritime Safety 1998 Edition,* http://www.kaiho.mlit.go.jp/e/tosho/apoms1.pdf (accessed 3 March 2008).

[201] See, for instance, the MSA, *Heisei 9 nen-ban Kaijou Hoan Hakusho* (White Paper on Maritime Safety 1997 edition),
http://www.kaiho.mlit.go.jp/info/books/h9haku/mokuji.htm (accessed 10 March 2008).

[202] The MSA, *Heisei 10 nen-ban Kaijou Hoan Hakusho* (White Paper on Maritime Safety 1998 edition); *Heisei 11 nen-ban Kaijou Hoan Hakusho* (White Paper on Maritime Safety 1999 edition); *Heisei 12 nen-ban Kaijou Hoan Hakusho* (White Paper on Maritime Safety 2000 edition).

[203] The JCG, "Message from the Commandant" in *Kaijo Hoan Report 2001* (2001 Japan Coast Guard Annual Report),
http://www.kaiho.mlit.go.jp/info/books/report2001/message/index.html (accessed 18 February 2008).

[204] The JCG, *Kaijo Hoan Gyomu Suiko Keikaku* (Maritime Safety Task Implementation Plan), April 2001, http://www.kaiho.mlit.go.jp/seisakuhyoka/h16.4.8/keikaku.pdf (accessed 20 February 2008).

---

[205] The JCG, *Kaijo Hoan Gyomu Suiko Keikaku* (Maritime Safety Task Implementation Plan), April 2001, http://www.kaiho.mlit.go.jp/seisakuhyoka/h16.4.8/keikaku.pdf (accessed 20 February 2008); The JCG, *Dai Ni-ji Kaijo Hoan Gyomu Suiko Keikaku* (Second Maritime Safety Task Implementation Plan), April 2006, http://www.kaiho.mlit.go.jp/seisakuhyoka/no2keikaku.pdf (accessed 20 February 2008).

[206] The JCG, "*Junshi-sen/tei Koku-ki no Seibi* (Acquisition of Patrol Ships/Boats and Aircrafts)," http://www.kaiho.mlit.go.jp/shisaku/soubi.htm (accessed 3 February 2008).

[207] The JCG, "*Tatkokukan Renkei* (Multinational Collaboration)" in *Kaijo Hoan Report 2006 nen-ban* (Japan Coast Guard Annual Report 2006), http://www.kaiho.mlit.go.jp/info/books/report2006/tokushu/p019.html (accessed 5 March 2008).

[208] *Ibid.*

[209] Samuels, Richard J., *Securing Japan: Tokyo's Grand Strategy and the Future of East Asia* (Ithica: Cornell University Press, 2007), 77.

[210] The JCG, "*Shiryohen: Sentei Koukuki* (Appendices: Ships/boats and aircrafts)" in *Kaijo Hoan Report 2007 nen-ban* (Japan Coast Guard Annual Report 2007), http://www.kaiho.mlit.go.jp/info/books/report2007/siryou/p126.html (accessed 10 March 2008).

[211] The JCG, "*Junshi-sen Kouku-ki no Keinen Taisaku* (Addressing the aging of JCG fleet and aircrafts)" in *Kaijo Hoan Report 2005 nen-ban* (Japan Coast Guard Annual Report 2005), http://www.kaiho.mlit.go.jp/info/books/report2005/sonota/p148-1.html (accessed 15 March 2008).

[212] The JCG, "*Kaijo Hoan-cho ho no Kaisei* (Revision of the JCG Law)" in *Kaijo Hoan Report 2002 nen-ban* (Japan Coast Guard Annual Report 2002), http://www.kaiho.mlit.go.jp/info/books/report2002/topics/01_2.html (accessed 15 March 2008).

[213] The Ministry of Defense, *Wagakuni no Bouei to Yosan: Heisei 20 Nen-do Yosan no Gaiyo* (Our Country's Defense and Budget: Overview of FY 2008 Budget), http://www.mod.go.jp/j/library/archives/yosan/2008/yosan_gaiyou.pdf (accessed 1 April 2008).

[214] The National Police Agency, *Heisei 19 nen-ban Keisatsu Hakusho* (2007 Police White Paper), http://www.npa.go.jp/hakusyo/h19/honbun/index.html (accessed 3 February 2008).

[215] The National Police Agency (NPA), "Police of Japan: Organization," http://www.npa.go.jp/english/kokusai/pdf/Poj2007-3.pdf (accessed 2 February 2008).

[216] *Ibid.*

[217] The NPA, "Organization and Resources," http://www.npa.go.jp/english/kokusai/pdf/Poj2007-9.pdf (accessed 5 February 2008).

---

[218] *Ibid.*

[219] The National Police Agency, *Heisei 19 nen-ban Keisatsu Hakusho* (2007 Police White Paper), http://www.npa.go.jp/hakusyo/h19/honbun/index.html (accessed 3 February 2008).

[220] *Ibid.*

[221] The Ministry of Defense of Japan, "*Noto Hanto Oki Fushin-sen Jian ni okeru Kyokun Hansei Jikou ni Tsuite: Youshi* (Regarding the "lessons learned" from the Unidentified Ship Incident Off of Noto Peninsula: Summary)," http://www.clearing.mod.go.jp/hakusho_data/1999/zuhyo/frame/az116009.htm (accessed 5 March 2008).

[222] Shikata, Toshiyuki, "*Nihon wa Konomama deha Ikinokorenai* (Japan cannot survive as is)" (Tokyo: PHP Kenkyujo, 2007): 101–107.

[223] An interview with a MOD official, Tokyo Japan: 8 May 2008.

[224] Tamura, Shigenobu and Tadahisa (CHECK) Sato. *Kyokasho Nihon no Bouei Seisaku* (Textbook: Japan's Defense Policy) (Tokyo: Fuyo Shobo, 2008).

[225] Ebata, Kensuke, Joho *to Kokka* (Intelligence and the Nation) (Tokyo: Kodan-sha, 2004): 3.

[226] *Ibid.,* 233.

[227] Aoki, Osamu, *Nihon no Koan Keisatsu* (Japan's Public Security Police) (Tokyo: Kodan-sha, 2000).

[228] *Joho Kino Kyoka Kentou Kaigi no Secchi ni tsuite* (Regarding the Establishment of the Exploratory Committee for the Enhancement of Intelligence Capabilities) Cabinet Decision, 1 December 2006.

[229] Answers by Shinichi Isajiki, Deputy Director, CIRO, in response to the questions by Honorable Takeshi Matsumoto. Transcripts of the House of Representatives Committee on National Security, the 162nd Session, 8 April, 2005, http://www.shugiin.go.jp/index.nsf/html/index_kaigiroku.htm (accessed 12 April, 2008).

[230] *Ibid.*

[231] Public Security Investigation Agency (PSIA), "*Koan Chosa-cho Shokai* (Introduction to the PSIA)," http://www.moj.go.jp/KOUAN/shoukai2.html#03 (accessed 31 March 2008).

[232] PSIA, *op. cit.,* http://www.moj.go.jp/KOUAN/shoukai2.html#03 (accessed 31 March 2008).

[233] Oros, Andrew L., "Japan's Growing Intelligence Capability" in *International Journal of Intelligence and Counterintelligence* Vol. 15, No. 1 (2002), 8.

[234] PSIA, *op. cit,*. http://www.moj.go.jp/KOUAN/shoukai2.html#03 (accessed 31 March 2008).

[235] PSIA, *op. cit.,* http://www.moj.go.jp/KOUAN/shoukai2.html#03 (accessed 31 March 2008).

[236] Prevention of Destructive Activities Law (*Hakai Katsudo Boshi-ho, Habo-ho*), Article Eleven, http://www.houko.com/00/01/S27/240.HTM#s3 (accessed 1 April 2008); Law concerning the Restrictions against the Organizations that have engaged in Indiscriminate, Large-scale Murder (*Musabetsu Tairyo Satsujin Koui wo Okonatta Dantai no Kisei ni kansuru Houritsu*) Article Twelve, http://www.moj.go.jp/KOUAN/HOREI/ho03.html (accessed 31 March 2008).

[237] Constitution of Japan (*Nihonkoku Kempo*), Article 10-40, enacted 3 May 1947, http://www.houko.com/00/01/S21/000.HTM#s3 (accessed 1 April 2008).

[238] Law concerning the Restrictions against the Organizations that have engaged in Indiscriminate, Large-scale Murder, Article 2, enacted 27 December 1999, http://www.moj.go.jp/KOUAN/HOREI/ho03.html (accessed 31 March 2008).

[239] Aoki, *Nihon no Koan Keisatsu,* 219-220. It also should be noted that the PSIA's request was turned down in 1997.

[240] Aoki, *Ibid.,* 211–212.

[241] Oros, "Japan's Growing Intelligence Capability," 8.

[242] Aoki, *Nihon no Koan Keisatsu,* 220–221.

[243] Oros, "Japan's Growing Intelligence Capability," 8.

[244] PSIA, "*Heisei 17-nen Naigai Josei no Kaiko to Tenbo* (2005 Review and Prospect of International and External Situations)," http://www.moj.go.jp/KOUAN/NAIGAI/NAIGAI17/naigai17-05.html (accessed 2 April 2008); "*Heisei 18-nen Naigai Josei no Kaiko to Tenbo* (2006 Review and Prospect of International and External Situations,)" http://www.moj.go.jp/KOUAN/NAIGAI/NAIGAI18/naigai18-05.html (accessed 2 April 2008); "*Heisei 19-nen Naigai Josei no Kaiko to Tenbo* (2007 Review and Prospect of International and External Situations,)" http://www.moj.go.jp/KOUAN/NAIGAI/NAIGAI19/naigai19-05.html (accessed 2 April 2008); "*Heisei 20-nen Naigai Josei no Kaiko to Tenbo* (2008 Review and Prospect of International and External Situations,)" http://www.moj.go.jp/KOUAN/NAIGAI/NAIGAI20/naigai20-06.html (accessed 2 April 2008).

[245] National Police Agency (NPA), "*Heisei 16-nendo ni okeru Keisatsu-cho no Soshiki Kaihen Koso ni tsuite* (Concept for NPA Reorganization for FY 2006)," Uploaded 15 January 2006, http://www.npa.go.jp/seisaku/soumu3/kousou.pdf (accessed 4 April 2008).

---

[246] Oros, "Japan's Growing Intelligence Capability," 11; Aoki, *Nihon no Koan Keisatsu,* 21-22; NPA, *Ibid.* http://www.npa.go.jp/seisaku/soumu3/kousou.pdf (accessed 4 April 2008).

[247] NPA, "*Heisei 19-nen no Kokusai Kyoryoku nado no Joukyou* (Situation regarding the International Cooperation and Other Related Activities in 2007)," March 2008. http://www.npa.go.jp/kokusaikyoryoku/kyoryokujokyo/20080312.pdf (accessed 4 April 2008).

[248] Oros, "Japan's Growing Intelligence Capability," 11.

[249] Aoki, *Nihon no Koan Keisatsu,* 20–24.

[250] Oros, "Japan's Growing Intelligence Capability," 9.

[251] Defense Intelligence Headquarters of Japan, *Saiyo Pamphlet* (Recruiting Brochure), 3, http://www.mod.go.jp/dih/bosyu.pdf (accessed 2 April 2008).

[252] Defense Intelligence Headquarters of Japan, "*Joho Honbu no Gaiyo* (DIH Overview)," http://www.mod.go.jp/dih/gaiyou.html (accessed 10 April 2008).

[253] Defense Intelligence Headquarters of Japan, *Ibid.,* http://www.mod.go.jp/dih/gaiyou.html (accessed 10 April 2008).

[254] Defense Intelligence Headquarters of Japan, "*Kakubu no Gyomu* (Tasks of each directorate)," http://www.mod.go.jp/dih/busyo.html (accessed 9 April 2008).

[255] Defense Intelligence Headquarters of Japan, *Ibid,.* http://www.mod.go.jp/dih/busyo.html, (accessed 9 April 2008).

[256] Defense Intelligence Headquarters of Japan, *Ibid,.* http://www.mod.go.jp/dih/busyo.html (accessed 9 April 2008).

[257] Wikipedia, *Bouei-sho Joho Honbu* (Ministry of Defense, Defense Intelligence Headquarters), http://ja.wikipedia.org/wiki (accessed 2 April 2008).

[258] Defense Intelligence Headquarters of Japan, *"Saiyo Pamphlet* (Recruiting Brochure)," 4, http://www.mod.go.jp/dih/bosyu.pdf (accessed 2 April 2008).

[259] Oros, "Japan's Growing Intelligence Capability," 9.

[260] "*Joho Honbu Secchi Sono Jittai wo Saguku: Kunimi Masahiro Joho Honbu-cho Interview* (Establishment of the Defense Intelligence Headquarters: Interview with DIH Director General Masahiro Kunimi)" *Securitarian* (March 1997), http://www.bk.dfma.or.jp/~sec/1997/03/t_kunimi.htm (accessed 13 April 2008).

[261] Interviews with MOD officials, 1–2 February 2007.

[262] Interviews with MOD officials, 9–12 July 2007.

[263] For instance, Director of Signals Directorate is always a seconded NPA official.

[264] Private conversation with a MOD officials,13 May 2008.

[265] Oros, "Japan's Growing Intelligence Capability," 12.

[266] Ministry of Foreign Affairs of Japan, "*Gaimusho Kaikaku no Genjo: Heisei 16-nen 7-gatsu izen oyobi 8-gatsu ikou no Gaimusho Kikou-zu* (The Current Status of MOFA Reform: Organizational Chart prior to July 2004 and after August 2004)."

[267] Ministry of Foreign Affairs of Japan, *Saihen/Kyoka no Mokuteki* (The purpose of reorganization and enhancement (of Intelligence and Analysis Service), http://www.mofa.go.jp/mofaj/annai/honsho/kai_genjo/pdfs/koku_j.pdf (accessed 11 April 2008).

[268] Ministry of Foreign Affairs of Japan, "*Saihen/Kyoka no Mokuteki* (The purpose of reorganization and enhancement (of Intelligence and Analysis Service),"http://www.mofa.go.jp/mofaj/annai/honsho/kai_genjo/pdfs/koku_j.pdf (accessed 11 April 2008).

[269] See, for example, Ota, Fumio, "*Joho to Anzen Hosho* (Intelligence and Security)," *Anzen Hosho* (Security) Vol. 100 No. 3 (June 2005) http://www.kokubou.jp/books-100-3.html (accessed 12 April, 2008).

[270] Oros, "Japan's Growing Intelligence Capability," 13.

[271] Wikipedia, *Naikaku Joho Chosa-shitsu* (Cabinet Intelligence Research Office), http://ja.wikipedia.org/wiki (accessed 5 April 2008).

[272] Unclassified briefing material on Japan's information-gathering satellite (IGS) provided to the author by a former Cabinet Secretariat official; Interview with a former Cabinet Secretariat official, 8 July 2008.

[273] Interview with a former Cabinet Secretariat official, 8 July 2008.

[274] *Ibid.*, Sunohara, Tsuyoshi., *Tanjo Kokusan Supai Eisei* (Birth of Indigenous Spy Satellite) (Tokyo: Nihon Keizai Shimbun-sha, 2005): 209–210.

[275] Wikipedia, "*Naikaku Joho Chosa-shitsu* (Cabinet Intelligence Research Office)," http://ja.wikipedia.org/wiki (accessed 14 April, 2008).

[276] Statement by Isajiki, Shinichi, Deputy Director, CIRO, in response to the questions by Honorable Takeshi Matsumoto. Transcripts of the House of Representatives Committee on National Security, the 162nd Session, 8 April, 2005, http://www.shugiin.go.jp/index.nsf/html/index_kaigiroku.htm (accessed 12 April, 2008).

[277] Oros, "Japan's Growing Intelligence Capability," 6.

[278] Oros, "Japan's Growing Intelligence Capability," 5.

[279] "Japan to Acquire Spy Satellite?" *Jiji Press,* 10 September 1982.

[280] "Japan Worried by North Korean Spies," *Jiji Press*, 5 April 1985.

[281] Tase Yasuhiro, "Intelligence gap weakens diplomatic effort" *Nikkei Weekly*, 7 September 1991.

[282] Sasajima, Masahiko, "Information is power when responding to the emergencies," *Daily Yomiuri,* 23 April 1998.

[283] The Council on Enhancing Intelligence Function *(Joho Kino Kyoka Kento Kaigi*), "*Kantei ni okeru Joho Kinou Kyoka no Kihon-teki na Kangae-kata* (Basic Concepts for Enhancing the Cabinet's Intelligence Capability)," 28, February 2007, http://www.kantei.go.jp/jp/singi/zyouhou/070228kettei.pdf (accessed 20 April 2008).

[284] *Ibid.*

[285] The Council on Enhancing Intelligence Function, "*Counter-intelligence Kinou no Kyouka ni kansuru Kihon Houshin (Gaiyou)* (Basic Principles for Enhancing Counter-intelligence Capability: An Overview)" August 2007, http://www.cas.go.jp/jp/seisaku/counterintelligence/pdf/basic_decision_summary.pdf (accessed 1 April 2008).

[286] The Council on Enhancing Intelligence Function, *Kantei ni okeru Joho Kinou no Kyouka no Houshin* (Principles of Enhancing Cabinet's Intelligence Capability), 14 February 2008, http://www.kantei.go.jp/jp/singi/zyouhou/080214kettei.pdf (accessed 1 March 2008)

[287] The Council on Enhancing Intelligence Function, *Ibid.*

[288] Omori, Yoshio, "*Intelligence wo Hitosaji* (A spoonful of intelligence)" (Sentaku Agency, 2004): 41, 86–90.

[289] See, for instance, Hoye, Isamu. "Lack of Espionage Law Pits Spy Against Spy" *Asahi News Service*, 3 June 1987.

[290] "Officials used secret funds to entertain each other" *Japan Weekly Monitor,* 26 February 2001.

[291] For the details of the charge, see the Ministry of Foreign Affair of Japan, *Matsuo Katsutoshi Zen-Youjin Gaikoku Houmon Shien Shitsu-cho ni yoru Koukin Ouryo Giwaku ni kansuru Chosa Hokoku-sho* (Investigation Report on the Embezzlement of Public Funds by Katsutoshi Matsuo, former Director, VIP Foreign Visit Support Office) 25 January 2001. http://www.mofa.go.jp/mofaj/press/kaiken/gaisho/0101chosa.html (accessed 15 January 2008).

[292] Ebata, Kensuke. *Joho to Kokka.* 233–238.

[293] The Constitution of Japan, http://homepage1.nifty.com/gyouseinet/kenpou/eiyaku.htm (accessed 3 April 2008).

[294] Lind, Jennifer, "Pacifism or Passing the Buck?" *International Security.* Vol. 29, No. 1 (Summer 2004); Richard L. Armitage and Joseph S. Nye, Jr., *The US-Japan Alliance: Getting Asia Right Through 2020* (Washington: Center for Strategic and International Studies, 2007).

[295] Tamura, Shigenobu, Kenichi Takahashi and Kazuhisa Shimada, editors. *Bouei Housei no Kaisetsu* (Commentary on National Defense Legislation) (Tokyo: Naigai Shuppan, 2006): 13–14.

[296] Tamura, et. al. *Ibid.* 17.

[297] See, for instance, the answer by Mimura, Osamu (Director, Cabinet Legislative Bureau) at the Cabinet Affairs Committee of the House of Representatives, 20 November 1986. Cited from *Bouei Handbook Heisei 19 nendo-ban* (Handbook for Defense 2007) (Tokyo: Asagumo Shimbun-sha, 2007): 586.

[298] Statement by then foreign minister Nakayama, Taro at the floor session of the House of Representatives, 18 October, 1990. Cited from *Bouei Handbook Heisei 19 nendo-ban* (Handbook for Defense 2007) (Tokyo: Asagumo Shimbun-sha, 2007): 592.

[299] *Ibid.*

[300] The Self-Defense Forces (SDF) Law, Article 3, http://law.e-gov.go.jp/htmldata/S29/S29HO165.html (accessed 2 April 2008).

[301] The SDF Law, Article 76, http://law.e-gov.go.jp/htmldata/S29/S29HO165.html (accessed 3 April 2008).

[302] The SDF Law, Article 77, http://law.e-gov.go.jp/htmldata/S29/S29HO165.html (accessed 3 April 2008).

[303] *Buryoku Kougeki Jitai nado ni okeru Wagakuni no Heiwa to Dokuritsu narabini Kuni oyobi Kokumin no Anzen no Kakuho ni Kansuru Houritsu* (Law on Ensuring the Nation's Peace and Independence, as well as the Security of the Nation and its People in case of Armed Attack, etc) Article 9, http://www.kantei.go.jp/jp/singi/hogohousei/hourei/kakuho.html (accessed 5 April 2008).

[304] The SDF Law, Article 88, http://law.e-gov.go.jp/htmldata/S29/S29HO165.html (accessed 16 April 2008).

[305] The SDF Law, Article 80, http://law.e-gov.go.jp/htmldata/S29/S29HO165.html (accessed 16 April 2008).

[306] *Buryoku Kougeki Jitai nado ni okeru Kokumin no Hogo no tameno Sochi ni kansuru houritsu* (Law Concerning the Measures to Protect the People in case of Armed Attack, etc.), Article 15, http://www.kantei.go.jp/jp/singi/hogohousei/hourei/hogo.html (accessed 16 April 2008).

[307] The SDF Law, Article 77-4, http://law.e-gov.go.jp/htmldata/S29/S29HO165.html (accessed 16 April, 2008).

[308] The SDF Law, Article 82-2, http://law.e-gov.go.jp/htmldata/S29/S29HO165.html (accessed 20 April 2008).

[309] Tamura, et. al. *Bouei Housei no Kaisetsu,* 85.

[310] *Ibid.* 85, 90.

---

[311] The SDF Law, Article 78, http://law.e-gov.go.jp/htmldata/S29/S29HO165.html (accessed 16 April 2008).

[312] *Ibid.*, Article 78-2, 78-3, http://law.e-gov.go.jp/htmldata/S29/S29HO165.html (accessed 16 April 2008).

[313] The SDF Law, Article 79, 79-2, http://law.e-gov.go.jp/htmldata/S29/S29HO165.html (accessed 16 April 2008).

[314] The SDF Law, Article 80, http://law.e-gov.go.jp/htmldata/S29/S29HO165.html (accessed 16 April 2008).

[315] The SDF Law, Article 81-1, 81-2, http://law.e-gov.go.jp/htmldata/S29/S29HO165.html (accessed 16 April 2008).

[316] The SDF Law Article 81-3, 81-4, http://law.e-gov.go.jp/htmldata/S29/S29HO165.html (accessed 16 April 2008).

[317] Tamura, et. al. *Bouei Housei no Kaisetsu,* 101.

[318] The SDF Law, Article 82, http://law.e-gov.go.jp/htmldata/S29/S29HO165.html (accessed 16 April 2008).

[319] Tamura, et. al. *Bouei Housei no Kaisetsu.* 100–101.

[320] The SDF Law, Article 84, http://law.e-gov.go.jp/htmldata/S29/S29HO165.html (accessed 17 April 2008).

[321] Tamura, et. al. *Bouei Housei no Kaisetsu,* 128–129.

[322] Tamura, et. al. *Bouei Housei no Kaisetsu,* 110.

[323] The SDF Law, Article 83, http://law.e-gov.go.jp/htmldata/S29/S29HO165.html (accessed 17 April 2008).

[324] The SDF Law, Article 83-1, http://law.e-gov.go.jp/htmldata/S29/S29HO165.html (accessed 17 April 2008).

[325] Tamura, et. al. *Bouei Housei no Kaisetsu,* 112.

[326] The SDF Law, Article 83-2 addendum, http://law.e-gov.go.jp/htmldata/S29/S29HO165.html (accessed 17 April 2008).

[327] The SDF Law 83-3, http://law.e-gov.go.jp/htmldata/S29/S29HO165.html (accessed 17 April 2008).

[328] *Daikibo Jishin Tokubetsu Taisaku Sochi-ho* (Special Measures Law in response to Large-scale Earthquakes, *Dai-shin Ho*) Article 9, 10, http://www.bousai.go.jp/jishin/tokai/houritsu/taishin/contents.htm (accessed 15 April 2008).

[329] *Ibid.,* Article 13-2, http://www.bousai.go.jp/jishin/tokai/houritsu/taishin/contents.htm (accessed 15 April 2008).

[330] *Genshiryoku Saigai Taisaku Tokubetu Sochi-ho* (Special Measures Law regarding the Response to Nuclear Disaster, *Gen-sai Ho*), Article 20-4, http://www.bousai.go.jp/jishin/law/002-1.html (accessed 10 April 2008).

[331] *Ibid.,* Article 28-1, http://www.bousai.go.jp/jishin/law/002-1.html (accessed 10 April 2008).

[332] The SDF Law Article 95, http://law.e-gov.go.jp/htmldata/S29/S29HO165.html (accessed 25 March 2008).

[333] The SDF law Article 81-2-1, http://law.e-gov.go.jp/htmldata/S29/S29HO165.html (accessed 25 March 2008).

[334] The SDF Law, Article 81-2-2, 81-2-3, http://law.e-gov.go.jp/htmldata/S29/S29HO165.html (accessed 25 March 2008).

[335] House of Concillors of Japan, *Jieitai No Kaigai Shukkin wo NasazaruKkoto ni Kansuru Ketsugi* (The resolution that prohibits overseas activities by the SDF), 2 June 1954, Cited in Maeda and Iijima eds. *Kokkai Shingi kara Bouei-ron wo Yomitoku* 138.

[336] The SDF Law, Article 100-4, 100-5, http://law.e-gov.go.jp/htmldata/S29/S29HO165.html (accessed 25 March 2008).

[337] The SDF Law, Article Ninety-Nine, http://law.e-gov.go.jp/htmldata/S29/S29HO165.html (accessed 25 March 2008); Masumi Ezaki, at the Committee on Foreign Affairs, House of Representatives, 24 May 1972. Cited in Maeda and Iijima, eds. *Kokkai Shingi kara Bouei-ron wo Yomitoru* (Understanding the Discussion on Defense from the Debate in the Diet (Tokyo: Sanseido, 2003): 154–155.

[338] *Kokusai Kinkyu Enjo Tai no Haken ni Kansuru Houritsu* (International Disaster Relief Law), Article 2, 3, http://law.e-gov.go.jp/htmldata/S62/S62HO093.html (accessed 22 March 2008); The SDF Law, Article 100-6.), http://law.e-gov.go.jp/htmldata/S29/S29HO165.html (accessed 25 March 2008).

[339] *Kokusai Rengou Heiwa Iji Katsudou Nado ni Taisuru Kyoryoku ni Kansuru Houritsu* (The UN Peacekeeping Cooperation Law), Article 3, http://law.e-gov.go.jp/htmldata/H04/H04HO079.html (accessed 15 October 2007).

[340] Tatsumi, Yuki, "The Political and Legal Environments Surrounding the Self-Defense Forces' Overseas Deployments" in Yuki Tatsumi and Andrew L. Oros ed. *Japan's New Defense Establishment: Institutions, Capabilities, and Implications* (Washington: The Henry L. Stimson Center, 2007) 52.

[341] *The Daily Yomiuri,* 2 September 1999.

[342] See, for instance, Yoichi Funabashi. "Japan has a Duty to Help an Independent East Timor" *Asahi News Service.* 27 September 1999; Keizo Nabeshima. "Agenda for the New Cabinet" *The Japan Times,* 16 October 1999.

[343] Japan Defense Agency, *Heisei 17-nendo bouei hakusho* (Defense of Japan 2005), 241-242.

[344] The SDF Law, Article 3, Sentence 2-2, http://law.e-gov.go.jp/htmldata/S29/S29HO165.html (accessed 15 February 2008).

[345] *The Japan-US Joint Declaration for Security—Alliance for the 21st Century,* http://www.mofa.go.jp/region/n-america/us/security/security.html (accessed 10 December 2007).

[346] *Shuhen Jitai ni Saishite Waga Kuni no Heiwa to Anzen wo Kakuho Suru Tame no Sochi ni Kansuru Houritsu* (The Law to Ensure Japan's Peace and Security in the Situations in the Areas Surrounding Japan) Article 2, 3, http://law.e-gov.go.jp/htmldata/H11/H11HO060.html (accessed 15 December 2007).

[347] *Ibid.,* Article 2, 11, and Appendixes, http://law.e-gov.go.jp/htmldata/H11/H11HO060.html (accessed 15 December 2007).

[348] *An Agreement to Revise the Acquisition and Cross-Service Agreement between Japan and the United States*, Article 3, http://www.mod.go.jp/j/library/treaty/acsa/acsa2.html. (accessed 1 March 2007)

[349] *Iraku Jindo Fukko Shien Tokuso Ho* (Special Measures Law Regarding Humanitarian Reconstruction Assistance Activities and the Activities to Support Ensuring Safety), http://law.e-gov.go.jp/htmldata/H15/H15HO137.html (accessed 16 December 2007).

[350] *Tero Taisaku Tokubetsu Sochi Ho* (Anti-Terror Special Measures Law) Article 1, http://www.cas.go.jp/jp/hourei/houritu/tero_h.html (accessed 1 November 2007).

[351] *Ibid.*

[352] *Ibid.,* Article 2.

[353] *Ibid.,* Article 2, http://www.cas.go.jp/jp/hourei/houritu/tero_h.html (accessed 1 November 2007).

[354] *Ibid.*

[355] *Ibid.*

[356] See, for example, "Gov't. Ministers deny MSDF fueled ships for Iraq war" *The Daily Yomiuri* 8 October 2007.

[357] "Diet passes anti-terror bill: Passage to enable refueling mission to resume in mid-February," *The Daily Yomiuri,* 12 January 2008.

[358] *Tero Taisaku Kaijo Soshi Katsudo ni taisuru Hokyu Shien Katsudo no Jisshi ni kansuru Tokubetu Sochi Ho* (Special Measures Law regarding the Replenishment Support Activities for Counter-Terrorism Maritime Intervention Activities) Article 2-3-1, 2-3-2, http://www.cas.go.jp/jp/hourei/houritu/kyuuyu_sinpou.pdf (accessed 1 April 2008).

[359] *Ibid.,* Article 1, Article 3-2.

---

[360] *Ibid.*, Article 5-5.

[361] *Ibid.* Article Eight, 8-4.

[362] Maeda and Iijima eds. *Kokkai Shingi kara Bouei-ron wo Yomitoku* 306.

[363] "4 in 5 Japanese oppose military attack on Iraq: Kyodo poll," *Kyodo News,* 16 March 2003.

[364] Statement by the Prime Minister Junichiro Koizumi, Tokyo: 20 March 2003, http://www.kantei.go.jp/jp/koizumispeech/2003/03/20danwa.html.

[365] Maeda and Iijima, *Kokkai Shingi kara Bouei-ron wo Yomitoku*, 306.

[366] "4 in 5 Japanese oppose military attack on Iraq: Kyodo poll" *Kyodo News,* 16 March 2003.

[367] Ministry of Foreign Affairs of Japan, *Nichi-bei shuno kaidan no gaiyou* [Overview of Japan-US Summit], 26 May 2005, http://www.mofa.go.jp/mofaj/kaidan/s_koi/us-me_03/us_gh.html (accessed 4 June 2008)

[368] Special Measures Law Regarding Humanitarian Reconstruction Assistance Activities and the Activities to Support Ensuring Safety Article 2, http://law.e-gov.go.jp/htmldata/H15/H15HO137.html. (accessed 5 July 2007)

[369] *Ibid.*, Article 3, http://law.e-gov.go.jp/htmldata/H15/H15HO137.html. (accessed 5 July 2007)

[370] *Ibid.*

[371] *Ibid.*, Article 4, http://law.e-gov.go.jp/htmldata/H15/H15HO137.html. (accessed 5 July 2007)

[372] *Ibid.*, Article 6, http://law.e-gov.go.jp/htmldata/H15/H15HO137.html. (accessed 5 July 2007)

[373] *Ibid.*, Article 8, http://law.e-gov.go.jp/htmldata/H15/H15HO137.html. (accessed 5 July 2007)

[374] *Ibid.*

[375] *Ibid.*

[376] *Ibid.*, Article 17, http://law.e-gov.go.jp/htmldata/H15/H15HO137.html. (accessed 2 March 2008)

[377] Japanese government's answer to the question by Kiyoshi Mori (Member, House of Representatives) 27 September 1985, Cited from *Bouei Handbook Heisei 19 nendo-ban* (Handbook for Defense 2007) (Tokyo: Asagumo Shimbun-sha, 2007): 587.

[378] Tamura, et. al. *Bouei Housei no Kaisetsu,* 157.

---

[379] *Keisatsukan Shokumu Shikkou Ho* (the Law regarding the Policemen Carrying Out Duties), http://www.houko.com/00/01/S23/136.HTM (accessed 2 March 2008).

[380] *Ibid.*

[381] Tamura, et. al. *Bouei Housei no Kaisetsu,* 157-158.

[382] *Keiho* (Criminal Code) Article 37, http://www.houko.com/00/01/M40/045.HTM#037 (accessed 10 March 2008).

[383] *Buryoku Kougeki Jitai ni okeru Gaikoku Gunyou-hin nado no Kaijou Yusou no Kisei ni kansuru Houritsu* (the Law Regarding the Control of Maritime Transport of Foreign Military and Other Items at the time of Armed Attack), Article 37, http://www.mod.go.jp/j/library/law/yuji/houritu/002b.htm (accessed 5 March 2008).

[384] Tamura, et. al. *Bouei Housei no Kaisetsu,*. 160.

[385] Tamura, et. al. *Bouei Housei no Kaisetsu,* 161-162.

[386] The Law regarding the Policemen Carrying Out Duties, Article 2, 4, 5 and 6, http://www.houko.com/00/01/S23/136.HTM (accessed 2 March 2008).

[387] Tamura, et. al. *Bouei Housei no Kaisetsu,* 98.

[388] The Japan Coast Guard Law, Article Sixteen, 17-1, and 18, http://www.houko.com/00/01/S23/028.HTM (accessed 10 March 2008).

[389] Tamura, et. al. *Bouei Housei no Kaisetsu,* 116-126.

[390] The Law regarding the Policemen Carrying Out Duties, Article Four, 6-1, 6-3, 6-4, http://www.houko.com/00/01/S23/136.HTM (accessed 2 March 2008); the Japan Coast Guard Law Article 16,
http://www.houko.com/00/01/S23/028.HTM (accessed 10 March 2008); *Saigai Taisaku Kihon Ho* (The Basic Law for Disaster Response), Article 63, 64, 65, 76-3, http://law.e-gov.go.jp/htmldata/S36/S36HO223.html (accessed 12 March 2008).

[391] Press conference with Prime Minister Junichiro Koizumi, 19 September 2001, http://www.kantei.go.jp/jp/koizumispeech/2001/0919sourikaiken.html (ccessed 15 November 2007).

[392] Press conference with Prime Minister Junichiro Koizumi, (27 April 2001), http://www.kantei.go.jp/jp/koizumispeech/2001/0427kisyakaiken.html (accessed 2 April 2008).

[393] *Abe Naikaku Souri Daijin Nento Kisha Kaiken* (New Year's Press Conference with Prime Minister Shinzo Abe),
http://www.kantei.go.jp/jp/abespeech/2007/01/04kaiken.html (accessed 5 March 2008).

[394] "*Anzen Hosho no Houteki Kiban no Sai-kouchiku ni kansuru Kondankai no Kaisai ni tsuite* (Regarding the Establishment of the Advisory Council on Re-establishing the Legal

Foundation for National Security)," 17 April, 2007, http://www.kantei.go.jp/jp/singi/anzenhosyou/konkyo.pdf (accessed 20 April 2007)

[395] A comment by a former senior MOD official, Tokyo, Japan: 13 May 2008.

[396] *Nihonkoku Kenpou no Kaisei Tetsuduki ni kansuru Houritsu* (Law regarding the Procedures for Revising the Constitution of Japan), http://law.e-gov.go.jp/announce/H19HO051.html (accessed 1 October 2007).

[397] Liberal Democratic Party of Japan (LDP) *Seiken Koyaku 2005* (Policy Manifesto 2005) http://www.jimin.jp/jimin/jimin/2005_seisaku/120yakusoku/120_theme05.html (accessed 1 December 2007).

[398] "*Aso Shushou Shudan-teki Jiei-ken Younin he `Kenpou Kaishaku Kaerubeki da* (Prime Minister Aso Looking to Allow the Right of Collective Self-Defense 'We Should Change the Constitutional Interpretation')" 26 September 2008, http://www.asahi.com/politics/update/0926/TKY200809260073.html (accessed 4 October 2008).

[399] Liberal Democratic Party of Japan, "*News: Kokusai Heiwa Kyoryoku no Ippan-ho ni kansuru Goudou Bukai ga Hatsu-kaigou* (News: the Joint Committee for the General Law for International Peace Cooperation Meet for the First Time"), 13 February 2008, http://www.jimin.jp/jimin/daily/08_02/13/200213b.shtml (accessed 25 February 2008).

[400] Liberal Democratic Party of Japan, "*News: Kokusai Heiwa Kyouryoku no Ippan-ho ni tsuite Yoto PT no Setsumei Ukeru; Kokusai Heiwa Kyouryoku no Ippan-ho ni kansuru Goudou Bukai* (News: Joint Committee receives a Briefing on a General Law on International Peace Cooperation from the Ruling Party's Project Team)" 20 June 2008, http://www.jimin.jp/jimin/daily/08_06/20/200620b.shtml (accessed 1 July 2008).

[401] Ministry of Defense of Japan, *Heisei 17-nendo ikou ni Kakawaru Bouei Keikaku no Taiko ni Tsuite* (National Defense Program Guideline, FY 2005), http://www.mod.go.jp/j/defense/policy/17taikou/taikou.htm (accessed 1 October 2008).

[402] Council on Security and Defense Capabilities, *Japan's Vision for Future Security and Defense Capability,* October 2004.

[403] The Constitution of Japan, (*Nihon koku Kenpou*) enacted 3 November 1945, Articles 67-68, 72, 74, http://law.e-gov.go.jp/htmldata/S21/S21KE000.html (accessed 1 March 2007).

[404] The Cabinet Law (*Naikaku Ho*), Enacted 16 January 1947, Article 4-9, http://law.e-gov.go.jp/htmldata/S22/S22HO005.html (accessed 3 May 2008).

[405] Iio, Jun, *Nihon no Touchi Kouzou* (Governing Structure of Japan) (Tokyo: Chuo Koron Shin-sha, 2007): 26-32.

[406] The Cabinet Law, Article 4, http://law.e-gov.go.jp/htmldata/S22/S22HO005.html (accessed 3 May 2008).

[407] Honda, Masatoshi, *Gendai Nihon no Seiji to Gyosei* (Government and Politics in Contemporary Japan) (Tokyo: Hokki Shuppan, 2001): 55.

---

[408] Honda, *Ibid.* 61.

[409] Honda, *op. cit.* 63–64.

[410] Honda, *op. cit.* 79–80.

[411] *Chuo Shouchou nado Kaikaku Kihonho* (Basic Law regarding the Reform of the Central Agencies and Other Organizations), Article 8, enacted June 1999, http://law.e-gov.go.jp/htmldata/H10/H10HO103.html (accessed 3 February 2008).

[412] Shinoda, Tomohito, "The Emergence of Cabinet Secretariat as Core Executive." *Asian Survey* (September/October 2005): 816.

[413] Interviews with the officials from the Cabinet Secretariat and Ministry of Defense. Tokyo, Japan: 8-17 May 2008.

[414] Yomiuri Research Institute, "*Kokka Anzen Hosho Kaigi to Nihon no Senryaku: America no Kyokun wo dou Ikasuka* (National Security Council and Japan's Strategy: How to Learn from American's Lessons)" 19 June 2007, http://info.yomiuri.co.jp/yri/o-forum/of20070619.htm (accessed 2 July 2007).

[415] Interview with a political correspondent with Yomiuri Shimbun, Tokyo, Japan: January 2008.

[416] Administrative Reform Council, *Saishuu Houkoku* (Final Report), 3 December 1998, http://www.kantei.go.jp/jp/gyokaku/report-final/II.html (accessed 2 February 2007)

[417] The Basic Law regarding the Reform of the Central Agencies and Other Organizations, Article 8-2.

[418] The Cabinet Law, Article 18, 12-2-6.

[419] Honda, *Gendai Nihon no Seiji to Gyosei:* 66.

[420] The Cabinet Law, Article 18.

[421] Ishiba, Shigeru, *Kokubo* (National Defense) (Tokyo: Shincho-sha, 2005): 123–125.

[422] Interview with a MOD official. Tokyo, Japan: 9 May 2008.

[423] An interview with MOFA official. Tokyo, Japan: 13 May 2008.

[424] Interviews with Cabinet Secretarial officials, Tokyo Japan: 9 and 13 May, 2008.

[425] Morimoto, Satoshi, *Kokubou no Ronten: Nihonjin ga Shiranai Hontou no Kokka Kiki* (Points of Discussion in National Defense: Real National Crises that Japanese Do Not Know) (Tokyo: PHP Kenkyujo, 2007).

[426] Liberal Democratic Party of Japan (LDP), "*Kenpou Kaise no Pointo: Kenpou Kaisei ni Mukete no Omona Ronten* (Points of the Constitutional Revision: Main Discussion Points in Constitutional Revision) 2004,

http://www.jimin.jp/jimin/jimin/2004_seisaku/kenpou/index.html (accessed 13 April 2008); Democratic Party of Japan (DPJ), "*Minshuto Kenpou Teigen* (DPJ Proposal for the Constitution)" 31 October 2005, http://www.dpj.or.jp/news/files/SG0065.pdf (accessed 10 April 2008)

[427] Komeito, "*Komeito Manifesto 2007 Seisaku-shu* (Komeito Manifesto 2007 Policy Priorities)" 2007, http://www.komei.or.jp/policy/policy/pdf/jutenseisaku2007.pdf (accessed 10 April 2008).

[428] Tatsumi, Yuki, "The Political and Legal Environment Surrounding the Self-Defense Forces' Overseas Deployments" in Tatsumi and Oros eds. *Japan's New Defense Establishment: Institutions, Capabilities and Implications*: 48.

[429] Tatsumi, Yuki. "The Political and Legal Environment Surrounding the Self-Defense Forces' Overseas Deployments" in *Ibid.* 52.

[430] *Koizumi Naikaku Souri Daijin Kisha Kaiken* (Press Conference with Prime Minister Koizumi) 27 April, 2001, http://www.kantei.go.jp/jp/koizumispeech/2001/0427kisyakaiken.html (accessed 2 March 2008).

[431] *Naikaku Souri Daijin no Danwa* (Statement by the Prime Minister) 9 December 2003, http://www.kantei.go.jp/jp/koizumispeech/2003/12/09danwa.html (accessed 1 June 2008).

[432] "Japan and NATO: Toward Further Collaboration" Speech by Prime Minister Shinzo Abe to the North Atlantic Council. 12 January 2007, http://www.mofa.go.jp/region/europe/pmv0701/nato.html (accessed 14 February 2008).

[433] Cabinet Affairs Office, "*Chosa Kekka no Gaiyou* (Executive Summary of the Poll Results)," *Jieitai Bouei Mondai ni Kansuru Yoron Chosa* (Public Opinion Poll on the JSDF and Defense Issues), February 2006, http://www8.cao.go.jp/survey/h17/h17-bouei/2-4.html (accessed 20 September 2008).

[434] *Ibid.*

[435] *Sankei Shimbun,* 27 July 2008.

[436] *Asahi Shimbun,* 18 July 2008.

[437] *Nikkei Weekly*, 17 September 2001.

[438] Tatsumi, "The Political and Legal Environment Surrounding the Self-Defense Forces' Overseas Deployments" in Tatsumi and Oros eds. *Japan's New Defense Establishment: Institutions, Capabilities and Implications*: 48–58.

[439] Tatsumi, "The Political and Legal Environment Surrounding the Self-Defense Forces' Overseas Deployments" in *Ibid.* 69–71.

[440] Comment of a former senior US Department of State official, Washington DC. 29 July 2008.

---

[441] Interviews with former and current senior MOD officials, Tokyo, Japan: 10–15 2008.

[442] Ministry of Foreign Affairs of Japan, *Japan-US Joint Declaration on Security: Alliance for the 21st Century,* 17 April 1996, http://www.mofa.go.jp/region/n-america/us/security/security.html (accessed 13 September 2008).

[443] Ministry of Foreign Affairs of Japan, *The Japan-US Alliance for the New Century,* 29 June 2006, http://www.mofa.go.jp/region/n-america/us/summit0606.html (Accessed 15 September 2008).

[444] "Three basic points stated by Supreme Commander to be 'musts' in constitutional revision," 4 February 1946, SCAP File of Commander Alfred R. Hussey, Document No. 5, http://www.ndl.go.jp/constitution/shiryo/03/072/072tx.html (accessed 12 April 2008).

[445] Iokibe, Makoto, *Senryo-ki: Shushou tachi no Shin Nippon* (Occupation Period: New Japan for the Prime Ministers) (Tokyo: Yomiuri Shimbun-sha, 1997).

[446] Tanaka, Akihiko, *Anzen Hosho* (Security) (Tokyo: Yomiuri Shimbun-sha, 1997).

[447] The Security Treaty between Japan and the United States of America. 8 September 1951, http://www.ioc.u-tokyo.ac.jp/~worldjpn/documents/texts/docs/19510908.T2J.html (accessed 10 May 2008).

[448] Satoshi Morimoto, *Nihon Bouei Saiko-ron* (Reconsideration of Japan's Defense) (Tokyo: Kairyu-sha, May 2008): 281.

[449] The Mutual Security and Cooperation Treaty between Japan and the United States of America, Signed 19 January 1960, Articles 2 and 5, http://www.ioc.u-tokyo.ac.jp/~worldjpn/documents/texts/docs/19600119.T1J.html (accessed 15 May 2008).

[450] Sotooka, Hidetoshi, Masaru Honda, and Toshiaki Miura, eds. *Nichi-Bei Doumei Han-Seiki: Anpo to Mitsuyaku (Half Century of the US-Japan Alliance: Security and Secrete Agreements)* (Asahi Shimbun-sha, 2001) 89–102.

[451] Sotooka, Honda, and Miura, eds. *Ibid.* 127–141.

[452] Richard Nixon, "Address to the Nation on the War in Vietnam," 3 November 1969, http://www.presidency.ucsb.edu/ws/print.php?pid=2303 (accessed 3 May 2008).

[453] Fukuda, Takeshi, "*Nichi-bei Bouei Kyouryoku ni okeru 3-tsu no Tenki: 1978 nen Gaidorain kara 'Nichi-Bei Doumei Henkaku' madeno Michinori* (Three Junctures in the Japan-US Defense Cooperation: Road from the 1978 Guidelines to 'Transformation of the Japan–US Alliance,)" Reference National Diet Library of Japan, July 2006; 143–172, http://www.ndl.go.jp/jp/data/publication/refer/200607_666/066607.pdf (accessed 3 October 2008).

[454] Fukuda, *Ibid.*

[455] *Ibid.*

[456] Kissinger, Henry A, "Speech to the Japan Society Annual Dinner," 18 June 1975, http://www.ioc.u-tokyo.ac.jp/~worldjpn/documents/texts/JPUS/19750618.S1J.html (accessed 1 June 2008).

[457] "Address of President Gerald R. Ford at the University of Hawaii," 7 December 1975, http://www.ford.utexas.edu/library/speeches/750716.htm (accessed 5 June 2008).

[458] "Joint Communiqué: Productive Partnership for the 1980s (Visit of Prime Minister Ohira of Japan)" 2 May 1979, http://www.ioc.u-tokyo.ac.jp/~worldjpn/documents/texts/JPUS/19790502.D1E.html (accessed 2 June 2008).

[459] Ministry of Finance in Japan, "*Nihon no Taibei Keijou Shushi no Doukou* (Japan's Current Account Balance vis-à-vis the United States)," https://www.mof.go.jp/kankou/hyou/g460/460_a.pdf (accessed 3 July 2008).

[460] "Joint Communiqué of Japanese Prime Minister Zenko Suzuki and U.S. President Reagan," 8 May 1981, http://www.ioc.u-tokyo.ac.jp/~worldjpn/documents/texts/JPUS/19810508.D1E.html (accessed 1 July 2008).

[461] "Remarks of the President and Prime Minister Yasuhiro Nakasone of Japan Following Their Meetings in Tokyo," 10 November 1983, http://www.ioc.u-tokyo.ac.jp/~worldjpn/documents/texts/JPUS/19831110.O1E.html (accessed 2 July 2008).

[462] *Ibid.*

[463] *U.S.--Japanese Negotiations on the Development of the FSX Support Fighter: The President's News Conference,* 28 April 1989, http://www.ioc.u-tokyo.ac.jp/~worldjpn/documents/texts/JPUS/19890428.S2E.html

[464] *Joint Communiqué: Productive Partnership for the 1980s (Visit of Prime Minister Ohira of Japan),* 2 May 1979. http://www.ioc.u-tokyo.ac.jp/~worldjpn/documents/texts/JPUS/19790502.D1E.html (accessed 6 June 2008).

[465] *Speech By US Secretary of State to George Shultz to the Pacific Cooperation Council,* 2 May 1985, http://www.ioc.u-tokyo.ac.jp/~worldjpn/documents/texts/JPUS/19850202.S1J.html (accessed 1 June 2008).

[466] For Nakasone's remarks at G7 Summit, see "*Dai 9-kai Shuyoukoku Shunou Kaigi (Williamsburg) Kanren Bunsho* (Related Documents for the Ninth G7 Summit (Williamsburg)," http://www.mofa.go.jp/MOFAJ/gaiko/bluebook/1984/s59-shiryou-405.htm (accessed 1 August 2008).

[467] *Remarks of the President and Prime Minister Yasuhiro Nakasone of Japan Following Their Meetings in Tokyo,* 10 November 1983, http://www.ioc.u-tokyo.ac.jp/~worldjpn/documents/texts/JPUS/19831110.O1Ehtml (accessed 10 June 2008).

---

[468] Oros, Andrew L, "The United States and 'Alliance' Role in Japan's New Defense Establishment" in Tatsumi and Oros eds; *Japan's New Defense Establishment: Institutions, Capabilities and Institutions*: 73–83.

[469] Morimoto, Satoshi, "*Nichi-bei Bouei Kyouryoku Gaidorain to Shuhen Jitai Ho* (Japan-US Defense Cooperation Guidelines and the Law regarding the Situations in the Areas Surrounding Japan)," http://www.qiuyue.com/gendai/guideline.htm (accessed 3 June 2008).

[470] Morimoto, *Ibid.* 170–171.

[471] Ministry of Foreign Affairs of Japan, "Korean Energy Development Organization (KEDO)," June 2006, http://www.mofa.go.jp/mofaj/gaiko/kaku/kedo/ (accessed 1 September 2007).

[472] William J. Perry's remarks at the Brookings Leadership Forum "Crisis on the Korean Peninsula: Implications for US Policy in Northeast Asia," The Brookings Institution, 24 January 2003, http://www.brookings.edu/comm/events/20030124.pdf (accessed 25 January 2007).

[473] Jimbo, Ken, "*Dando Misairu Bouei to Nichibei Doumei: Nichi-bei Kyodo Kenkyu no Seisaku Katei to Doumei no "Senryaku Chosei,"* (BMD and the US-Japan Alliance: Policy Process in the US-Japan Joint Research and "Strategic Adjustment" within the Alliance)," *Kokusai Anzen Hosho* (Journal of International Security). No. 29 Vol. 4 (March 2002).

[474] Morimoto, "*Nichi-bei Bouei Kyouryoku Gaidorain to Shuhen Jitai Ho* (Japan–US Defense Cooperation Guidelines and the Law regarding the Situations in the Areas Surrounding Japan)," in *Asia Chiiki no Anzen Hosho to Genshiryoku no Heiwa Riyou* (Security in Asia region and the Peaceful Use of Nuclear Power) (Council for Nuclear Fuel Cycle, 2000), http://www.qiuyue.com/gendai/guideline.htm (accessed 22 November 2007).

[475] US Department of Defense, *The United States Security Strategy for East Asia–Pacific Region,* 10 February 1995, http://www.dtic.mil/cgi-bin/GetTRDoc?AD=ADA298441&Location=U2&doc=GetTRDoc.pdf (accessed 1 July 2008).

[476] Ministry of Foreign Affairs of Japan, *Japan–US Joint Declaration on Security: Alliance for the 21st Century.* 17 April 1996, http://www.mofa.go.jp/region/n-america/us/security/security.html (accessed 13 September 2008).

[477] Ministry of Foreign Affairs of Japan, *The Guidelines for Japan–US Defense Cooperation,* 23 September 1997, http://www.mofa.go.jp/region/n-america/us/security/guideline2.html (accessed 20 June 2008).

[478] See, for example, Prime Minister Keizo Obuchi's answer to the Honorable Gotaro Yoshimura at the Special Committee on the Guidelines for Japan-US Defense Cooperation, House of Councillors, the 145th Session, 24 May 1999. http://kokkai.ndl.go.jp/cgi-bin (accessed 15 July 2008).

[479] Statement by Honorable Keigi Kajiwara (Social Democratic Party of Japan) at the floor session of the House of Councillors, 22 January 2000, http://kokkai.ndl.go.jp/cgi-bin (accessed 15 July 2008).

[480] Institute for National Strategic Studies (INSS), "The United States and Japan: Advancing Toward a Mature Partnership," *INSS Special Report* October 2000, http://www.ndu.edu/inss/strforum/SR_01/SR_Japan.htm (accessed 15 October 2007).

[481] INSS, *Ibid.*

[482] *Souri Daijin Seimei* (Prime Minister's Statement), 12 September 2001, http://www.kantei.go.jp/jp/koizumispeech/2001/0911seimei.html (accessed 19 July 2008).

[483] *Naikaku Souri Daijin Kisha Kaiken: Beikoku ni Okeru Douji Tahatsu Tero Jiken* (Press Conference with the Prime Minister: Simultaneous Multiple Terrorist Incidents in the United States), 12 September 2001, http://www.kantei.go.jp/jp/koizumispeech/2001/0912sourikaiken.html (accessed 19 July 2008).

[484] *Koizumi Naikaku Souri Daijin Kisha Kaiken-roku* (Transcript for the Press Conference with the Prime Minister Koizumi) 19 September 2001, http://www.kantei.go.jp/jp/koizumispeech/2001/0919sourikaiken.html (accessed 25 July 2008).

[485] *Koizumi Souri Daijin Kisha Kaiken* (Press Conference with Prime Minister Koizumi), 20 March 2003, http://www.kantei.go.jp/jp/koizumispeech/2003/03/20kaiken.html (accessed 5 June 2008).

[486] *Naikaku Souri Daijin no Danwa (Iraq Jindo Fukko Shien Tokuso-ho ni motoduku Taiou Sochi ni kansuru Kihon Keikaku)* (Statement by the Prime Minister: Basic Plan regarding the Iraq Reconstruction Assistance Special Measures Law), 9 December 2003, http://www.kantei.go.jp/jp/koizumispeech/2003/12/09danwa.html (accessed 1 June 2008).

[487] *Dando Misairu Bouei Shisutemu no Seibi nado nit suite* (Regarding the introduction of ballistic missile defense system, etc.), Cabinet Decision, 19 December 2003, http://www.kantei.go.jp/jp/kakugikettei/2003/1219seibi.html (accessed 13 November 2007).

[488] Council on Security and Defense Capability, *Japan's Visions for Future Security and Defense Capabilities*, October 2004, http://www.kantei.go.jp/jp/singi/ampobouei/dai13/13siryou.pdf (accessed 10 January 2007).

[489] *Heisei 17-nendo ikou ni kakawaru Bouei Keikaku no Taiko* (National Defense Program Guideline in FY 2005 and after) 10 December 2004, http://www.mod.go.jp/j/defense/policy/17taikou/taikou.htm (accessed 1 February 2007).

[490] *Joint Statement: US–Japan Security Consultative Committee,* 19 February 2005, http://www.mod.go.jp/j/news/youjin/2005/02/0219_2plus2/04.pdf (accessed).

---

[491] *US–Japan Alliance: Transformation and Realignment for the Future* 29 October 2005, http://www.mod.go.jp/j/news/youjin/2005/10/1029_2plus2/29_e.htm (accessed 30 October 2007).

[492] *United States–Japan Roadmap for Realignment Implementation,* 1 May 2006, http://www.mod.go.jp/j/news/youjin/2006/05/0501-e02.html (accessed 15 May 2006).

[493] Comment at a closed conference in Washington, DC: 27 March 2008.

[494] Baker, Howard H. Jr. "US–Japan Relationship in 2004" Remarks to the Japan National Press Club, Tokyo, Japan: 14 December 2004, http://www.state.gov/p/eap/rls/rm/2004/40478.htm (accessed 25 February 2007).

[495] Bloomfield, Lincoln Jr. "The Strategic Landscape in US–Japanese Relations" Remarks before the Nikkei–CSIS Forum, Tokyo, Japan: 16 December 2004, http://www.state.gov/t/pm/rls/rm/39978.htm (accessed 19 May 2007).

[496] Deming, Rust M, "Japan's Constitution and Defense Policy: Entering a New Era?" *Strategic Forum* No. 213 (Institute for National Strategic Studies, November 2004), 8. http://www.ndu.edu/inss/Strforum/SF213/SF213_Final.pdf (accessed 1 March 2008).

[497] Przystup, James J, "US-Japan Relations. Progress Toward a Mature Partnership," *Occasional Paper No. 2* (Institute for National Strategic Studies, June 2005) 4, http://www.ndu.edu/inss/Occassional_Papers/Przystup_OP_072005/Przystup_OP_072005.pdf (accessed 10 June 2007).

[498] Armitage, Richard L. and Joseph S. Nye, Jr., *The US-Japan Alliance: Getting Asia Right* (Washington: Center for Strategic and International Studies, 16 February 2007): 18-19, 21-22, http://www.csis.org/media/csis/pubs/070216_asia2020.pdf (accessed 1 March 2007).

[499] *Abe Naikaku Souri Daijin Kisha Kaiken* (Press Conference with Prime Minister Abe) 26 September 2006, http://www.kantei.go.jp/jp/abespeech/2006/09/26press.html (accessed 14 April 2007).

[500] *Abe Naikaku Souri Daijin Kisha Kaiken: Dai 165-kai Rinji Kokkai Shuryo wo ukete* (Press Conference with Prime Minister Abe: Following the Conclusion of the 165th Extraordinary Session of the Diet) 19 December 2006, http://www.kantei.go.jp/jp/abespeech/2006/12/19kaiken.html (accessed1 March 2007).

[501] Armitage and Nye. *The US-Japan Alliance: Getting Asia Right.* 31.

[502] Comments made by a former US government official to a group of Japanese government officials visiting Washington, DC: March 2007.

[503] "*Nihon-ban NSC Sousetsu wo Miokuri Fukuda Shushou* (Giving up on Creating Japanese-version of NSC: Prime Minister Fukuda)" *Sankei News* 24 December 2007, http://sankei.jp.msn.com/politics/policy/071224/plc0712241823006-n1.htm (accessed 28 December 2007).

[504] "*Ku-ji Iraq kara Nennai Tesshu he* (JASDF to withdraw from Iraq by the end of the year)," *Sankei News*, 29 July 2008,

http://sankei.jp.msn.com/politics/policy/080729/plc0807290116001-n1.htm (accessed 1 August 2008).

[505] "*Seifu Jieitai no Afghan Hondo Katsudo Dannen Chian Akka Komei Hantai* (Government Gave Up on Dispatching JSDF troops to the mainland Afghanistan: Worsening Security, Opposition from Komeito)," *Iza! News,* 20 July 2008, http://www.iza.ne.jp/news/newsarticle/162701/ (accessed 22 July 2008).

[506] *Bouei-sho Kaikaku Kaigi* (The MOD Reform Council), *Houkokusho: Fushoji no Bunseki to Kaikaku no Hoko-sei* (Report: Analyses of the Scandal and the Direction for Reform) 15 July 2008, http://www.kantei.go.jp/jp/singi/bouei/dai11/pdf/siryou.pdf (accessed 24 July 2008).

[507] For instance, "*Fukuda Shushou Bouei-Sho Kaikaku Wo Kyocho Bouei-Dai de Sotsugyo-shiki* (Prime Minister Stressed the MOD Reform: at the Graduation Ceremony of the National Defense Academy) 18 March, 2008. http://www.asahi.com/special/080219/TKY200803230248.html (accessed 1 May 2008).

[508] The MOD Reform Council, *Report: Analyses of the Scandal and the Direction for Reform* 41.

[509] *Ibid.,* 42–43.

[510] "*Kenpou Kaisei Hantai 43 paacento: Sansei wo Uwamawaru* (43 Percent Opposed the Constitutional Revision: Opposition Bigger than Support)" *The Yomiuri Shimbun,* 8 April 2008, http://www.yomiuri.co.jp/feature/20080116-907457/news/20080408-OYT1T00041.htm (accessed 10 April 2008).

[511] *Ibid.*

[512] The comment by a MOD official at an off-the-record roundtable discussion on Japanese experience in Iraq, Washington, DC: June 2006.

[513] Cabinet Affairs Office, "*Chosa Kekka no Gaiyou* (Executive Summary of the Findings)" in *Jieitai Bouei mondai ni kansuru Yoron Chosa* (Public Opinion Poll on the JSDF and Defense Issues), February 2006, http://www8.cao.go.jp/survey/h17/h17-bouei/2-4.html (accessed 1 March 2007).

[514] Ueki, Koji, "*Iraku Jieitai Haken to Kokumin Ishiki* (JSDF Diepatch to Iraq and Public Opinion)" April 2004, http://www.nhk.or.jp/bunken/research/yoron/shakai/shakai_04040101.pdf (accessed 1 July 2008).

[515] *Ibid.*

[516] "*Kita Chosen Tero-kokka Shitei Kaijo 'Nattoku Dekinu' Hachiwari* (De-listing of North Korea from the State Sponsors of Terrorism: 80 percent 'Unconvinced,'" *Yomiuri Shimubn,* 14 July 2008, http://www.yomiuri.co.jp/feature/20080116-907457/news/20080714-OYT1T00529.htm (accessed 20 July 2008).

---

[517] "*Tero Shitei Kaijo Gimon no Ooi Jikko-teki na Kensho* (North Korea De-listed from the State Sponsors of Terrorism: Many Questions about the Effectiveness of Verification)," *The Yomiuri Shimbun,* 12 October 2008, http://www.yomiuri.co.jp/editorial/news/20081011-OYT1T00781.htm (accessed 13 October 2008).

[518] "*Nichibei Kankei no Hyoka Akka Ryokoku de 2000 nen Ikou Saitei* (The Evaluation of US–Japan Relationship Worsening: Worst in Both Countries Since 2000)," *The Yomiuri Shimbun,* 14 December 2007. http://www.yomiuri.co.jp/feature/fe6100/news/20071213i217.htm (accessed 13 July 2008).

[519] *Ibid.*

[520] A comment by a former US government official, Washington, DC: 15 September 2008.

[521] Ministry of Foreign Affairs in Japan, *Japan-Australia Joint Declaration on Security Cooperation,* 13 March 2007, http://www.mofa.go.jp/region/asia-paci/australia/joint0703.html (accessed 10 June 2008); Ministry of Defense of Japan, *Heisei 19-nen-ban Bouei Hakusho* (Defense of Japan 2007); 308.